Moth alchemy

"**The great story-teller Frank O'Connor** said that every good story should end, in spirit, with the exact same words: *And everything that ever happened to me afterwards, I never felt the same about again.* (He actually got to use that ending, once.) In this new book of Moth stories, that test of significance, of meaning, is – once more – met again and again. There are very few of these well-told tales that don't have those words as an invisible addition. You can mouth them to yourself as the story ends: *Jesus, she could never have felt the same about anything after that ...*

And if *I'll never feel the same* is the moral of every good story, *We're all in this together* is the moral of every Moth occasion. Of all the alchemies of human connection – sex and childbirth and marriage and friendship – the strangest is this: You can stand up and tell a story that is made entirely, embarrassingly, of I's, and a listening audience somehow turns each I into a me. This is the alchemy of all literature and it is **what makes The Moth fly.**"

Adam Gopnik

First published in Great Britain in 2017 by
SERPENT'S TAIL:
3 Holford Yard, Bevin Way
London WC1X 9HD

www.serpentstail.com

1 3 5 7 9 10 8 6 4 2

Typeset in Lino Letter to a design by Henry Iles.

Printed and bound in Great Britain by
Clays, Bungay, Suffolk

A CIP catalogue record for this book is available from the
British Library.

ISBN 978-1781256633
eISBN 978-1781256657

MIX
Paper from
responsible sources
FSC
www.fsc.org   FSC® C104740

All These Wonders

True stories about facing the unknown from

THE MOTH

EDITED BY
Catherine Burns

Contents

An Icy Cold Patch

Grace Rushes In

To Be a Boy

CONTENTS

To Face the Fear

By Every Claim of Love

Afterword

Introduction

Word of Moth

Lemn Sissay

I admit it. I'm a Mothaholic. I became an addict after the first taste and if this is your first then you are in luck. It's a sweet addiction. And if you've come to this after listening to the Moth podcast or after a live Moth then you already know what's coming.

Eight years ago, my friend Hannah suggested I listen to the obscurely named Moth podcast. After listening to the first story I needed another. Immediately. If you've seen me on a street corner laughing out loud or on a tube or plane shaking at the shoulders (trying not to weep) blame The Moth. A stranger asked "Are you okay?" I told her, "I'm listening to a story on The Moth". Her eyes widened "The Moth podcast? I love the Moth podcast," she said. I'd love to say we got married. We didn't.

There are more stories passing between more people in more ways now than at any other time in human existence. The migratory nature of stories has never created such beautiful and terrifying formations to so many. The Moth is one of the best ways. I'd say it was a market leader if the term market leader didn't kill the spirit of The Moth. The Moth is a migratory species of storytellers. We cross all borders. There are no visas. We all have a story. So it was gobsmackingly bonkers to receive a call from Meg Bowles of The Moth inviting me to tell a story at The Moth live at The Union Chapel in London.

Imagine being a fan of star wars then receiving a call "Hi, it's George Lucas here. We'd like you to be in our next film." Bring. It. On. My enthusiasm and excitement turned slowly to anxiety and melting panic as Meg's weekly calls encouraged my story to take shape. That's what The Moth do. They tease out the story from the teller. A moth is drawn to the light of the flame, so the idiom goes. Were The Moth's directors trying to draw me to the warm flame inside the story?

Sometimes we are not aware what the real story is but when it hits us we know. That's what happens with The Moth stories. They hit you. That is why they call. They wanted me to find the flame. The stories don't need to be grand. They don't need to be serious. They can begin as simple as "I was walking home". One of the most incredible stories I've heard on The Moth is about a guy walking home.

The day came. The Moth event in London sold out in twenty-four hours by word of Moth. See what I did there? The Moth community around the world is all by word of mouth. Hundreds of people gathered in one giant room to listen to strangers tell an unpublished true story. (I said unpublished not unpolished.) This is London. There's a book launch by a world class author nearly every night, American superstars are on the West End theatre, there's a cookery class by a Michelin Star chef somewhere. There's probably a Beckett play performed by Lisa Dwan somewhere. Everything is here, and yet this audience wants to listen to a true story by a series of strangers. That is the power of The Moth. There will be a story in

The Moth which will move you to tears or laughter or more likely both.

I am so nervous I could eat my knuckles. The woman who created the hair style of David Bowie walks off stage after telling the magnificent tale of a girl from the 'burbs whose life changed by chance. The familiar applause that I hear on The Moth podcasts fills the room.

You have got the right book at the right time. The book is the venue. In holding this book you are in the audience. The speakers are waiting for you to turn the page.

Imagine The Moth to be an encampment in the desert. Take a seat. Someone will make space for you. It's dusk in the land of story. What's happening? Who knows? Someone's gonna stand up and speak? Something about their life – something that means something to them, something that may mean something to you. The sun dips and fires, rising stars spill across the sky like shoals of silver fish. You see there are as many small fires as there are stars. This is not an encampment. It is the world. The air is perfect body temperature. It is. The Moth is by the people for the people. That's you.

Now listen. Look. Now read.

The Eternal Music of the Spheres

Tara Clancy

◇◇

The Moon and Stars Talks

I am a fifth-generation native New Yorker. And while there is certainly something cool about that, there is also actually a downside. There was a moment when it occurred to me that while many other American families also first landed in New York, for the most part, at some point, *they kept going* – pioneering their way west with little more than the rags on their backs and all of that.

Meanwhile, it's like my own family got off a boat, took two steps, and were like, "Good enough for me. Forever."

All of that is to say I come from people to whom "discovering the great unknown" means . . . New Jersey.

But seriously, it didn't take me too long to realise that the reason for that was mostly fear, and that that fear pervades everything: where you live, what you do for a living. You find the first solid thing, and you don't risk going any further.

But as it would wind up, my mother was something of a pioneer herself, although not without her share of false starts. At twenty years old, she had hardly been outside of Brooklyn, and when she did finally leave a year later, it was only because she married a cop from Queens, which she then called "the country."

They had a baby – me – but by the time I was two, they had divorced. So to make a little extra money afterwards, she had to take on a weekend job cleaning apartments.

The very first was this duplex with Manhattan-skyline views, filled with antiques and artwork. But as it winds up, it would be her last. Because over the course of a year, she would go from being the cleaning lady to the secretary to the girlfriend of the multimillionaire who owned it, named Mark.

They never wound up living together full-time. They were both divorced, so it was sort of *been there, done that*. But also my mom had this philosophy, which was if you take someone's money, you have to take their advice.

"When it came to raising you," she said, "I wanted to do it my way, which had to mean on my dime."

So she would go on to spend every weekend with him, and then every weekday back home in Queens, living this dual life . . . for the next twenty-two years. On the weekends when I wasn't with my dad, I was right there with her. Together, Mom and I became like superwomen: able to jump social strata in a single bound!

Because of my mom's plan, my life was never very different from anybody else around me. I wasn't sent to some elite private school or moved to a penthouse. So I grew into your typical Queens teenager. I smoked blunts, and I drank 40s, and one of my best friends had a baby in high school. I was a walking cliché in every way, except for the fact that I still spent every odd weekend talking with this art-collecting, croquet-playing, brilliant (if pretty intimidating) man at his mansion in the Hamptons.

When I say "talking," I actually really mean it. I don't just mean we made a little chitchat. I mean that after dinner every odd Saturday night for twenty years, he would ask me some enormous question.

He would say, "If I told you that the universe was infinite – that it had no end – how would that make you feel?" (And for that one I was, like, five years old.)

But I lived for it, really. We would go on for hours and hours. My mother would just kind of leave us to it.

Eventually she'd come back in, and she'd be like, "Are you two gonna talk about the moon and the stars all night?" That's actually what she came to call them, our moon and stars talks.

At sixteen, like all teenagers, I didn't want to be away from my friends for five minutes, let alone a whole weekend. So I called Mark, and I asked if I could bring them to the Hamptons.

Ring. "Mark speaking."

"Hi, it's Tara. Could I bring some of my friends next weekend?"

"That would be fine." Click.

He wasn't one for small talk.

But there was a problem. What the problem was, was that some of my friends had no idea about any of this. Now, that's not because I was trying to hide it. It's really because the details weren't exactly easy to slip into conversation.

They'd be like, "Hey, Tara, you want to go smoke and drink on the corner?"

"Well, I had been thinking of discussing the Hudson River School painters over dinner in Bridgehampton, but what the hell!"

Truly, I was nervous about telling them. The only thing I can kind of compare it to is like coming out: "I have to tell you something, and I hope you find it in your heart to accept me . . . *but I know a rich guy!*"

But truly, it was awkward, because I really wanted them to come, but I also didn't want them to be embarrassed, so I had to explain. So literally, here we'd be in the schoolyard, and on one side kids would be beatin' the crap out of each other – that's how we do recess in Queens – and then on the other side I'd be huddled up with my friend Lynette, trying to explain *antiquing*.

Before you know it, there we were – me, Lynette, her boyfriend, Rob – piled into the back of his red hoop-tie, flying down the highway heading from Hollis to the Hamptons. For brevity's sake let's just say that Rob is like Eminem and Lynette's like an Italian Rosie Perez. They're in the front, and I'm in the back.

Now as we're getting closer, I'm getting a little more nervous, and I'm thinking of all these things to explain.

I'm like, "Oh, shit! Did I tell you about the ketchup?"

"The what?"

"You can't put the ketchup bottle on the table."

"Where do you put it, on the floor?"

"No, listen. You gotta take the ketchup out of the bottle and you gotta put it in a little bowl with a spoon first. Remember that."

"Oh, and I didn't tell you this: there's no TV there."

"Dear God!" That always got the biggest reaction. "What does he do all day?"

It's like in Queens, the most diverse place in the world, the one thing everybody has in common is a perpetually blaring TV set. So that would lead me to have to explain what we did after dinner instead of watching TV, which was the talks – the moon and stars talks.

Like I said, I really loved them, but they weren't for the faint of heart, meaning that Mark did not care if you were some kid unaccustomed to this type of thing. He talked, and he argued with you like you were his peer, and he fully expected you to keep up. So I was not sure if my friends were gonna be into that, or if he was gonna be into them, but too late. There we were pulling in to the driveway.

The most shocking thing you first saw at Mark's place wasn't the hand-laid stone pool, or even the regulation croquet court, or the five-bedroom historic farmhouse. It was Mark himself. He was six foot ten. Again, *six foot ten*. Everyone just sort of looked at him like, *Is that a man or is that an oak tree wearing chinos?*

Likely because my friends ignored my stupid paranoia and were just themselves, the day went without a hitch. But still, that night as we finished up dinner, I couldn't help but be a little nervous again, as I knew the questions were coming.

So Mark says, "Presuming we can fix all of the societal ills right here and now, where would you begin? Go."

Really, you have to understand that nobody is asking us these kinds of questions. Maybe, sure, we're at an age where you may be starting to think bigger picture, starting to think about what you are gonna do for a living. But we come from a place where it always felt like there were only two job options: cop . . . not a cop. It was what your parents did: you took the first solid city job that came along, and you held on for dear life. And you were proud, and you did your best, and you did it forever.

Solving society's ills doesn't get you a pension. We weren't thinking about these kind of things.

So I kind of look away, I look down. But then I hear Rob say something, and I look up, and then I see Lynette kind of disagrees with that. Then I see that Mark is nodding along, and *it's on,* just like that, and not just that one time.

There would be many more moon and stars talks over the years. And it was a beautiful thing, because I think what most of us would tell you now is that those talks forever changed the way we thought of ourselves. Those talks made us think that maybe there was a little more to us than we knew.

For some of my friends, certainly not all, but for some, and definitely for me, they even made us think, *Well, shit, if (a) I like talking about these big things, and (b) the universe is infinite, then (c) there's gotta be more job options than cop.*

But really, I think that when we stood at that same crossroads as our parents had, it was this experience that gave us something that unfortunately they didn't have, and that's just the confidence to know that we had a choice.

And so here I am today, living in a whole other world: Manhattan, a whopping twenty minutes away from where I grew up.

But that is not because of fear. That's my choice.

TARA CLANCY is the author of *The Clancys of Queens.* Her writing has appeared in the *New York Times Magazine,* the *Paris Review Daily,* and the *Rumpus.* She is a Moth GrandSLAM winner, and her stories have been featured on *The Moth Radio Hour,* as well as NPR's *Snap Judgment* and *Risk!* Tara lives in New York City with her wife and two sons. www.**taraclancy**.com

THIS STORY WAS TOLD ON FEB 10, 2014 AT **COOPER UNION, NEW YORK CITY.** THE THEME OF THE EVENING WAS *FLIRTING WITH DISASTER: STORIES OF NARROW ESCAPES.* **DIRECTOR: JENIFER HIXSON.**

Ishmael Beah

<><><><><><><><><><><><><><><><><><><><><><><><><><><><><><><><><>

Unusual Normality

I came to New York City in 1998. I was seventeen. I entered the United States with just a passport in my hand, because somehow the baggage that I'd checked when I boarded the flight from Ivory Coast (which was tattered in ways unimaginable) didn't make it.

I stood there at the luggage rack, watching all these huge bags go by, and mine didn't come. This bag held all my possessions at this point: two pairs of pants and two shirts – one long-sleeved and one short. So I just started laughing, and I didn't even bother going to the lost-baggage section to claim it.

I just walked right out to meet my new adoptive mother, who was standing there with a beaming smile, waiting for me. And I explained to her what had happened, and we laughed some more.

We left and went into Manhattan, and that evening we went to Kmart. (After we had had Chinese food and a fortune cookie that said, "You're about to have new clothes.")

And I thought to myself, *What a great omen. Fresh new start to everything.*

I was coming from a country called Sierra Leone. At age eleven, a war had started in my country. At twelve I had become an orphan, because my mother, father and two brothers had been killed in that war. At thirteen I was fighting as a soldier in that same war. At sixteen, after three years of war, I'd been removed from all that and had gone through rehabilitation, where I began learning how to deal with the memories of the war.

So from this experience, I had come to the United States. To have a new home, and to live with a mother who was willing to take me into her life when most people at the time were afraid of somebody like me.

It was a chance at living again, because all I had come to know, since I was eleven, was how to survive. I didn't know how to live. All I knew, really, up until this point in my life, was struggle. This was what I had come to expect from life, and I didn't trust in happiness or any kind of normality at all.

So here I was in New York, with my new mother. We needed to step into that normality.

But we had a lot of things to deal with, and one of the most pressing ones was that I needed to get into school. You see, the visa that I had been given was a prospective-student visa. This meant that when I arrived in the United States, I had three months to get into a school. If I didn't, I would be returned to my war-torn country, Sierra Leone.

Now, when I arrived, it was in the summer, so all the schools were closed. But my mother got on the phone and called every school principal she could think of in Manhattan, and tried to get them to grant me an interview.

When I went to some of the interviews, I was immediately denied because of the following conversation:

"Do you have a report card to show that you had been in school?"

I would say, "No, but I know I have been in school."

And then my mother would interject to explain the context.

I would sit there thinking to myself, *What do these school principals think? Do they really think that when there's a war in your village or when your town is attacked, and people are gunned down in front of you, and you're running for your life, you're thinking to yourself, "You know, I must take my report card and put it in the back of my pocket."*

At some of these interviews, I was able to say some of these things, thinking that it would be funny. But the school principals didn't find it funny. I learned a new American term for what they *did* find it. They were "weirded out" by the strange sense of humour that I had about this.

So I decided that I was going to write an entrance essay about this, and the essay was simply titled "Why I Do Not Have a Report Card."

With this essay, along with exams that were given to me, I was accepted to the United Nations International School and placed in the eleventh grade.

Thus began my two years of high school and making other teenagers confused about who I was. You see, I didn't fit into any box. I didn't have the same worries about what shoes or clothes I wore. And so my teenage counterparts always wanted to find out why I was like that. Why I didn't worry about my essays or exams or things.

And of course I couldn't tell them, because I felt that they were not ready to hear the truth. What was I going to say?

During a break from class, "Hey, you know, I was a child soldier at thirteen. Let's go back to class now."

So I was silent, mostly. I didn't say much. I would just smile. And this made them more curious.

They would say to me, "You're such a weird kid."

And I would respond by saying, "No, no, no. I'm not weird. *Weird* has a negative connotation. I prefer the word *unusual*. It has a certain sophistication and gravitas to it that suits my character."

And of course when I was finished saying this, they would look at me and say, "Why don't you speak like a normal person?"

The reason I spoke like this was because of my British-African English that I'd learned, which was the only formal English that I knew. So whenever I spoke, people felt ill at ease, particularly my fellow teenagers. They thought, *What is wrong with this fellow?*

Some of them, though, didn't find it as strange. They thought maybe my English was like this because I was from some royal African family.

So throughout my high-school years, I tried to make my English less formal, so that my friends would not feel disturbed by it. (However, I did not dispute the fact that I was from some royal African family or that I was a prince. Because, you see, sometimes some stereotypes have their benefits, and I certainly took advantage of that.)

But I needed to be silent about my background, because I also felt like I was being watched. When I got into the school, some of the other parents were not very happy that somebody with my background was in school with their children. And I realised that the way I conducted myself would determine whether they would ever let another child who had been through war into such a school.

But even with all of these attitudes, and with my silence, I started making friends. To them it was sufficient that I was just some kid who lived in the East Village, who was from an African country.

And these kids were tough (they told me). Because they lived in a tough city, New York. And therefore *they* were tough.

They had been to the Bronx. They had been to Bed-Stuy. They had taken the train there. They had gotten into fights and won.

So they would say things to me like, "If you want to survive the streets of New York City, we need to teach you a few things."

And I'd be like, "Okay, sure. I'm open to learning."

And they would tell me things about how to be tough and stuff, and I would say, "Well, thank you very much. I truly appreciate this advice that you're giving me."

They were like, "No worries, our African brother. Anytime, anytime."

Truth was, I'd been to some of these places that they spoke about, these neighbourhoods, and I knew that the people who lived there didn't glorify violence the way they did. They didn't have time to pretend, because they lived in it, just like I had.

I noticed that these kids had a sort of *idea* of violence that they'd never really *lived*. They glorified it in a way, because they'd never actually experienced it at all.

When I walked with them, I observed that I paid more attention to the people who walked past us – how the person walked, which way they were coming from. I didn't take the same route twice, because I didn't want to develop a predictable path. These were all habits that were formed from my experiences, but I noticed that my new friends didn't do that at all. So I knew they were just saying these things to seem tough to me.

Now, I did enjoy listening to my new friends that I had made. I enjoyed listening to them tremendously, because I wished, when I listened to them, that the only violence I knew was the violence that I imagined. And listening to them allowed me to experience childhood in a way that I hadn't known was possible. It let me be a normal kid.

So I listened to them, and we hung out all the time, and through that I participated in what was left of my childhood. I got to be a child again with them; the only worries that we had were when we went Rollerblading without any protective gear. We took our brakes off, and sometimes we would avoid hitting an old lady by falling into a trash can on the street, and we laughed about it.

These things meant a lot to me.

After about a year of being friends with these boys, one of them decided to invite a group of us, about ten of us, to upstate New York. His family had property up there, and he said we were going there for the weekend to play a game called paintball.

I said, "Well, what is that?"

And he said, "Oh, man, you've never played paintball? You're gonna love it. It's a great game. The fellows and I, we always play it. And don't worry, we'll teach it to you, and we'll protect you. You use these balls of paint, and you shoot people," and he explained the basics of the game to me.

I said, "Okay, that sounds interesting."

And I thought, *If these guys who only pretend about violence can play it, it must not be that difficult a game.*

But of course I didn't say this. I just thought these things. So I went with them upstate to a humongous property that had trees and creeks that ran into a bigger river – this beautiful open place.

But as soon as we arrived, I began to memorise the terrain immediately, and this was from habit. I knew how many paces it took to get to the house, how many paces it took to the first tree, to the first bush, to the shed. I learned the spaces between the trees.

Overnight, while everybody was sleeping, I tried to replay some of these things in my head – to memorise the terrain. And this was all out of habit, because where I came from, in my previous life, this kind of skill set could determine whether you lived or died.

In the morning, at breakfast, they were pumped up.

Everyone was saying, "Yeah, the game is gonna be awesome today."

And so after we finished breakfast, I was introduced to the game of paintball. They showed me the weapon, how you can shoot it. And I allowed them to teach me to shoot things.

They were very macho about it. They said to me, "This is how you shoot, you aim like this."

I said, "Okay." I tried it a few times. I deliberately missed.

Then they showed me the camouflage and the combat gear and everything.

And then everybody was ready to go, and they were amped up, and all like, "Yeah, we're gonna go out! We're gonna DO THIS!!"

They decided we were going to play one-on-one. And then, after, we would play team games.

So they started painting their faces, getting into this idea of war that they knew.

I declined putting the face paint on, and I wanted to give them a hint about my past, but then I thought, *You know what? I'm going to have fun with this.*

So we went off into the bush, and when one of them shouted, "Yeah, let the war begin! I'm going to bring pain to all of you! I'm going to show you how it's done!" I thought to myself, *First rule of warfare, you never belittle your opponent.*

But I didn't say this. I went into the bushes. I already knew where to go, because I had memorised the layout of the place.

And so I would hide. I would wait for them. I would climb a tree here. I would hide under certain shrubs. And they would come rolling around, jumping, doing all kinds of things, things they'd probably seen in movies about how people act in war.

I would just wait for them. And after they were done exhausting themselves, I would come up behind them, and I would shoot the paintball at them.

This went on all day. And when we came back that night, during dinner, they talked about it.

You know: *How come you're so good? You're sure you've never played paintball before?*

I said, "No, I have never played paintball before. I'm just a quick learner, and you guys explained the game to me, and you are really great teachers. This is why I'm able to play so well."

But they said, "That can't be all."

Some of the kids' parents were there, and the kids said to them, "This guy, he comes up on you. You can't even hear him coming at all."

And I said, "Well, you know, I grew up in a village. And I used to be a hunter when I was a boy, so I know how to blend into the forest, like a chameleon. I know how to adapt to my environment."

And they looked at me and said, "You're a very strange fellow, man. But you're *badass* at paintball."

I said, "Well, thank you. Thank you very, very much."

So this went on. We never got to play the group game. We played as individuals all throughout the weekend, because they wanted to beat me, and so they started to team up with each other. I would see them doing this, and then I would come up with a kind of watered-down version of another guerrilla tactic, just to play with them.

For example, sometimes I would walk backwards and then stand where my footsteps "began" and hide. They would follow my footprints, and then I would come up behind them.

Anyway, at some point I decided that I was going to sit out the game, just so that they could enjoy it. And I saw a sense of relief on all of their faces. They were like, *Oh, well, FINALLY!*

When I returned, I told my mother about this game. And my mother, being a mother, was immediately worried. She said, "Oh, did that bring up something for you?"

And I said, "No, it didn't, absolutely."

Because I know the difference between pretend war and real war.

But it was interesting for me to observe how my friends perceived what war is.

The next day at school, these friends of mine talked about the awesome weekend of paintball we'd had. But they never said how I'd won all the games. And I said nothing at all.

They never invited me back to play paintball with them. And I didn't ask to be invited back.

I so wanted to talk to them about the war while we were playing the game. I wanted to explain certain things, but I felt that if they knew about my background, they would no longer allow me to be a child. They would see me as an adult, and I was worried that they would fear me.

My silence allowed me to experience things, to participate in my childhood, to do things I hadn't been able to do as a child.

It was only years later that they learned why I had won the game.

But I wish I had been able to tell them early on, because I wanted them to understand how lucky they were to have a mother, a father, grandparents, siblings. People who annoyed them by caring about them so much and calling them all the time to make sure they were okay.

I wanted to tell them that they were so lucky to have this naïve innocence about the world. I wanted them to understand that it was extremely lucky for them to only play *pretend* war and never have to do the real thing. And that their naïve innocence about the world was something for which I no longer had the capacity.

ISHMAEL BEAH, born in Sierra Leone, West Africa, is the *New York Times* bestselling author of *A Long Way Gone: Memoirs of a Boy Soldier* (2008) and *Radiance of Tomorrow: A Novel* (2015).
www.ishmaelbeah.com

THIS STORY WAS TOLD ON MAY 6, 2016, AT THE **BAM HARVEY THEATER, BROOKLYN.** THE THEME OF THE EVENING WAS *DON'T LOOK BACK: STORIES FROM THE TEENAGE YEARS,* PRODUCED IN CONJUNCTION WITH RADIO DIARIES WNYC'S RADIOLOVEFEST. **DIRECTOR: JENIFER HIXSON.**

Arthur Bradford

◇◇◇

The Quest for Chad

I'm kneeling on the floor of a cheap roadside motel, somewhere in western Tennessee. Next to me, leading me in prayer, is a large, middle-aged man with cerebral palsy named Ronnie Simonsen.

He says, "Bless my mother, my brothers and sisters, and my pastor back home in New Hampshire. God, bless Bob Hope and Cher . . . and all three of Charlie's Angels. Especially Jaclyn Smith."

And then Ronnie says, "And, Lord, please help us get to California quickly, where I know I'm going to meet my spiritual brother, Mr Chad Everett, the star of CBS's drama *Medical Center.*"

And here I interrupt Ron. I say, "Ron, you know, we might not meet Chad Everett. We're not sure that's going to happen."

He says, "Yeah, yeah, I know, but keep praying. Keep praying."

I first met Ronnie about eight years before that. I was working at a summer camp for people with disabilities. I was a counsellor there, and I had brought along a video camera, because I was also interested in making films.

Ronnie was drawn to that camera. He came right up to me and wanted to talk about movies and TV. He had cerebral palsy in his legs, but he also had an interesting combination of autism and obsessive-compulsive disorder. It manifested itself in this extreme fascination with television and movie stars from the 1970s, which is when he was a kid.

He spent most of his childhood in hospitals, and he became particularly obsessed with the people who would play doctors on television. He took comfort in their calm voices.

And there was one man, above all, who he held as sort of like a god, and that was Chad Everett, who played Dr Joe Gannon on CBS's *Medical Center*.

I really liked Ron. He was fun. He was great on camera – he loved to be on camera. We made lots of videos together at the camp.

Some of the most popular videos were these newscasts we would do. (We made our own news show.) Ronnie was fantastic at that, especially when we could go downtown, and he would interview people on the street. He was this large man, and when he would talk to people, he couldn't stand up for too long, so he would lean on them for balance while he was asking them questions. And he would get them to do skits. He had this real ability to bring people out.

These films that we made, they had kind of developed this underground popularity. Eventually I was able to get some funding to make a film outside the camp. The idea was, we were going to drive across country with five people with disabilities from this summer camp.

We were going to go from their houses in New England all the way to Los Angeles, California. Everyone on the trip had their own hopes and dreams for going to California, a place they'd never been. But Ronnie's dreams overshadowed everybody else's.

To him, California was the Holy Land. It was the place where he was destined to meet Mr Chad Everett, his spiritual brother. It was his biggest dream. (He told everybody, "It's my biggest dream.")

He took this biggest-dream mission very, very seriously. It kind of stressed him out. He had this skin condition called psoriasis, and he would get these rashes on his arms when he got stressed out, and he would itch at them. And I felt like this whole situation was mainly my responsibility as the director of this ridiculous film, and I decided I would be Ronnie's roommate across the country.

So every night, in these hotels, I would help Ronnie apply the medication to his rashes, and then we would say a prayer. And that's how I ended up in this hotel room in Tennessee, praying with Ronnie Simonsen.

As Ronnie prays, I say my own little prayer. I'm not a very religious person. I had never really prayed much before. I'm twenty-nine years old, but this is the first time I pray in earnest. I say, *Please, help us get to California safely. And please, when we get there, give me some guidance. Help me to solve this mess that we're going to have when we get to California.*

Because I have this secret that I haven't shared with Ron. I probably should have shared it with him, but I just can't.

I'd gotten in touch with Chad Everett's agent before we went on the trip, and I'd asked if we could set up a meeting between these two people. I knew it was going to be a fantastic moment on film.

But his agent made me understand that Chad Everett was a very busy man, and that he wasn't going to have time for something like that. In fact, he didn't really wanna encourage his obsessive fans.

I probably should have told Ronnie that, but he didn't take disappointment very well.

I'd helped Ronnie write letters to numerous celebrities over the years, and we had written to Chad Everett. One year Ronnie had called me up. He was so excited, 'cause he got this head shot in the mail. It was a smiling picture of Chad Everett. Ronnie memorised every word that Chad Everett had signed on this picture.

It said, "To Ron, life's not meant to be lived in reruns. Watch me in the new show *Love Boat*! Walk in the light, Chad Everett."

And so all the way across the country, as we were driving from across Texas to the Grand Canyon, Ronnie would go over the contents of that letter with me.

He would say, "What does that mean, 'life's not meant to be lived in reruns?' And what does that mean, to 'walk in the light'? I'm walking in the light, right?"

And I would say, "Yeah, Ron, you're walking in the light."

When we reach California, it's a wonderful moment. We all go swimming in the ocean, and everybody's really happy. Except for, of course, Ron. Because he's on a higher mission.

Ron and I come to this agreement: everyone else involved with the film is going to fly home, and he and I are going to spend a few more days in Los Angeles.

So everyone goes home, and Ronnie and I end up in this hotel room together, putting on his psoriasis medicine. And I have no plan at all.

Along the trip, someone, who I believe was very well-meaning, had said to Ronnie, "Hey, Ronnie. You shouldn't be so self-conscious."

And Ronnie, for about the 150th time that trip, asked me, "What does that mean, self-conscious?"

I tell him, "Well, Ronnie, to be self-conscious, that means to worry about yourself too much."

Then he says, also for the 150th time, "I'm not being self-conscious right now, am I?"

And I'm kind of fed up at this point. I just wanna say, "You know, by definition, you asking me that question? That means you're being self-conscious, right?"

But I don't say that. I know better.

"No, Ronnie. You're not being self-conscious at all."

On our last day in California, we hatch a plan out of desperation. We go to this town near Malibu, out in the hills, where Ronnie had heard that Chad Everett lived. We go to a shopping center, and Ronnie gets really excited because he interviews this kid who apparently had bagged Chad Everett's groceries. Then someone else tells us that they know the street that Chad Everett lives on.

Ronnie says, "I just wanna see what his house looks like."

So we go up, and it's a gated community. And then I find myself sneaking past as the guard's not looking, and we get to what we think is his house.

Ronnie says, "I just wanna take a picture in front of his house."

So Ronnie gets out, and it's not until we're hiding in the bushes, and we've been there for over an hour, that I realise that this is a terrible idea. Why are we here? What did I think was going to happen? I had this crazy idea that Chad Everett would see Ronnie, and he would under- stand that this was someone that he should get to know.

But of course if Chad Everett walked out of that house, Ronnie was going to rush towards him, and someone was going to call the police. It was going to be a disaster.

So it was a certain sense of relief that I felt when a security guard came up and told us that we had to leave.

So we did leave. And that film ends with Ronnie kiss- ing Chad Everett's star on the Hollywood Walk of Fame.

It's a good ending, but of course it's not the ending that Ronnie and I wanted for that film.

As we took the film to film festivals around the country, Ronnie became a little bit of a celebrity, and it was funny, because that didn't mean anything to him, to be a celebrity himself. He would ask anybody in the audience at the festivals if maybe they knew a way to get this film into Chad Everett's hands. That's all he cared about.

Throughout that year Ronnie would call me up and he'd say, "You need to send a tape to this person, because they might know Chad Everett's daughter."

I was starting to get kind of annoyed, to be honest. I was like, *Man, we went all the way to California. Why can't he just drop this whole thing?*

And I was kind of annoyed with myself, too, because I had become tethered to this dream of Ronnie's.

On top of that, I had a version of the dream that was a nightmare for me, which was this: that Ronnie would somehow meet Chad Everett . . . and I wouldn't be there.

That kept me up at night. If Ronnie were to meet him, and I wasn't there, I didn't think I could live with myself. I honestly felt that way. I was in this state.

Then one day I got a phone call. There was a deep voice on the other end of the line, and it said, "Hello, this is Chad Everett."

I said, "No it's not."

And he said, "Yes it is." And it *was* Chad Everett. He had seen our film, and he liked it. He liked it a lot. In fact, he agreed that if we could get Ronnie to California, he would meet Ronnie. And he would do an interview with him.

I hung up the phone, and I drove three hours to Ronnie's house, and I said, "Ronnie, Chad Everett saw the film, and he wants to meet you."

And Ronnie said, "Oh, boy!!!"

For two weeks straight, Ronnie couldn't sleep. All he could do was call me up and talk about exactly what was going to happen.

Eventually we got on a plane and we flew out to California. The whole way, Ronnie's clapping his hands and rocking back and forth. Everyone he meets, he tells them that he's going to achieve his biggest dream – he's going to meet Chad Everett.

I said, "We're going to do this on a beach, because it's wide open. It's a big, wide-open space, and there's lots of room."

I think this is a good plan until we get to the beach, and I'm walking with Ron on the sand. At this point Ronnie's legs are really kind of giving out, and he can hardly walk on solid ground without assistance.

And he can't even stand up on the sand.

I realised it was a bad idea, to do this on a beach. We sit him down on a beach chair, and I'm trying to think, *Where else could we do this?* – when this convertible pulls up, and the license plate says SIR CHAD.

Down at the other end of the beach, this handsome older man steps out, and he starts walking across the beach. He's a hundred yards away, and Ronnie spots him.

He yells, "Is that Chad Everett?"

And Chad Everett yells back, "Yes it is! You betcha!"

And Ronnie hoists himself up out of this chair, and he starts running across the beach. He's running. I've never seen Ronnie run *ever* in my life. And he is running across the beach. He's kicking up the sand.

He's going, "Chad Everett! Chad Everett!"

I think he's going to fall and wipe out, and Chad Everett's going, "Slow down! Slow down! Slow down!"

Ronnie's running towards him, and he looks like a little boy. He does. He looks like a little boy.

And when he reaches Chad Everett, he throws his arms around him, and he says, "Chad, I'm so happy to see you!"

They have a wonderful time. They do skits together on the beach. Ronnie interviews him. And they say a prayer. It's a wonderful meeting.

We take the red-eye home that night, and Ronnie's exhausted. He's a man who hasn't slept for weeks.

He says to me, "Well, Arthur, we did it." And then he finally goes to sleep.

After that trip I didn't hear from Ronnie for quite a while, and that was strange, because he would call me so often. When I finally did hear from Ron, he had some bad news. He had been diagnosed with leukaemia, and his mother told me privately that he was given six months to live.

Ron said to me, "Look, I know that Chad Everett's a really busy man. But do you think you could tell him about this?"

I said, "Sure, Ron. I can let him know."

So I did. I told Chad Everett.

And an amazing thing happened then. Chad Everett started calling Ronnie every Sunday, and they would talk. Without fail, he called Ronnie every Sunday.

And Ronnie outlived that diagnosis by months and months. He lived for over two years. In fact, he went back to California and saw Chad and had a party to celebrate.

Eventually Ronnie did die of that disease. And after his death, I thought a lot about the lessons I had learned from Ronnie Simonsen. About the importance of having a biggest dream, no matter how silly it is.

But I often wondered, *Did I spend too much time chasing this other person's dream, that wasn't really my dream?*

Then, recently, we were putting together a compilation of tapes that we'd made with Ronnie.

The editor called me up and said, "Hey, I've got this audio track I want you to hear. I think you'll find it funny." So he plays it for me, and it's this person breathing really hard. It sounds like it's someone who's going up the stairs or really out of breath. And then I hear my voice going, "Oh, my God. Oh, my God. Oh, my God."

It's the audio track from my camera as I'm filming Ronnie running towards Chad Everett. I'd never heard that. I'd always heard Ronnie's mic, not my mic. And I'm saying, "Oh, my God, oh, my God." And as they hug, I swear, you can almost hear my heart beating out of my chest. I'm so excited by this meeting.

If you had asked me ten years ago, "What's your biggest dream?" It would *not* have been "to meet the star of CBS's *Medical Center*." But through Ron that had become my dream. And I've always wanted to thank Ron for sharing that with me and for making it come true.

ARTHUR BRADFORD is an O. Henry Award-winning writer and Emmy-nominated filmmaker. He is the author of *Dogwalker* (2002) and *Turtleface* (2015), and creator and director of *How's Your News?*, which features a team of news reporters with mental disabilities. He is currently shooting a documentary about Matt Stone and Trey Parker, creators of *South Park* and *The Book of Mormon*. He lives in Portland, Oregon, and works with incarcerated youth.

THIS STORY WAS TOLD ON JULY 10, 2013, AT THE **PLAYERS, NEW YORK CITY.**
THE THEME OF THE EVENING WAS *PULLING FOCUS: STORIES OF INSIGHT.*
DIRECTOR: JENIFER HIXSON.

Kate Braestrup

◇◇

The House of Mourning

Nina's mother came up to me, and she said, "Chaplain, I think I have a problem. It's Nina. She says she wants to go and see Andy, her cousin."

Well, I looked over at Nina, who was hanging by her knees from the swing set in her backyard, little pigtails brushing the ground.

I said, "How old is Nina, again?"

And her mom said, "Five."

"Wow."

I should probably mention that cousin Andy was dead. Which isn't the unusual part.

I've been chaplain to the Maine Warden Service for about thirteen years now. And in Maine, game wardens enforce fish and wildlife law. But they also respond to a whole variety of outdoor calamities: snowmobile accidents, freshwater drownings, all-terrain-vehicle accidents. The occasional alfresco homicide or suicide. And when they think the outcome is likely to be fatal, they ask their chaplain to go along.

I also teach baby game wardens in the academy about how to support bereaved people, which they're often called upon to do. The example I usually use for them is personal.

My first husband, Drew, was a state trooper. And he was killed in the line of duty in 1996. As soon as I was told that he was dead – he died instantly when his cruiser was T-boned by a truck – as soon as I was told that fact, I knew I wanted to go see him and take care of him.

So I told the funeral director that. And the funeral director responded using a special voice that I think funeral directors learn in funeral-parlour school.

He said, "Yes. I understand." And then he went back to the funeral parlour, and he called the Maine State Police.

He said, "I think you should know that your trooper's widow wants to see and dress and take care of the body herself."

And the state police freaked out.

So all night long, phone calls were ricocheting back and forth across Maine between the state police command staff and the funeral parlour and Tom, the trooper who had been specifically assigned to manage me.

In the morning Tom arrived, and he said, "Kate, we're gonna let you do this thing. But you have to take me with you. And we're going to bring Sergeant Drake and Sergeant Cunningham along as well."

My mom said, "I'll go, too." Good ol' Mom.

And Tom said, "Because if we don't like what we see, we're going to take you out." And I pictured three troopers all drawing their sidearms and taking aim in the funeral parlour.

I said, "I think it's gonna be okay."

Mom was reassuring. She said, "You know, she grew up on a farm. She's used to dead things."

I had to fake absolute confidence in this. I didn't have absolute confidence. Because I'd never done this before. But I faked it. I took my mother by the hand, and she and I, surrounded by troopers, did a weird sort of perp walk up the street to the funeral parlour, where we were welcomed by the funeral director in his "special" voice. And they were all watching me as I walked into this cool room where Drew's body lay.

And he was dead. But that's all. He was just dead.

And it was okay. *I* was okay.

So the troopers and my mother and the funeral director all left. And I had about twenty minutes alone with my husband's body. Then they all came back, and we got him dressed in his Class-A uniform – his dress uniform.

And it was hard. (I mean, if you've ever tried to get someone into a Class-A uniform when they're not cooperating, you know what I mean.)

But it was fine. Actually, it was better than fine. It was actually kind of great. It was beautiful and sad and funny, and it was okay.

But there are baby game wardens who need a less personal, more biblical example. So I remind them that Mary Magdalene went to see and touch and anoint the body of Jesus, and she didn't have to overcome the protective scepticism of the disciples to do that. When she got to the tomb and found it empty, she didn't have to justify her distress at finding the body gone.

Well, nowadays we're persuaded that it's the presence of the body, not its absence, that is most distressing. But in my experience – and I have a lot of experience by now – people are far more likely to regret not having seen the body than they are to wish they hadn't.

So in the warden service, we're actually training our wardens to be pretty proactive about this. To really try to make space within our operations for the family to be with the body. Give them a moment where all the strangers and officials get out of the way and let them take care of their own.

And let me tell you, the mourners are gorgeous. They're gorgeous. They are brave and tender. A mother will smooth the hair back from her drowned son's forehead, and the dad will hold his hand. A spouse will bring a flower and put it on his breast and murmur endearments. They're beautiful.

But okay. Nina was five. She was five.

And her cousin, her best friend Andy . . . was *four*.

Nina – she didn't grow up on a farm. Maybe there's a dead goldfish in her background somewhere. But if you're five, there's not a lot of background to work with.

Suffer the little children to come unto me. That was this biblical phrase that kept going around in my head. Although, as the wardens and I kept assuring each other, the one good thing you could say about Andy's death was that he didn't suffer. He was killed instantly when an all-terrain vehicle driven by a neighbour rolled over on him.

When we had cleared the scene that day, they had taken his body to a funeral parlour, and that was where Nina wanted to go, to visit him.

"We want to protect her," her dad said.

But her mom kept saying, "I know, but she's so sure."

And finally I said, "You know, you're her parents. You know her. You know what's right for her much better than I do. But I do believe it would be okay. I believe it would not hurt her more to see him."

So three days later, I went back up to this little town, because Andy's family had asked me to preside over the service. I got to the church a little early, and Nina's mom was there, and she was arranging stuff on the altar table – photographs and Tonka trucks and teddy bears, flowers.

She said, "I have to leave room for the box containing his ashes, but it's not a very big box."

I said, "So what did you do about Nina? Did Nina go see Andy?"

"Let me tell you," Nina's mom said.

"Got in the car, drove her to the funeral parlour. Soon as we pull in, Nina's out of the car, striding across the parking lot. We had to scramble to keep up with her.

"She goes in through the front door, past the funeral-parlour guy. And we stopped her at the door of the cool room where Andy's little body lay.

"We said, 'Nina, we just want to make sure that you understand that Andy's not gonna be able to talk to you.'

"'Yup,' said Nina.

"'Well, and you understand, he's not gonna move or get up.'

"'Yeah, yeah.'"

And she opened the door, and in she went, and she walked right up to the dais where Andy's body lay, covered by a quilt that his mom had made for him when he was a baby.

She walked right up to him, and she walked all the way around the dais, putting her hands on him to make sure he was all there. Then she put her head down on his chest and talked to him.

After about ten minutes of this, her parents were awash in tears, and they'd kind of had enough, so they said, "Nina, you ready to go?"

"No. I'll tell you when I am."

So she sang him a song, and she put his Fisher-Price plastic telescope in his hand, so that he could see anyone he wanted to see from heaven. And then she was okay, and she was done.

She said, "But he's not gonna be getting up again, so I have to tuck him in." So she walked all the way around the dais again, tucking in the quilt.

And then she put her hand on him and said, "I love you, Andy Dandy. Good-bye."

You can trust a human being with grief. That's what I tell the wardens.

I tell them, "Just walk fearlessly into the house of mourning, for grief is just love squaring up to its oldest enemy. And after all these mortal human years, love is up to the challenge."

But I don't have to fake confidence in this anymore, because I have Nina. And now, with the gracious permission of Nina's family, so do you.

KATE BRAESTRUP spent her childhood in Algiers, New York City, Paris and Bangkok, as the daughter of a foreign correspondent. She published a novel, *Onion*, in 1990, before entering the Bangor Theological Seminary. Since 2001 she has served as chaplain to the Maine Warden Service, and has published three bestselling memoirs – *Here If You Need Me* (2008), *Marriage and Other Acts of Charity* (2011) and *Anchor & Flares* (2016) – and *Beginner's Grace: Bringing Prayer to Life* (2011). She is married to artist Simon van der Ven and between them they have six children. **www.katebraestrup.com**

THIS STORY WAS TOLD ON MAY 30, 2015, AT THE **STATE THEATRE, PORTLAND**, MAINE. THE THEME OF THE EVENING WAS *INTO THE WILD: STORIES OF STRANGE LANDS*. **DIRECTOR: CATHERINE BURNS.**

Suzi Ronson

The Girl from Beckenham

I was born a few years after World War II and lived with my parents in a nice house in a suburb southeast of London – Bromley, in Kent. My parents got married after the war simply because that's what everybody did. The government gave a generous allowance for children; we used to get free milk and great lunches at school. Both my parents worked: my father was a long-distance lorry driver, delivering meat, and my mother was an assistant at a dress shop in Beckenham. I don't think my parents expected too much from me. I think they thought I would, you know, leave school, grow up, get a job, possibly get married, and live 'round the corner.

Well, the Swinging Sixties in London changed all of that. It was a great time to be a teenager in London. We had the best music – the Beatles and the Rolling Stones; we had the best fashion – the miniskirt – and we had the pill. The model of the day was Twiggy. She was a tall, slim thing with a flat chest and flat hair. I was challenged. I mean I was completely out of style. I had this thick, frizzy hair I couldn't do anything with, and even thicker glasses, and a waist and hips. I wasn't good at school, I didn't like school, and by the time I was fifteen, I'd had enough.

So I left school and enrolled in the Evelyn Paget College of Hair and Beauty in Bromley. I wouldn't say that hairdressing was my dream job, but with my education it was my best option, and as it turns out I was quite good at it. So at the end of my course, I was transferred to the flagship salon, Evelyn Paget's in Beckenham.

It was here I met Mrs Jones. Mrs Jones was my quarter-to-three shampoo and set on a Thursday afternoon. Once in a while, she'd have a trim, and every now and again a chocolate-kiss rinse. As I'm doing her hair she would talk to me about her son, David.

She would say, "He was such an artistic child," and "He's a singer in a band."

And she was so proud of him, you know? I would nod and smile and listen, as you do, and it wasn't until she mentioned "Space Oddity" that my ears kind of pricked up. I said, "'Space Oddity'?"

She said, "Yes."

I said, "Well I've heard that song on the radio." It was a hit.

I said, "Are we talking about *David Bowie*?"

"Yes," she said, "I'm his mum."

Well, I was surprised about that. There was a buzz about David in Beckenham. He played the local pub, the Three Tuns – albeit folk music – but he'd had the hit "Space Oddity." It had been a while ago, so I thought he might have been a one-hit wonder.

The first time I actually saw David, he's walking down Beckenham High Street in a dress, and he's with this girl who had these skinny black pants on. I met the girl – Mrs Jones brought her into the salon. It turned out it was Angie, David's wife.

Well, I liked her immediately. She was so cool and confident, and she looked so great – she certainly didn't shop in Beckenham. She talked to me a little bit about her life. She did lights for David's shows, and they would hang out all night in London at the clubs and just have the best time. It all sounded so glamorous.

The next time I saw her, she was coming in for an appointment. It was Christmas week. Well, every self-respecting salon is full Christmas week.

I took her to one side, and said, "I can't do your hair here, but here's my telephone number, give me a call. I'll come to your house."

Off I went to Haddon Hall. It was about a mile out of town, one of those huge mansions. It was divided into flats. David and Angie had the middle floor.

It wasn't the sheer size of the place that was over-whelming, it was the way it was decorated: a midnight blue carpet, midnight blue walls, and a silver ceiling. There wasn't much furniture: a couch, a couple of chairs, a long, low coffee table, tons of album covers all over the place, and a guitar in the corner.

David and Angie were sitting in the middle of a bay window discussing the merits of cutting his hair short – he had this long, blond, wavy hair at the time. They asked me my opinion.

I said, "Well, no one's got short hair" – because nobody did. "You would be the first."

He stood up and walked over and showed me this photograph in a magazine. It was of a Kansai Yamamoto model with short, red, spiky hair.

He said to me, "Can you do that?"

As I'm saying yes, I'm thinking to myself, *That's a little weird. It's a woman's hairstyle, and how am I going to actually do this?*

Inside, however, I'm excited – this is a chance to be very creative. He was rock-star thin, white skin, a long neck, a great face – if I could pull it off, it would look fantastic!

Well, it took me about a half an hour to cut, and when I finished, his hair didn't stand up. It kind of flopped.

I looked at David, and he's panicking, and I'm not feeling too bright, and I said to him, "Listen, David, the second we tint your hair, the colour will change the texture and it will stand up." I prayed I was right.

I found the colour, Schwarzkopf "Red Hot Red" with 30 volume peroxide to give it a bit of lift. There was no product in those days, nothing to help me make it stand up. So I used GARD. GARD was an anti-dandruff treatment that I used to use on the old girls at the salon – it set hair like stone.

The second David saw himself in the mirror with that short, red, spiky hair, all doubts disappeared. Angie and I looked at him in awe, he looked so good.

A huge wave of relief washed over me: I'd done it, you know, I'd done it! I hadn't known it was going to work until I felt that texture changing in my hands as I was drying it, and it stood up.

He looked *amazing*.

I started gathering my things together to leave, and Angie said, "Oh, how much do we owe you?"

I think I said, "Two pounds, please."

I left, and a week or so later Angie called me and said, "You know, the band are playing in London, why don't you come and see them?"

I said, "Well, I'd love to."

It was at a college, so I went there, and I'm still not quite sure what to expect, you know? I walked in, and the place is sold out – it's completely full – and I stood in the audience, and the lights went down, and some music came on, and it was a real *Oh, my God* moment for me.

When the band came on the stage, David was in full makeup – his red hair blazing in the lights. He'd turned himself into Ziggy Stardust. The band were all in costumes that looked like curtain material: flat pastel velvet tucked into lace-up boots. They looked incredible. And when they played, the place rocked, it was so good – so unbelievably good.

I went home thinking to myself, *Oh, my God, that wasn't folk music!* I didn't know what to expect, but it wasn't that.

Well, Angie called the next day and said, "Did you like it, and will you come up to Haddon Hall again?" And off I went. I met Freddie Burretti. Freddie Burretti was a friend of David and helped design the costumes. He was so fabulous. He minced, and lisped, and was just gorgeous. I was fascinated with Freddie. I'd never met a gay man before. Sometime during that evening, David leaned over and kissed Freddie full on the lips. I didn't know which way to look, you know?

I looked at Angie, and she's laughing, and suddenly I felt completely out of my depth. I wasn't like these people. I didn't know who Nietzsche was. I'd never heard of Lou Reed and the Velvet Underground or Andy Warhol. I'd certainly never seen two guys kissing before. I was from Beckenham!

Later that evening, Angie takes me to one side and she says, "You know, David and I have been speaking, and we'd like you to come and work for us full-time. Come on the road. Go up to the MainMan offices, and sort out your wages, and come and work with us."

Off I went to the MainMan offices, heart in hand. I met David's manager, Tony Defries, and by the end of the afternoon I'd got the job. It's not till I'm driving home, I'm realising, *My life's going to really change. I'm going on the road with a rock and roll band!* I was so excited.

I went down to Evelyn Paget's the next day to give in my notice to my boss, and he looked at me and said, "You know, Suzanne, you should think twice before giving up a well-paying, secure job."

I said, "Yeah, I have."

Of course, after that my confidence knew no bounds. I took the drummer and turned him into a blond Ziggy, and chopped Trevor's hair off and made it spiky on top with silver sideburns. The only holdout was Mick Ronson, the guitar player – he didn't want to look like David.

I started doing shows with them. We did *Top of the Pops* – David played "Starman," and when he draped his arm around Mick Ronson during the chorus, I think it shook Britain to its core. Nobody did stuff like that in those days, they just didn't. (It certainly shook my parents.)

David was always thinking of the next thing to do, he was always very ambitious, and he wanted to do rock and roll theatre. So we hired a theatre in London, in Finsbury Park, and he built a set – scaffolding and dry ice and lights – and it was amazing. We were all working eighteen hours a day to put this show together, and he was saying, "Don't talk to anybody, don't tell anybody what it's about, no recording equipment, no cameras."

Of course, the more you make of these things, the more interesting it becomes, and we opened to a fanfare of press. All the celebs came.

Kids were coming with Ziggy haircuts at that point, and it was a great show. I think the only person that didn't like it was Elton John. He walked out halfway through, saying, "This isn't rock and roll."

But it *was* rock and roll, because we were then running up and down England in buses, and shows were being added, the gigs were getting bigger, and everything was selling out. And I was with David and the boys all the time during this period, doing everybody's hair, looking after the costumes, doing the dry cleaning, making sure everything was right.

There were many costume changes, so David would come to the side of the wings, and I would be standing there with a glass of red wine, a Gitane cigarette, and while Mick is wailing ten feet from me, I'm changing David's clothes. We got quite good at it.

We went to America and stayed in the Plaza in New York. It was an amazing hotel.

We had a great advanced team. Cherry Vanilla, who's a famous groupie, and Leee Black Childers, who was a Warhol actor. They would go to the next town, go to the gay clubs, and create fervour. It was really a good idea, because it got the kids to the gigs.

I met Iggy Pop in California. We stayed at the Beverly Hills Hotel, and Iggy wanted me to dye his hair blue, and I obliged. I said to him, "You know, you might want to wash that a couple of times before going back in the pool."

Of course he paid me no mind, and by the end of the afternoon there was a blue streak from one end to the other of the Beverly Hills Hotel pool. (I think he was asked to leave after that.)

We went to Japan, and I met Kansai Yamamoto, and I picked up some more wonderful costumes for David. It was exciting. Suddenly I was cool: the girl with the thick hair and the thicker glasses was in a world where everybody wanted to be.

I went back to Beckenham, and I walked up and down the High Street, looked through Evelyn Paget's windows – my God, it looked so small, I was so glad I wasn't there.

Nothing had changed in Beckenham, nothing had changed at home, but I was so changed, I was a million miles from here.

The last show that David ever did as Ziggy Stardust was at Hammersmith Odeon in July 1973, and he just stood on the front of the stage and said, "This is the last show we're ever going to do." Then he played "Rock 'n' Roll Suicide."

I was sad to say good-bye to Ziggy, I think we were all sad to say good-bye to Ziggy, but I didn't go home. I went to Italy and fell in love with a guitar player and moved to London with him.

I'm so grateful for my luck. I'm grateful I met Mrs Jones and Angie, grateful I gave Angie that telephone number – otherwise somebody else might have been living my life. Thrilled that I met and married the late, great Mick Ronson and had a lovely daughter with him.

And, of course, I'm so grateful to David. He took a chance on me, changed my life completely. My haircut's on British currency now – the Brixton ten-pound note. Now, who would have thought I could have done that?

SUZI RONSON has worked as a household manager, music producer, and consultant for a number of well-heeled individuals in New York City, the Hamptons, Florida and the British Virgin Islands. She is a singer-songwriter who performs for friends, and a horse enthusiast. Currently, she lives in the West Village of New York City, while her daughter and the rest of her family live in London. She swears she'll go back one day.

THIS STORY WAS TOLD ON APRIL 11, 2016, AT THE **UNION CHAPEL, LONDON**. THE THEME OF THE EVENING WAS *COMING HOME*. **DIRECTOR: MEG BOWLES**.

Christof Koch

◇◇

God, Death and Francis Crick

It was the 1990s, and I was course director at the Marine Biological Lab in Woods Hole on Cape Cod, directing a class on how computers can be used to learn about the brain.

We were celebrating with a boisterous evening – a big dinner party and a live rock and roll band. And I'd really indulged in dancing and drinking.

But then I grew restless. I'd spent my previous evenings reading the German philosopher Friedrich Nietzsche writing about how modernity had killed God, divine putrefaction, and how we're all God's gravediggers. This had reawakened this long-simmering conflict I'd had between my religious upbringing and my profession as a scientist.

So I left the party, and I wandered off through the forest to the beach. When I arrived at the beach, there was a crescent moon, which was partly obscured by the clouds that were being chased across the sky by the wind, which had picked up.

The storm had also driven the white of the waves towards the land, and it was this desolate, empty beach with just a couple of boulders. In the background there were trees, and they were swaying – very menacing.

And I went through this existential crisis, and I shouted out to the sky, *"Gott, wo bist Du?"*

See, God speaks German, of course.

I was shouting for God to reveal himself. Here I was, trying for many years to desperately believe in him, but I never had a sign of his existence. So I was debating with him, in what was a very one-sided debate.

I wanted him to show himself. I needed a booming voice from the sky. I wanted a burning bush. I wanted some *sign*. And because I had drunk a lot, I was increasingly insistent and bellicose, shouting into the wind at the top of my voice for God to show himself.

Then suddenly the earth erupted in front of me, and there was this bright light that dazzled me. A very angry form materialised right in front of me.

And it was shrieking and yelling, "Get the fuck off this beach!"

God had metamorphosed into an angry camper who was trying to sleep there. I hadn't noticed him before, and I'd awakened him.

I grew up happy, raised by my parents in the best liberal Catholic tradition, where, by and large, science – including evolution by natural selection – was accepted as explaining the facts of the world.

I was an altar boy. I learned to say the prayers in Latin, and I loved the Masses and the passions and the requiems of Orlande de Lassus, Verdi and Bach.

When I was a teenager, my dad gave me a five-inch reflector telescope, and I still very viscerally remember the night when I – on the top of my house – calculated where the planet Uranus should be in the sky.

I pointed the telescope at the azimuth and the elevation, and *right there* it appeared, and I remember this incredible feeling of elation. What a terrific confirmation of order in the cosmos. I felt this lawful universe that I found myself in, where I could actually compute things like the position of this blue planet that gently drifted into view.

Over the years I began to reject a lot of the things that the Catholic Church told me. I was taught one set of values by my parents and by my Jesuit teachers, but I heard the beat of a very different drummer in books, lectures and the laboratory.

I had one explanation for things in the world for Sunday, and then I had another explanation for the rest of the week. There was a sacred explanation, and there was this profane explanation.

On the one hand, I was told my life was given meaning by putting it in the context of the large scale: there's this large creation of God, and I'm just a puny part of it. On the other hand, science actually explained facts about the real universe I found myself in. And so for many decades, I had this profound split of reality.

And then I met Francis Crick. I first encountered Francis under an apple tree doing what he loved best, which was discussing biology. Francis Crick was the physical chemist who together with James Watson discovered the double-helical structure of the molecule of heredity, DNA, the discovery for which he was given the Nobel Prize.

It was really to him and his guiding intellect that the field of molecular biology looked for guidance in the giddy race to discover the universal code of life. And when that goal was achieved in the late sixties, he shifted his interest from molecular biology to trying to understand how consciousness arises out of the physical brain.

That's when I encountered Francis, and we grew quite close and fond of each other. We worked together for close to two decades. We published two books. We wrote two dozen papers, and he dedicated his last book to me.

Francis also epitomised the historical animosity between religion and science. This grew legendary in 1961, when Francis resigned from Churchill College at Cambridge University in England to protest plans to add a chapel to the college grounds. Francis felt that a new college dedicated to science and mathematics and engineering was no place for superstition.

Winston Churchill, in whose name the college had been founded after the war, tried to appease Francis, and wrote him a letter pointing out that the financial means for the construction of the chapel would be raised entirely by private means. It would be open to people of any faith, and nobody would be forced to attend.

Francis replied by return post, proposing the construction of a brothel – a bordello. The construction of the bordello would be financed entirely by private means. It would be open to all men, no matter what their religious conviction, and no man would be forced to attend. Included in his letter was a check for a down payment.

So ended the correspondence between the two great men.

By the time I knew Francis, his animosity vis-à-vis religion had become muted. Although he knew I was raised Catholic, and I sporadically attended Mass, he never probed. I think he was a kind man, and he wanted to spare me the embarrassment of groping for an explanation – especially since my belief didn't interfere with our quest to understand how the conscious mind arises out of the brain within an entirely natural framework.

For emotional reasons I wasn't ready to give up my faith, but I was afraid that his searing intellect couldn't be matched by anything I could say to explain why I believed certain things.

Many years into our collaboration, when I visited him in San Diego, where he lived, he told me in a very matter-of-fact tone that his colon cancer – he had a previous bout with colon cancer – had probably returned. He was expecting a call from his oncologist later on that day to discuss the results of some tests they'd run.

I was actually with him in the study – that's how we worked, in his study at home – when the call came confirming that the cancer had indeed returned with a vengeance. He put down the phone and stared off into space for a minute or two, and then he returned to our conversation about brains.

At lunch he discussed his diagnosis with his wife, talking about what needed to be done to accommodate him. But for the rest of the day, we worked.

That was it. There was no doom and gloom. There was no gnashing of teeth. There were no tears. It impressed me immensely, this living embodiment of an ancient stoic dictum: *accept what you can't change.*

A couple of months later, when again I visited him, we went, as usual, through his large correspondence pertaining to consciousness. There was a personal letter from a famous British philosopher confessing to Francis his abject fear when faced with the idea of his own mortality.

The philosopher wrote, "I feel like an animal cornered, absolutely terrified, panicky, unable to think clearly when contemplating my own demise."

I finally found the strength to ask him, apropos that letter, "Francis, how do you feel about your diagnosis?" (Studiously avoiding any mention of the word *death*.)

Here again he was very much down-to-earth. He said something like, "Everything that has a beginning must have an end. Those are the facts. I don't like them, but I've accepted them, and I will not take any heroic measures to prolong my life beyond the inevitable. I'm resolved to live my life out with intact mind."

And so he did. Over the next two years, as the cancer weakened his body, but never his spirit, we continued to write. We finished my book. I was just immensely impressed by how he could deal with this. I, of course, reflected on my own future demise, and whether I would be able to have this calmness, this composure, to meet my own end.

When he was suffering from the debilitating effect of chemotherapy, I overheard him one day on the phone talking with somebody who was trying to convince him to sign off on the construction of a bobblehead of him. (Because Francis Crick is a very famous figure, they wanted to construct a bobblehead doll of him.)

At some point I heard him put down the phone. He shuffled past me on the way to the bathroom. When he returned several minutes later to resume the conversation, he just sort of dryly remarked to me in passing, "Well, now I can truly say this idea made me throw up."

Then one day he called me to say, "Christof, the corrections to our paper we're working on – they're going to be delayed. I have to go to the hospital for a couple of days, but don't worry."

In the hospital he continued to dictate corrections to this paper to his assistant. Two days later he passed away, and his wife, Odile, told me how on his deathbed he had this hallucinatory conversation with me involving neurons and their connection to consciousness.

A scientist literally to his last breath.

Given the forty-year age difference, we fell into this very natural father/son relationship. We became very close intellectual companions, and he became my hero for the unflinching way he dealt with mortality and aging.

With a view towards the inevitable, he gave me a huge life-size portrait of himself sitting in a wicker chair, gazing out at me with a twinkle in his eyes, signed, "For Christof – Francis – keeping an eye on you."

And so it does today in my office.

I've never had another encounter with God, nor do I expect to, for the God I now believe in is much closer to Spinoza's God than the God of Michelangelo's painting or the God of the Old Testament.

I'm sort of saddened by the loss of my belief in religion. It's like leaving forever the comfort of your childhood home, suffused with the warm glows and fond memories. But I do believe we all have to grow up.

It's difficult for many. It's unbearable to the few. But we have to see the world as it really is, and we have to stop thinking in terms of magic.

As Francis would have put it, "This is a story for grown men, not a consoling tale for children."

And so here I am seven years later. I'm a highly organised pattern of mass and energy, one of 7 billion. In any objective accounting of the universe, I'm practically nothing, and soon I'll cease to be. But the certainty of my own demise, the certainty of my own death, somehow makes my life more meaningful, and I think that is as it should be.

I find myself born into this universe. It's a wonderful place. It's a strange place. It's also a scary and sometimes lonely place.

And every day in my work, I try to discern through its noisy manifestation, its people, dogs, trees, mountains, stars – everything I love – I try to discern the eternal music of the spheres.

CHRISTOF KOCH was born in the American Midwest but grew up in Holland, Germany, Canada and Morocco. He studied physics and philosophy at the University of Tübingen in Germany and was awarded his PhD in biophysics in 1982. In 1986 he joined the California Institute of Technology as a professor of biology and engineering. In 2013 he left academia to become chief scientific officer and later president of the Allen Institute for Brain Science in Seattle, leading a ten-year effort to build brain observatories to map, analyse and understand the cerebral cortex. He has authored more than three hundred scientific papers and articles, eight patents and five books. Together with his longtime collaborator, Francis Crick, Christof pioneered the scientific study of consciousness. His latest book is *Consciousness: Confessions of a Romantic Reductionist* (2012). **www.christofkoch.com**

....

THIS STORY WAS TOLD ON JUNE 1, 2013, AT **THE PLAYERS, NEW YORK CITY**. THE THEME OF THE EVENING WAS *WHAT LIES BENEATH: STORIES OF DISCOVERY AT THE WORLD SCIENCE FESTIVAL*. **DIRECTOR: MEG BOWLES**.

Things I've Seen

Jung Chang

◇◇

Where are you going?

I have always wanted to be a writer. But when I was growing up in China, under Mao, in the 1950s and the '60s and '70s, it was impossible even to have this dream, because in those years nearly all writers were condemned – sent to the gulag, driven to suicide. Some were even executed.

To write for oneself was impossible in the Cultural Revolution. I remember, I wrote my first poem on my 16th birthday, in 1968. I was lying in bed, polishing my poem, then I heard the door banging.

The Red Guard had come to raid our flat. If they saw my poem, I would get into trouble and my family would get into trouble. So I had to quickly rush to the toilet to tear up my poem and flush it away.

That ended my first venture in writing.

But the desire to write never left me. In the following years, I was exiled to the edge of the Himalayas, and worked as a peasant and as a barefoot doctor. Then I went into the city and worked as a steel worker, and then electrician. When I was spreading manure in the paddy fields, and when I was checking electricity supplies on top of the electric post, I was always writing in my head with an invisible pen. But I couldn't put pen to paper.

Then, in 1976, Mao died, and China began to change. In 1978, for the first time, scholarships for going abroad were awarded on academic basis. I sat for a national exam, did reasonably well, and so I became one of the first group of 14 people to come and study in Britain.

And as far as I know, I was the first person to get out of Szechuan province, a province then of 90 million people, to come and study in the West. So when I got my doctorate in linguistics from the University of York, I was so lucky. I became the first person from communist China ever to get a doctorate from a British university.

When I first arrived in London, of course, it was like landing on Mars. Everything was so different. In those days, we were still wearing the Mao uniform, which was, a blue, ill-fitting kind of thing. We were not allowed to go out on our own. We had to move in a group. We were quite a sight in the London streets.

Before I arrived in England, the only foreigners I had spoken to were some sailors in a port in south China, where we as English-language students were sent to practice our English. We were so keen to talk to these sailors, because they were our only chance, and we were only there for two weeks.

So we would be sitting in the only restaurant, eagerly awaiting our sailors. We would grab them as soon as they came onshore. (And of course, we had no idea what must have been on their minds.)

Even our teachers had never seen foreigners themselves. So our textbooks were direct translations of Chinese texts. I always remember the lesson, "Greetings," because in those days, in China, when we bumped into each other, we said *Nǐ yào qù nǎlǐ?* and *Chīle ma?* – which means, "Where are you going?" And, "Have you eaten?"

Those were the English greetings I learned. So when I arrived in London, I used to go around and ask people where they were going and whether they had eaten.

We were under a lot of strict rules – not to do this and that and the other. One thing in particular we were told not to do was to go into an English pub, because the Chinese translation for pub, *Jiŭguǎn*, suggested somewhere indecent with nude women gyrating. So we were particularly warned.

But I was filled with curiosity, of course. I spotted a pub across the road from the college, and one day I sneaked out of the college. I darted across the road, and I pushed the door of the pub open, and of course I saw nothing of the kind. Only some men sitting there drinking beer.

I was rather disappointed.

So I was having a fantastic time, and writing was the last thing on my mind. In fact, I positively didn't want to write because to write, for me, would be to look inward and look back into a past I simply wanted to forget all about. In the Cultural Revolution, my father was arrested, tortured and driven insane, because he was one of the few who spoke up against Mao and against the Cultural Revolution. He was exiled to a camp and died tragically and prematurely.

My mother was under tremendous pressure to denounce my father, but she refused. And so she was put through over a hundred of those ghastly denunciation meetings, which were an everyday feature in the Cultural Revolution.

Like other victims, she would be put on a stage. Their hands were twisted to the back, and their heads were ferociously pushed down, and they were kicked and beaten. My mother was made to kneel on broken glass. She was paraded in the streets where children spat at her and threw stones at her. Then, she was exiled to a camp, but she survived. And today, she still lives in Chengdu, in China.

My grandmother, who really brought us up, also died in the Cultural Revolution. So their deaths were a very painful spot in my heart, and I just wanted to forget all about the past.

Then in 1988, my mother came to London to stay with me.

For the first time, she told me the stories of her life, and stories of my grandmother, and her relationship with my father. Once she started, she couldn't stop. She stayed with me for six months, and she talked every day.

When I was listening to my mother, I kept saying to myself, I've got to write all this down. And then I realised how much I wanted to be a writer, and how much I had always wanted to be a writer. My mother seemed to know I had long cherished this dream, and she was helping me to fulfill this dream.

When I was out working, my mother would talk into the tape recorder – she was interviewing herself. By the time she left London, she had left me 60 hours of tape recordings.

And so after my mother left, I sat down, and I transcribed the tapes. I did more research, and I wrote Wild Swans. Wild Swans changed both our lives.

My mother first started talking because she wanted her daughter to understand her. And now she has understanding from tens of millions of readers, all over the world.

And I, at last, have become a writer.

JUNG CHANG was born in Yibin, Sichuan Province, China, in 1952. She was a Red Guard briefly at the age of fourteen and then worked as a peasant, a 'barefoot doctor,' a steelworker and an electrician before becoming an English language student and, later, an assistant lecturer at Sichuan University. She left China for Britain in 1978 and was the first person from the People's Republic of China to receive a doctorate from a British university. Chang is the author of *Wild Swans: Three Daughters of China*, and, with her husband Jon Halliday, of the biography, *Mao: The Unknown Story*. Her books have been translated into more than 40 languages and sold more than 15 million copies, in addition to millions in pirated editions and computer downloads in mainland China where both books are banned. Her latest book, *Empress Dowager Cixi: The Concubine Who Launched Modern China*, was published in 2013.

THIS STORY WAS TOLD ON APRIL 13 2015 AT THE **UNION CHAPEL, LONDON**. THE THEME OF THE EVENING WAS *HIGH ANXIETY*. **DIRECTOR: MEG BOWLES**.

Dan Ilic

<><><><><><><><><><><><><><><><><><><><><><><><><><><><><>

The Most Hated Man in Australia

The most dangerous thing I've ever done in my career is use a pun. Comedians, we hate puns. Puns are comedy punctuation – they're good for getting to one place to the next, but they're kind of devoid of meaning.

In Australia, we have very lax pun control laws. And our puns are usually handed down by our fathers.

My dad's favourite pun is, "You know, I tried to be a trapeze artist once, but I couldn't get the hang of it."

It's doubly funny, because what you don't know about my dad is that my dad is quadriplegic, so when he sets it up, you know, it's "I tried to be a trapeze artist once. . . "

And you can just *see* people go, *Oh, is* that *why he's in the wheelchair?* But then when he says, "But I couldn't get the hang of it," they just laugh out of sheer terror.

It's amazing stuff to watch – that's what we call in show business an A-grade pun.

And the reason why I'm telling you this is because wrong jokes and dark humour are how I've learned to deal with tragedy my entire life – being facetious is a family trait.

So it was 2008 and I was not the well-established C-grade celebrity that stands before you tonight. I was putting together a fringe festival show at the Melbourne

Fringe Festival. Fringe festivals are great places for comedians and artists to try out new work that might not be quite ready for everyone to see. But any time you put on a fringe festival show, you put your heart and your art and your wallet on the line every time. And we were a few days out from opening our show, and we hadn't sold a ticket.

Now, my show was a musical comedy about a mine disaster in northern Tasmania in a town called Beaconsfield.

In April 2006, in Australia, the Beaconsfield mine disaster was *the only* story that existed. A mine collapsed, killing one man and trapping two men underground. But I was more interested in what was happening on the surface, *above ground* at Beaconsfield. The town had a population of about 50, but it grew to 500 overnight, and media and journalists started mining the local people for ratings gold.

Every TV show, every radio station, every magazine and journalist, anyone with a public profile, went to Beaconsfield to be seen to be "doing their part for the miners" (and to do their part for their careers at the same time.)

It was really weird. One breakfast show had a musical concert in a park next to the mine. The very next day, the rival breakfast show held a very similar musical concert.

I don't know if you remember, but Bill [Shorten], who was the head of the unions at the time, borrowed a billionaire's jet and flew to Launceston, just so he could be the face of tragedy. (Incidentally, he did such a great job of being the face of tragedy they made him Labor leader.)

Celebrity reporter Richard Carlton got an exclusive interview with the miners' families, and he actually had a heart attack and died in the middle of a press conference. One of our most famous TV presenters, David Koch, or

Kochie, as we call him in Australia, jumped over the media barricades and into the back of an ambulance to score an interview with one of the miners.

It was ridiculous. Watching at home, I was disgusted. I thought this was crazy. A whole bunch of assholes were basically making reality TV out of this tragedy, and it was abhorrent. I thought, *I need to write something about this. I need to write about the media exploitation of this disaster.*

So I did. In my mind it was like a Robin Hood affair – I thought I was doing a good thing, kind of like robbing from the rich and giving to the poor.

But for me, the pun came first:

Beaconsfield: A Musical in A-flat Miner.

I know what you're thinking: grade-A pun. (My dad loved it, so whatever.)

So I flew to Beaconsfield, and I spent a week in the mine, interviewing the locals and putting their stories in the show. Fast forward six months, we're three days out from opening night, and me and the director Luke were standing on the stage.

And we hadn't sold a single ticket.

Theatre is a strong word. It was like the living room of a 200-year old terrace in South Melbourne. And standing on that stage, looking at 30 empty seats, it might as well have been 3,000. I tried everything. I emailed every media outlet in Melbourne, tried to get them to write a story about the show. But no one in Melbourne wanted to touch it, and I was just at my end. I'd flown people from all over Australia to be part of this. I had a great director and a great musical director, people from Sydney and Melbourne were all part of it.

I was thinking, *There must be something I can do.*

And then I thought, *Well, I have one last idea.*

So I emailed the *Launceston Examiner,* the local paper in Beaconsfield. I thought, *Maybe someone will read about it in Launceston and pop over from Melbourne for the weekend and check out the play.*

Maybe. I don't know.

A couple of hours later, my phone rang, and it was a reporter from the Launceston *Examiner.* She was very serious, nonplussed, very professional. She wanted to know all about the show, and she asked if I had time. Standing on that empty stage in Melbourne, I had plenty of time in my schedule to talk to anyone about it.

I was so excited to talk to her about all these jokes I'd written. I was telling her about how Macquarie Bank ran the mine at a loss, and how we wrote this song about Richard Carlton's death called "The Carlton Cardiac." We said it was an *arresting* tune.

And it was *really exciting.* I was laughing and having a great time.

But she wasn't laughing.

She said, "Are you going to bring it to Beaconsfield?"

And I said, "Yeah, of course."

I lied. I wasn't going to.

She hung up, and I went to bed. I woke up about 11 o'clock that night, and my friend Chris was calling me.

"Uh, Dan, just to let you know, I was just listening to Tony Delroy's 'What the Papers Say.' Um. . . you're going to be on the front page of *The Age* tomorrow."

Oh my god, *The Age,* the most important and prestigious newspaper in Australia (according to people that live in Melbourne.)

Wow.

I went to bed. The first phone call the next day was at six o'clock in the morning. It was Matt and Joe from Fox FM. They're your standard Fox FM breakfast crew.

"Tell us about your show. What's it like? Whoa-ho-ho! Good luck! *Zing!*"

The next phone call was from Neil Mitchell on 3AW. He's a shock jock. According to his Wikipedia entry (written by his staff), he's Melbourne's most prominent thing.

He just yelled at me for five minutes straight: "You're the WORST PERSON in the WORLD. How DARE you? Would you write a musical about HITLER?"

I said, "Well, Mel Brooks has already done that."

"I'm not here to encourage your jokes."

And I was like, "Well, what *are* you here for? I don't really know what's going on."

So for about five minutes straight, it was the most abusive phone call I'd ever had. It was insane, and about a million people were listening.

Then, for the next two hours, 20 more phone calls from journalists and radio people all over Australia, just calling me up to tell me what an asshole I was.

My email inbox was filling up as well, with lots of emails from people telling me what a jerk I was, and random death threats and stuff like that.

There was one email that stood out, though. It was from Senator Guy Barnett. And the subject just said, "Call me."

I was like, "Oh, wow. This is important."

Now, the senator could either want one of two things. He could be just a massive fan of my sketch comedy work and wanted me to emcee his Liberal Party fundraise. (I assume a free chopper would be included in that.) Or he was excited that someone was talking about the media hypocrisy of the story. When I called him up, you would be surprised to figure out that it was neither. He was *frothing over* with rage.

He said, "If you come to Beaconsfield, you'll be hung, drawn, quartered, and dragged through the streets from the back of an ute." (I don't know if that's still Liberal Party policy. I think they just take your citizenship now – it's a lot easier.)

I was like, *wow, incredible*. TV shows were calling too, so I had to call a press conference.

I texted the cast and said, "Meet me at the theatre half an hour before for the press conference."

When I got to the theatre, there were two groups outside the theatre. One, the cast, who couldn't get inside the theatre because... Two, there were thirty journalists blocking the entrance.

I don't know who I was scared of most, the cast or the journalists. One of the cast members yelled at me, "Dan, what the fuck have you done?"

The lights went on, the cameras started rolling, the mics got shoved in my face. At that point, I thought, *Oh my goodness, if all of you had just bought a ticket, we wouldn't be in this problem.*

They started firing questions at me: "Why did you call the song 'The Carlton Cardiac'? Isn't that offensive to the family?"

I was like, "Well, I'm just stating his facts. You know, his name was Richard Carlton. He had a cardiac."

"You don't think *Beaconsfield: A Musical in A-flat Miner* is a little bit bad taste?"

And I said, "Do you have any idea how hard it is to write a musical in a-flat minor? It's very difficult."

"Why haven't you changed the name of the musical?"

"Because *Beaconsfield: A Rock Opera* would just set expectations far too high."

"What next? September 11 the sitcom?"

"I'll think about it."

I thought I was killing it. I was coming back with jokes, dark jokes, because that's what I'd always done growing up.

But that night, we went back to watch ourselves on TV. It was pretty much impossible to not watch ourselves on TV. *We were on every single channel that night.*

And I was far from killing it. I was nervous, I was a wreck. I was defensive. I was looking at me, thinking, *I hate this guy.*

I was the most hated man in Australia that day.

I had written a musical *about* media hysteria that was *causing* media hysteria. And every question I was asked, I just dug myself into a bigger hole.

The rest of the day was hard. I was emotionally and physically drained. It was exhausting. I was nervous about everything. Suddenly, our little play had a lot more attention on it than we ever dreamed of or wanted. We just needed to sell out a few shows, 30 seats. That night, I got drunk and went to bed, and just prayed it would all blow over. But I woke up to text messages and emails and voicemail messages from my friends supporting me, saying, "Keep your head up."

One message was from my brother, who at the time was a major in the army. He had 200 people under his command, and he said, "Uh, Dan, just letting you know that I've spoken to a few of the boys and they're quite happy to go around tonight if there's any problems."

The Australian army was going to be deployed to protect my thirty-seat theatre? Fantastic! (I politely declined.)

And then later that morning, there was one more phone call. I answered.

"Hello, Dan, it's James Carlton here." James Carlton is a broadcaster, a journalist who works at Radio National here in Australia, but he's also the *son* of the late Richard Carlton, the *60 Minutes* reporter who had died of the heart attack.

"Dan, I just want you to know that while the world is angry with you, no one ever spoke to us. The family's not angry with you. *I'm* not angry with you. And this kind of hypocrisy that you're pricking with your art is just the kind of thing Dad would have loved."

And I can't explain how that phone call made me feel. It was just magical. For the first time in about 48 hours, I felt okay.

We opened the show, we sold out the run, the reviews were absolutely extraordinary – the best I've had in my career so far.

But I changed the name of the musical. I changed it to *Beaconsfield, the Musical,* because puns are devoid of meaning, and they're just comedy punctuation.

Standing outside the theatre on closing night, drinking a beer, where just four days before I'd been in the wrath of the Australian media, I thought, *I will never use my jokes to hurt people again. . . unless they truly deserve it.*

DAN ILIC is one of Australia's most prolific comedic voices, appearing on television and radio in Australia for ten years. Most recently Dan was the senior producer of satire for AJ+ English (Al Jazeera's digital platform for millennials). He currently lives in Los Angeles where he is the Executive Producer of Satire for FUSION Network.

THIS STORY WAS TOLD ON SEPTEMBER 6, 2015 AT THE FESTIVAL OF DANGEROUS IDEAS AT THE **SYDNEY OPERA HOUSE**. THE THEME OF THE EVENING WAS *RAZOR'S EDGE*. **DIRECTOR: JENIFER HIXSON**.

Carl Pillitteri

<><><><><><><><><><><><><><><><><><><><><><><><><><><><><><><><>

Fog of Disbelief

For many years I worked along the northeast coast of Japan, and when assigned there I would frequent this one particular restaurant, five, six nights a week. Over the years I came to grow very fond of the older woman who owned and operated it. She didn't speak any English, and I didn't speak any Japanese, but we shared a friendship just the same.

Upon arrival I would always slide open her door, and take a half step in, and look at her as if to say, *Hey, Mom, I'm home!*

And she would greet me with this warm and welcoming smile, and she was always happy to see me. She knew what I was there for, the same thing every time – her amazing pan-fried chicken dish.

She was a motherly figure to me as well. She was always giving me extra things to eat, and was just genuinely a very nice woman. I would stop there so often after work just to rest and relax, yet I never knew her name or the name of her restaurant. We all referred to her fondly as the "Chicken Lady."

Her restaurant was located just south of the Fukushima Daiichi nuclear generating station, where in 2011 I was working as a field engineer.

When you walked through the gates of the Fukushima nuclear generating station, it resembled a botanical garden. The landscaping was immaculate. There were well-manicured lawns everywhere, and the trees were pruned to perfection to resemble these large bonsai. The reactor buildings themselves were painted sky blue with white clouds on them, and it was always my favourite place to work.

March 11, 2011, was a beautiful sunny day there. My crew and I were working inside of the Reactor One turbine building, a huge, rectangular-shaped building similar in size to an international airport hangar.

At 2:46 in the afternoon, I had a young man overhead in the crane as an operator. Ten of us, including myself, were in a very well-defined contaminated work zone, dressed from head to toe in our protective clothing, when suddenly it felt like someone took a very big hammer and hit the foundation of that very big building.

I turned to my crew and I said, "Earthquake!"

This powerful earthquake caused these massive upheavals of the earth, and then these dropping sensations. It was taking the entire structure we were in with it, it was very violent, and it was just starting. I was trying to navigate my way around my crew, the whole time keeping an eye on this young man in the overhead crane. He was taking the ride of his life as this crane hopped on its tracks and crabbed, and it was really difficult to watch.

The concrete floor and walls around us began to crack, and sections of ductwork were coming down, and the lights, the lights were dropping everywhere. The huge, vast space that we were in quickly filled with what I first thought was smoke, but was actually a thick cloud of dust that was being thrown airborne from this huge structure getting the living hell shook out of it.

We were all right there on the borderline of panic, and then the lights went out and we were in the pitch-black.

This really scared the crap out of all of us. Two young Japanese boys came to me, and grabbed a hold of me in the dark. I had this one tall kid on my left, and he had his arm around my shoulder, and I had my arm around his back. The other guy was on his knees, and he had his arms around my waist, and I had my hand on his shoulder.

We were squeezing each other with every jolt that this thing's throwing at us. And we were huddled up, three grown men like three little boys, and I began to pray earnestly aloud for all of us. It appeared that the Japanese boy on my left was praying in Japanese, and we were standing just yards in front of this massive turbine and generator that was spinning at 1,500 rpm, being driven by the steam coming right off the Unit One reactor.

It was at a hundred percent power, and the sounds that began to come out of this turbine caught my attention. I start to realise that it sounds like it wants to come apart, and it's going to explode and pepper us against the walls.

As if to confirm my fears, I hear my American co-worker from afar, in complete darkness, scream, "It's gonna blow! It's gonna blow!" And I recognise the terror in his voice.

I stopped praying, and I went to this Psalm, 23:4 – *though I walk through the valley of the shadow of death, I fear no evil* – but I couldn't get through it. I broke down in the middle somewhere, and I just surrendered, and I asked, *Just please make this quick.*

So we rode it out in the darkness. We were frozen there. We could feel it, and we could hear it, and we could smell it. We could even taste it. We just couldn't see it.

About five minutes into that first quake, we caught a break, and the light circuit came back on. There were only a handful of lights that had survived the quake, but it was enough light to see again. We were able to get the young man out of the crane, and he was in rough shape, but we headed for the door.

I made sure I was the last one out, because this was my crew, and I was responsible for them. I took one last look back at the millions of dollars' worth of equipment and tooling that I had cared for since 2008, and I just knew I wasn't going to see any of that again.

We finally get outside after many obstacles, and we're jumping across cracks in the roadway, and we get to a point where we have to split up. I have to head up this long stairway up the hillside to where my rental car is parked.

When I get up there, I realise that the power of this quake has shifted all the parked cars and pinned mine in. I take a time-out, and realise that my heart is beating out of my chest, and I'm not breathing. And I start concentrating on getting my heart and lungs back in sync.

I'm looking down the hillside, and there's a freighter in the harbor in front of Fukushima. There are deckhands running around it, and there's black smoke coming out of it.

I remember thinking, *Well, this must be their procedure during an event of this magnitude.* Then it struck me: *are they taking precautions against a possible tsunami?*

I watch them cast off, and get out of the harbor, and head out in the Pacific due east.

I'm on top of this hillside now, and I'm working on my breathing, and surveying the damage all around me, which was staggering.

These so-called aftershocks (which are actually earthquakes and high on the magnitude scale) were just ripping through and rattling my nerves. The earth around me was distorting like Jell-O, and I looked back out to sea to eyeball the freighter.

He was a mile or so out, and I saw this wall of water coming in from the horizon as far north and as far south as I could see, and it was just a perfect wall of water. I watched that freighter go up the face of it, and I thought he was going to roll and capsize to his starboard, but he cut over the top of it.

And I don't know who I was talking to – I was alone up there – whether I was talking to Mother Nature or God himself, but they both heard me when I shouted across the Pacific at this thing, "You've got to be fucking kidding me!"

I watched the wave crash into the coastline below me and the four reactor buildings. I stood there in horror as the tremendous power and force of the thing just snapped everything, taking everything in its path with it.

When it hit the coastline, it had nowhere to go but uphill towards me, because there was a lot of water behind it. It continued to push up, and I started revisiting that feeling of doom I had twenty minutes earlier in the turbine building.

My thoughts shifted to all the low-lying communities north and south of me there, the ones I was so familiar with. I was on top of this hill, but somebody certainly must be in trouble. And it was a feeling of helplessness.

Then something happened to me. I went into shock. I felt like I was in this glass bowl. I could see through it, but the inside of it was filled with this gaseous fog of disbelief, and I watched two more, smaller tsunamis come in on top of the first one, bringing the water up even higher.

Then finally it all started to recede back down. It got to the shoreline, and continued out into the Pacific. It receded out to sea a quarter of a mile, and that harbor completely drained in front of my eyes, and I was looking at seabed as far north and as far south as I could see.

But with that came this wild weather front from the highlands behind me. These big, black, ominous clouds came rolling in, tumbling real low, and they just whipped across me.

And behind it was this – it wasn't even a wind, it was like a vacuum. It was coming out to sea, and you could feel the temperature drop . . .

. . . And it began to snow.

I'm standing there thinking, *Am I witnessing the end of our world?* I truly pondered that.

I took this long, dazed walk off-site, and to this day I cannot remember the walk. But I got off-site to our office, and I started to recognise groups of my co-workers and familiar faces. And when I saw them, I stopped, and I turned around, and turned my back to them, and broke down.

We were eventually evacuated to this parking lot up in the hills, where we spent a very long night. The power was out, of course no water.

I tried in vain to call my wife for hours, but the network was busy. Around midnight I asked two friends to take me to town.

We slipped out of there, and I said, "Take me to the Chicken Lady's."

I wanted to check on her to see if she was there, if she needed help, if she was okay. We arrived, and her little building was cracked right down the face, and she wasn't there. She was nowhere to be found.

I tried calling my wife again, and this time it rang. And when I said her name, she just screamed and kept screaming.

I just kept saying, "Bad, very bad."

I eventually got home on March 16, five days later, and you would think that getting home would cure all that ails you. But it was there that everything started to manifest.

I learned about the loss of life in Japan. I saw the footage on TV. I learned about the reactors that I had serviced for twenty years exploding.

I was tired, and I was exhausted, and I had no energy, but I couldn't sleep. I was depressed, heartbroken, and guilty. And even though I was surrounded by my family, I was alone with these emotions. I found myself in my recliner like a vegetable for a month before I even realised a month had passed. And nothing was important. Nothing.

I was out of work for five months, and then I learned of a program set up by the Japanese government allowing residents back into their homes and apartments.

That was it – it was absolutely necessary that I go back. I *needed* to go back.

So a few months later, I returned to the Exclusion Zone, and after several checkpoints I was given protective clothing from head to toe again – not to go to work but to enter the community and neighbourhood where I lived.

I asked my escort to take me to the restaurant first, and when I pulled her door open this time, I was tearing cobwebs with it, and that was unsettling to me, because it was clear that no one had opened that door in nine months. It made me wonder and worry more about what had happened to her.

From there we went to my apartment. I opened that door for the first time since the morning of March 11 when I left for work, and it was in shambles. Everything was on the floor, and all the contents of the cabinets had been thrown out. The fridge was on its side. There were cracks in the wall. Even my fiberglass bathtub was shattered.

I started to clean up, and my escort said, "You don't have to do this."

But I said, "Yes, I do. I'm responsible for this space and this mess," and I cleaned it all up from end to end.

I found what I was hoping to find, which was my wedding ring. I also picked up my alarm clock, the one that woke me up that morning. The battery had popped out of the back, and the hands were frozen at 2:47, the same time as the earthquake. Time had stood still in that apartment for nine months.

When I finished there, I backed my way out and closed that door, literally closing that door behind me. And it was therapeutic, to say the least, and I had some relief, some closure.

But I still had one thing I needed to find out. I needed to learn the fate of the Chicken Lady.

That night I reached out to the *Japan Times* and asked them if they could help me find her. Is she with family, is she going to be okay, can I help her?

And eventually they *did* find her, and for the first time I learned her name. It was Owada. Owada is her family name, Mrs Owada-san. And they told me the name of her restaurant was Ikoi and that *ikoi* in Japanese means "rest, relax and relief."

And I'm thinking, *What a wonderful name for a little place. I used to stop there so often after work to rest and relax.* Now I had this relief in knowing that these disasters didn't take her, and that she was alive.

And then finally, on February 19, 2012, Mrs Owada-san sent me a letter:

I have escaped from the disasters and have been doing fine every day. Pillitteri-san, please take care of yourself. I know your work must be important. I hope you enjoy a happy life like you seemed to have when you came to my restaurant. Although I won't be seeing you, I will always pray for the best for you.

CARL PILLITTERI has spent over thirty years hard-servicing nuclear generating stations around the world. After the events in Japan, he took a short sabbatical, trying to regain focus and find a new path. Carl attempted a start-up company, installing residential-size wind turbines in the archipelago off the western coast of Taiwan, but those efforts have been thwarted by the Taiwan Power Company (TPC). While Carl waits for the TPC to see value in his project, he is back on the road, hard-servicing nuclear generating stations in the USA.

THIS STORY WAS TOLD ON NOVEMBER 6, 2013, IN THE GREAT HALL AT **COOPER UNION, NEW YORK CITY**. THE THEME OF THE EVENING WAS *DUCK AND COVER: STORIES OF FALLOUT*. **DIRECTOR: MEG BOWLES**.

Chenjerai Kumanyika

<><><><><><><><><><><><><><><><><><><><><><><><><><><><><><><><><>

The Two Times I Met Laurence Fishburne

On December 21, 2007, at 2:15 p.m., a colleague at my job told me the boss wanted to see me, and I should brace myself, because the boss wasn't pleased.

Now, when I say "my job," what y'all should know is this was a temporary job. And when I say it was a temporary job, what you should know is that my performance today determined whether I would be asked back tomorrow.

So when I went in the boss's office, here's what she said: "Hi, Chenjerai. Yesterday I asked you to make two hundred *Gilmore Girls Thanksgiving Day Special* DVDs. But the Excel spreadsheet that you made ordered more than that."

"Okay. How many more?"

"One million *Gilmore Girls Thanksgiving Day Special* DVDs. Can you explain that, please?"

I could. I have no idea how to use Microsoft Excel. And I lied about my skills to get this job. And, uh, my solution to the first two problems had been when in doubt, hit ENTER.

What I'm trying to explain to you is, on December 21, 2007, at 2:15 p.m., my life sucked.

And it didn't just suck because I had a job that I was no good at, and that few people wanted. It sucked because only two years ago I had a job that I was much better at, and that *everyone* wanted. I was a full-time hip-hop artist.

You see, in 1995 four friends and I decided that the music industry was missing something. What the game needed was a group that was kind of like the Fugees, but not quite as talented. Kind of like the Roots, but not quite as creative.

So we formed the Spooks. And after years of grinding out demos and everybody telling us we were never going to make it, we finally did the impossible. We came up to New York, and we signed a record deal.

One day the CEO of our record label called us into his office, and his assistant said he was very excited.

"Spooks!" (He liked saying it a little too much for a white guy – I'm just saying.) "I figured out how we're all going to make millions, and it comes down to two words: Laurence Fishburne."

I was like, "Wait a minute, you mean like the *movie star* Laurence Fishburne? Like *Apocalypse Now* Laurence Fishburne? Morpheus in *The Matrix* Laurence Fishburne?"

According to our CEO, *the* Laurence Fishburne had agreed to make our song the main theme song of the first film he ever directed. All we had to do was go to dinner with him and solidify the deal. Pfft. No problem.

We went up to New York, waited out in front of a restaurant, and sure enough, *the* Laurence Fishburne pulled up on a scooter.

Not only did he agree to put our song in his film, but he agreed to be in our music video. We figured the film was gonna be a hit, and when the film was a hit, our song would be a hit, launching us into hip-hop superstardom.

Awesome.

Things didn't go quite like that. We struggled in the US. But like many genius artists before us – Jimi Hendrix, James Baldwin . . . the Spice Girls – we blew up in Europe first. We got a gold album in the UK, then we got a gold single in France, then we got a gold single in Belgium, and we got a gold single in Sweden.

I was telling this to a friend of mine the other day, kind of bragging, and he said, "Wait a minute, doesn't it only take like three thousand albums to go gold in Belgium?"

I was like, "Well, yeah, that's true. But I mean, how many gold albums *you* got? Fuck you. Don't be a hater."

We were Top 10, you know what I'm saying? We were Top 10 all over Europe.

That meant we did all the TV shows. We did *Viva MTV, Jools Holland, Top of the Pops* – you name it. We were flying all over doing concerts and festivals.

I finally felt like we had made it the day my manager told me we had a problem. We had to do two shows in two different countries on the same day. The solution was simple: Sony rented a private jet. Eight o'clock show in Berlin, eleven-thirty show in London.

As we were flying across Europe from one set of screaming fans to another in a private jet, drinking specially procured Scandinavian pear ciders, I was sitting next to a record exec who I felt was kind of becoming my friend. Because a lot of people around us at this time were just telling us what we wanted to hear. They had a financial incentive to do that.

But this person was somebody I was starting to trust.

So I was like, "Susan, I got an idea. When we finish touring, let's all of us just meet up somewhere in Europe. In fact, maybe we could make it a yearly thing, pick a place somewhere in the world and just kick it."

We had been laughing up to that point. But suddenly she got really serious.

And she took my hand, and she said, "Listen, Chenjerai, I have to be honest with you. I don't know where you're going to be next year. Enjoy it while it lasts."

She kind of knocked the wind out of me with that one.

I was like, "What do you mean? We're going to be making music next year. We're good at this, and people like our songs. I like doing this. I thought we were finally part of the club. Look at this private jet. Look at these specially procured Scandinavian pear ciders."

But she was right. Two months later another marketing exec called us into his office, and said that, due to a poorly chosen third single, they had run out of money to promote our album, and it was over. We did make one more album, but a young UK record exec informed us that most of the singles weren't "gangster" enough, and that album died on the vine.

I moved to Los Angeles. I got married. And eventually I found myself in a cubicle producing *Gilmore Girls* DVDs.

But even then, I felt like I still had a foot in the game, and apparently my wife did, too, because she was like, "Honey, I have a job for you working with celebrities. Are you interested?"

I was like, "Of course. But if I'm going to be around my people, I'm probably going to need to go shopping."

She reached in her purse, pulled out the JCPenney card, and she said, "Get a suit. Not the most expensive one. You'll be working security."

I went to the gig. Now, this was a gathering of the black filmmaking elite. Spike Lee was there, Tyler Perry was there, the whole cast from *The Wire* was there. And then, coming out of a limousine, was *the* Laurence Fishburne.

Now, I'm not going to lie. At that point people weren't treating me too well as the security guard.

But I thought, *Now they're going to see.*

You know what I'm saying? I didn't just get Laurence Fishburne's autograph. He was *in my video.*

But as he got closer, I started to second-guess myself a little bit. I thought, *Wait a minute now. What if he wants me to go in? I can't. I'm working. How am I going to explain that?* And actually, *He's not going to ask me to go in. I'm sitting here in a JCPenney suit.*

I didn't even have dress socks on. I had sweat socks on.

And come to think of it, I haven't made music in months. I'm not really an artist anymore. I'm not in the rap game. I make Gilmore Girls *DVDs.*

And I'm not even good at that.

I got more and more nervous. And as Laurence Fishburne headed toward me, I actually turned my head to the side so he wouldn't see my face, because I just didn't want to have to explain what my situation was. He walked right by me without seeing me. I don't know if I felt more depressed or relieved at that moment.

I knew at that point that I had to face the reality of my life. A few weeks later, I interviewed for a full-time job as an administrative assistant. Now, this firm was in a cramped office, dimly lit – the kind of place where there's insidious pop music leaking out of the radio, but nobody hears it because they're hopelessly staring into their computer screens.

I was hopelessly staring at my résumé, trying to figure out how I was going to explain these gaps in it, and why a hip-hop artist was really excited about being a full-time administrative assistant.

But as I was listening to the music, suddenly, it started to sound familiar.

I thought, *I kind of recognise that song.*

And then I was like, *wait a minute, I WROTE that song. That's "Things I've Seen." That's the song that did it for us!*

One of the employees looked at his co-worker and was like, "Yo, remember this song, 'Things I've Seen'? I fuckin' love that shit. Song was so hot."

I got excited, like maybe somebody's going to recognise me. I started looking around. But no one did.

But it was kinda okay, because I realised at that moment that my music coming out this speaker was giving me a message, and what it was saying is, *You don't have to suffocate trying to pretend to be some rock star who hangs out with Laurence Fishburne. But these guys heard your song, and they liked it. And in a way, isn't that what making music is really about anyway?* What I always loved most about music was that you don't have to be a big, important person to make compelling songs that can reach out and touch somebody.

I also realised in that moment that maybe I have more to offer the world than Excel spreadsheets. I was looking for a third door, where I could do what I wanted, and at the same time make opportunities for other people to make music.

I found that door when I was offered the chance to run a studio for an incredible nonprofit organisation called Street Poets. Street Poets works with marginalised youth, to help develop them into artists and teachers and healers. After working at Street Poets, I was able to get my PhD and become a professor of media studies.

And now, sometimes when I'm sitting in my office, my students come in and they're so excited to tell me about their dreams and their fears.

And I know I should say to them, *Listen, y'all, it's hard out there. Life kicks your ass. Play it safe.*

But I never do.

I tell them, "Go for it. Enjoy it while it lasts, but brace yourself, because when it doesn't, sometimes you've got to figure out who you're *not* so you can become who you *are*."

DR CHENJERAI KUMANYIKA is a scholar, an activist and an artist who holds a creativity professorship at Clemson University, South Carolina. He is a board member for several youth-mentoring programs, including Street Poets Inc., and a news analyst for Uprising Radio. His livestream journalism at Black Lives Matter protests during 2014–15 has been viewed by tens of thousands of viewers. Chenjerai is also a founding member of the hip-hop group the Spooks, whose first album, *S.I.O.S.O.S. Vol. 1* (2000), produced singles on Top 10 charts around the world. **www.Chenjerai.net**.

THIS STORY WAS TOLD ON NOVEMBER 17, 2015, AT **BLUE MAN GROUP'S ASTOR PLACE THEATRE, NEW YORK CITY**. THE THEME OF THE EVENING WAS *THE MOTH AND BLUE MAN: TRIBES*. **DIRECTOR: CATHERINE BURNS**.

Louis C.K.

<<<<<<<<<<<<<<<<<<<<<<<<<<<<<<<<<<<<<<<<<>

Untitled

I went to Russia in 1994, and it had just become Russia again. It was the Soviet Union until really that year, but then everything started to crash down.

At the time I was a writer for the Conan O'Brien show. I had written there for two years, and I was burnt out, and I didn't want to do it anymore.

So I went to the head writer, and I said, "I have to quit, because I think I'm going to have a nervous breakdown."

He said, "Take two weeks off, and we'll pay you for the two weeks."

I said, "Okay. I'll do that."

I was in my twenties – I had no wife, nothing. I had no girlfriend, even. I was just this guy, and I had money from a TV job.

So I had nowhere to go, and I thought, *I'm going to go to Russia.* Because when I was a kid, I used to read Russian novels, and I loved them. I would open all the windows so I would be cold. I wanted to be cold like they were.

Also, somebody told me that the wall had just come down, and that Russia was a really crazy place at the time.

So I said, "I'm gonna go there."

I went to Russia in the middle of December, alone.

I speak no Russian. I can't even look at the alphabet and understand what I'm looking at. There was no place more foreign to me than Russia.

I went to Moscow, and when you land in Moscow, it's just forest all around, and then suddenly there's this city in the middle of a big forest. It's terrifying.

As the plane goes down you're like, *No, no, no, no. I didn't want to really do this!*

It was a country that was just broken in pieces. And the weirdest things happened to me there.

Like, I was in a restaurant one day, and a waiter came up to me – not my waiter – and he said, "Coca-Cola?"

I said, "Huh?"

He said, "Coca-Cola."

And I said, "Sure." I don't drink Coca-Cola, but I had learned by that point to just do what they're asking you to do. Sure.

So he went to the kitchen, and he got a Coke in a can, and he handed it to me, and he said, "Five dollars," because only dollars were worth anything there.

I said, "Okay, on my bill."

He said, "No. Five dollars, me. Now."

So I gave him five dollars, and he put on his coat, and he left. He sold me a Coke on the side, and then quit his job. Those are the kinds of confusing moments I was having there.

I couldn't talk to anybody, and I was so lonely. It was difficult. I'd just sit in my room. I tried to watch television, but the TV was all American shows like *Dynasty*.

The way they translated was, they lowered the sound a little, and there was one man saying all of the dialogue in Russian over the whole show. I was there for two weeks, and it just was crushing. I made no contact with anyone.

Then one day I went into the subway. Now, if you've never been to Moscow, the streets there were made wider during the Cold War, so that they could have missiles go down the middle of the street for the parades.

If you go behind the big buildings, you'll find out that they actually tore the buildings off of their foundations and dragged them back. A lot of the bigger buildings in Moscow, in the back, they're being held up by bricks. It's really unnerving how unsafe the whole city is.

So the streets are very wide, and you can't cross the street on a green light – you'll never make it. So they made tunnels so you can go under, and those are connected to the subway.

The subway in Moscow, you go down an escalator, and it just keeps going. You keep going until you think, *This is so deep. This is really upsetting.*

But everyone hangs out in these tunnels. And I'm standing in the subway, and I'm watching a violin player.

One thing about Russia, even still today, I think, is that no one has any money. So when you see a guy playing the violin in the subway, he's like the *first-chair violin* for the Russian Symphony Orchestra, because that doesn't pay shit, and at least he can get a few kopecks in the subway.

So I'm watching him, and there are other people sitting on the floor listening, and everybody's crying. Everybody. People are just watching, wiping away tears.

And there's a young fellow sitting there, and he looked my age. I was twenty-five at the time. He looked about twenty-five, too, and he was tattered and just watching this violin player.

Then this group of kids walked by, about eight children, ranging from five to ten years old. Their faces were dirty, like in *Oliver Twist* – like they were in a play and they had rubbed dirt on their faces.

They're all wearing men's coats, from the neck hanging down to the floor. None of them have their hands in their sleeves, so their sleeves are just flopping. They were street urchins, and the coats – you kind of knew all the men who owned those coats were dead, and at least one of these kids killed those guys. Like, I swear I looked at an eight-year-old's face and thought, *He has murdered.* That's what they looked like, just tough little kids. I had seen them before in Moscow. They work in groups.

The guy sitting below me that I identified with calls out to the head kid in the front. He's appealing to him. He needs something.

And the kid, with his hands in his sleeves, looked at him suspiciously and said, [mimics Russian], like, *What the fuck? Why? What do you want from me?*

The guy showed the kid that his shoe had come apart. His shoe was like a flap.

The kid shrugged and said, [mimics Russian], like, *Okay.*

The kid's hand appeared from out of the sleeve, and there was a tube of shoe glue in his hand. He didn't rummage for it – it was already there.

He handed it to the guy, and the guy fixed his shoe with the glue and gave it back to him. Then the kid – his other hand had a paper bag in it, and he put the glue in, and he huffed it. His eyes rolled back, and he got high.

Then the group kept going, but I couldn't believe what I just saw. That the misery in this country at that time was so palpable and so predictable, that this guy thought, *My shoe's broken. Oh, there's a child. He's sure to have some glue in his hand, because the state of our nation is so wretched.*

I looked at him, and he looked at me, and I was startled.

And then he laughed, and I laughed. He's the only person I had any contact with in the whole of the Soviet Union.

I realised this is why I came here – to find out how bad life gets. And that even when it's this bad, it's still fuckin' funny.

LOUIS C.K. is a six-time Emmy Award winner and one of the most honest and respected comedic voices of his generation, on stage, TV and film. He is perhaps best known as executive producer, writer, director, editor and star of FX's Peabody Award–winning hit show *Louie*. His other work includes writing, directing and starring in *Horace and Pete* – a drama he directly distributed through his website – and serving as co-writer and producer on FX's *Baskets* and *Better Things*. Throughout his career he has earned over thirty Emmy nominations and won five Comedy Awards, four Writers Guild Awards, two Critics Choice Television Awards, two Television Critics Association Awards, two Grammy Awards and a Screen Actors Guild Award.

THIS STORY WAS TOLD ON MAY 12, 2015, AT THE MOTH BALL AT **CAPITALE, NEW YORK CITY**.

Bliss Broyard

<<<<<<<<<<<<<<<<<<<<<<<<<<<<<<<<<<<<<<<<<<<<<<<<<<<

A Tale of Two Dinners

I'm at a dinner party in Charlottesville, Virginia. I've just moved to town, and I don't know anybody except for the second cousin of my ex-boyfriend, this woman named Whitney, who invited me to the party.

All I really know about her is that she's a huge WASP, which is fine, because I'm a WASP, too. I was born in Fairfield, Connecticut, which is the land of WASPs. So I feel like I know the drill.

They were going to have two black Labrador retrievers, a house full of eighteenth-century furniture, and then WASPs always have these really threadbare linen napkins. (It's this weird thing, like they just can't bear to throw them away.)

So we're at dinner, and Whitney turns to me and she says, "Oh, if you're free next weekend, you've gotta come fox hunting with us."

All right.

"It's really fun. We hunt all day, and then at night we have dinner, and then we go dancing at the club."

Okay.

Then Whitney's husband says, "Oh, just make sure you watch out for Chuck."

"Yeah, Chuck's a little annoying. Sometimes he attaches himself to single women, so you should avoid him."

At this point the hostess breaks in, and she says, "Who attaches himself to single women? I'm single, and nobody ever talks to me. Who's this Chuck guy?"

Whitney says, "You know who he is. He's got really curly hair. He's kind of got full features."

She goes on describing what he was wearing and what happened at the last party. The hostess still has no idea who they're talking about.

Then her husband John says, "Oh, just say it. Chuck was the black guy."

And this cry goes up around the table.

"Chuck's black? He's *black*? I didn't know he was black."

"Well, I mean, you wouldn't exactly call him black. He's more like a high yella."

The hostess says, "Wait a minute, I have photographs from that party."

She jumps up and then comes back with this photo album and is looking through it.

"Oh, him. Yeah, Chuck. Okay. God, he's black? It's so hard to tell."

Then she starts passing the photo album around the dinner table.

And people are like, "Oh, yeah, look at his hair. It *is* kind of kinky. I hadn't really noticed. Look at his lips. Yeah, they are kind of full. And I guess his nose is sort of wide."

And then the photo album gets to me.

I stand up, and I say, "You know, sometimes it *is* really hard to tell. Like, what would you say about my hair? It's curly, but would you say it's kinky? And what about my lips? I mean, the bottom one's kind of full, but the top one actually is really thin. How about my nose? You think my nose is wide? If you saw me on the dance floor, you'd know I've got natural rhythm, but I'm not very good on the basketball court, because I can't jump. What would you say about my skin? Would you call my skin a high yella?"

Actually, when this photo album came to me, I passed it to the next person. I didn't say anything.

And then about five minutes later, I said I felt sick – which I did – and I left.

Because four years before that, when my father was dying of prostate cancer, I found out that he had a secret. He said he would tell us what it was, but when we all gathered to talk to him about it, he couldn't bring himself to reveal it just then. One night a tumour broke through the wall of his bladder, and he had to go in for emergency surgery, and it looked like he wasn't going to live until morning.

My mother sat my brother and me down, and she said, "Look, kids, I've got to tell you what the secret is. Your father's black."

Now, I'd always known that he was a Creole from New Orleans, and I thought it meant that he was French and he spoke patois and ate jambalaya. What I didn't know is that it also meant he was black.

That night in the hospital, we were like, "Oh, *that's* the secret? Dad's *black*? Well, cool. Hey, that means that we're black, too, you know?"

My first question was, "How black is he?"

That's always everyone's first question to me, because he didn't look black.

And my mom said, "Well both of his parents were black, too. They were very light-skinned. In fact, they could pass for white, and when they moved up to Brooklyn, to Bed-Stuy, when they left New Orleans, they had to pass for white to get work in the thirties."

His grandparents had been black, too, she said, and they had also been light-skinned.

I had known that my dad's father had died a long time before I was born and that my grandmother had died when I was twelve. But we never saw her or my father's two sisters, although they lived in New York City, which was just an hour away from where we were living in Connecticut.

When I would ask my dad why not – why don't we see your family? – he would say, "Well, they don't interest me."

Which of course then put a lot of pressure on me to be interesting.

But honestly, with my father in the next room, about to go into this life-and-death surgery, it really didn't seem like a big deal.

He made it through the surgery, but he was never lucid again, and then he died a month later. So I never got a chance to talk to him about it. And pretty quickly the secret started seeming like a big deal.

First of all, why was it a secret in the first place? That was one thing I had trouble understanding.

My mom said that as a kid my dad had been picked on by black kids because he looked white, and had been ostracised by white kids because they knew his family was black. He would come home from school with his jacket torn, and his parents wouldn't ask him what happened. He didn't want his own children to go through the same pain and confusion that he did.

But as many questions as it answered, it raised a lot more. Like, for one, what did this make me? For the first twenty-three years of my life, I was a white girl from Connecticut. And you know, I didn't really feel white anymore, but I didn't feel black either.

I mean, I don't look black. I didn't really know anything about being black either, or anything about black culture.

At that point I didn't know anybody who *was* black. So I figured, well, I guess I should start with my own family.

I looked up my father's family, who I had met for the first time at his memorial service. And just as an interesting side note, out of four hundred people at the service, they were the only black people, except for one of my dad's colleagues from the *New York Times*.

I was so excited to meet them. I was twenty-four, I had just lost my father who I really loved, and it was starting to kind of feel like I had lost him twice. He had died, but also, I was learning all these things about him that I didn't know. And I realised in meeting them that they're not just my dad's family, they're my family, too.

So it turns out that my father's sister, my Aunt Shirley – her husband was this amazing civil-rights leader. He'd been the head of the NAACP for the whole western part of the country in the fifties. He'd started the first civil-rights division for the state of California. He was the second African-American person ever appointed to the UN, and then he was the US ambassador to Ghana.

He was this amazing guy, and I never even got to meet him, because he'd died a couple of months before my father.

I said to my Aunt Shirley, "You know, I don't really know what to do with this information. I don't know how to identify myself.

"I used to say, 'I'm French and Norwegian.' And now I would say, 'Well, I'm Norwegian and black,' but then people kind of look at me like, *Oh, hmmm. Really?*

"So then I say, 'Well, I'm Norwegian and Creole, which means French and black, but I didn't know about the black part until a couple years ago, and so that's why I don't seem more black.' I'll be going on and on, and they're like, 'Well, sorry I asked.'"

My aunt said, "Well, you know who you are. You're Bliss. That's who you are. And you have a whole life in front of you to figure out what that means. Look, the minute you let other people start to define you, you are just giving away your power."

So I thought, *All right, I'll try and figure out who Bliss is. That seems like a pretty good question.*

I started to read. I went to the library, and I looked up words like *passing* and *mulatto* and *mestizo* and *miscegenation* – words I'd never even heard of before. I learned about the "one drop" rule: if you have one drop of black blood, it makes you black.

I started reading all these books that we didn't really cover in my prep school in Connecticut. I was reading Ralph Ellison and Richard Wright and Toni Morrison, and I was learning all about this rich, interesting, and painful culture.

I went down to New Orleans. I tried to trace my roots. I was like, "So how did we get here anyway? Did we come from Africa?"

Then one night I was having dinner with my aunt, and I asked her this question that was really weighing on me. We were on the Upper West Side in this café. I remember the tables were really small and close together.

So I leaned forward, and in a whisper I said, "So, Shirley, is it possible that some of our ancestors had been slaves?"

And she kind of gave me a look, and she sat back in her chair, and she said, "Well, not too many black people came here as immigrants back in the 1700s, so they probably were."

I still had many, many more questions. So a family member put me in touch with the head of the Afro-American studies department at Harvard. I called him up, and he was interested in my story, because my father had been a well-known writer. And so we talked, and he gave me some more books to read, and he promised that he would put together a bibliography and put it in the mail.

The next time I heard from him, he called up and said, "Hey, I pitched the story of your father to the *New Yorker,* and I'm going to be doing a profile on him."

I was kind of upset about that. I mean, I'd always wanted to be in the *New Yorker,* but this really wasn't the way I'd imagined it would happen.

But he writes this article, and in it he says that my father never even told his kids – that his daughter didn't know until she was twenty-three. So I figured, well, I *really* need to work out this question of what my identity is, because now everybody's reading about it.

Then I got a phone call from a woman who said, "Hi, I'm your cousin, Claire Cooper, from Los Angeles, and I grew up down the street from your father in New Orleans, and I want to tell you that that article was full of lies. Your father is *not* black. The Broyards are white."

I said, "Are you sure? Because I went down to New Orleans, and I looked at some records, and it said 'coloured' on the birth certificate."

"No, no, no. That's a lie. Those are people that are just trying to pin something on us."

I said, "Well, you know, would it be all right if we were?"

And she said, "Well, it doesn't matter, because we're not. There's all these Broyards out here in California, and we're all white."

I'm like, "All right."

I was prepared to believe anything. I'd been told so many things.

But then I found this guy on the Internet, a writer named Mark Broyard, and he lived out in Los Angeles, too. He wrote this play called *Inside the Creole Mafia*. It's all about the politics of skin colour, and who's passing and who's not. So I called him up and said, "I think maybe we're cousins."

And he said, "Yeah, I bet we are."

I said, "So what's the deal? Are the Broyards black or not?"

He said, "Well, I'm a Broyard, and I'm black, and all the Broyards I know out here are black, too."

So I headed out to California. I thought, *I've got to see this for myself.*

So we all get together at a Creole restaurant called Harold & Belle's on Jefferson Boulevard in South Central. I've got Claire Cooper there, with her husband, representing the "white" side of the family, and then I have Mark Broyard and his family from the black side.

We're all having brunch. So once again I'm around this dinner table, and once again I'm with this group of people that I don't even really know, and lo and behold, once again there's a photo album coming my way.

This one belongs to Claire Cooper, and it's filled with pictures of my relatives, this whole family I didn't even know I had. All these ancestors, going back to the 1800s, these five brothers that came over from Morocco, somebody said.

Mark is sitting next to me, and he passes me the photo album, and he's like, "Hey, check out all these white Broyards."

I look at him. We both start laughing, because all these people looked black!

And we're like, "Claire, if you need to be white, all right, yeah, you know, whatever."

So I'm sitting there, and the silliness of so much of this situation hit me.

I thought, *Well, here I am, a WASP from Connecticut, having brunch with her black family in South Central.*

But the real truth of the matter is that I felt totally at home.

BLISS BROYARD is the author of the bestselling story collection *My Father, Dancing* (1999), which was a *New York Times* Notable Book, and the award-winning memoir *One Drop: My Father's Hidden Life – A Story of Race and Family Secrets* (2007), which was named a best book of the year by the *Chicago Tribune*. Her stories and essays have been anthologised in *Best American Short Stories*, *The Pushcart Prize*, and *The Art of the Essay*, and she has written for the *New York Times*, the *New Yorker* website and *Elle*. She is at work on a novel set on Martha's Vineyard, called *Happy House*, and blogged about a yearlong trip with her husband and two kids around the world at **www.4intransit.com**.

THIS STORY WAS TOLD ON APRIL 19, 1999, AT **LANSKY LOUNGE, NEW YORK CITY**. THE THEME OF THE EVENING WAS *WHO DO YOU THINK YOU ARE? AN EVENING OF STORIES ON GETTING AND KEEPING YOUR IDENTITY*. **DIRECTOR: JOEY XANDERS**.

Stephanie Peirolo

<><><><><><><><><><><><><><><><><><><><><><><><><><><><><><><><><><>

Walking with RJ

I was twenty-three years old when I had my first child. I was in labor for three days before my son, RJ, was born. So when I first laid eyes on him, I felt nothing but exhaustion.

I said, "This is it?"

It wasn't until about an hour later, when I woke up, and he was in my arms, wrapped up, that I felt it – that rush of maternal love, that primal adoration. And I thought, *This is it. This is how the species survives.*

I had another child, a daughter, Emma. And soon after Emma was born, their father and I divorced. He moved to Europe, and I raised the kids by myself.

Fast-forward. We're living in Seattle. The kids are both in high school, and they're doing great. They get straight A's.

The only thing RJ gets in trouble for is wearing his hair long, because he goes to Catholic school, and you're supposed to have your hair above your collar. But RJ plays the drums, he's in theatre, so he wears his hair long.

In the fall of his junior year, he's cast as the lead in the school play. He's going to be Atticus Finch in *To Kill a Mockingbird,* so he has to get his hair cut.

And I remember him walking out of the barbershop. He had a crew cut, and he was six feet tall and impossibly handsome.

He had this kind of shy smile, and I thought, *This is the man he is becoming.*

In January of his junior year, a cop showed up at our door, and he said, "Are you RJ's mom?" I said yes.

He said, "There's been an accident."

I said, "Is he dead?"

And he said, "Not yet, but we have to get to the hospital right away."

So the cop drove me to Harborview, which is not the closest hospital to our house, but it is the one with a trauma center. We went in the back way, where the ambulance bays are. Someone was hosing blood out of the back of the ambulance, all of this blood, and I remember thinking, *That's my son's.*

We walked in, and I saw RJ being wheeled away on a gurney just for a second, but I recognised his haircut.

It took a couple of hours for me to find out what had happened. RJ had been driving to his best friend's. He had his seat belt on. He didn't have any drugs or alcohol in his system, and he was hit from the side at a blind intersection.

He sustained a traumatic brain injury (or TBI), a number of broken bones, and he had broken his pelvis. At the time I didn't understand the gravity of a TBI, so I was worried about his pelvis.

I was the vice president of an advertising agency that was owned by a global conglomerate of advertising agencies. They had just changed their insurance plan.

Keep in mind it's the first week of January. So I don't have a list of my benefits, what's called a Summary Plan Description. What I have is an insurance card with a phone number on the back. So while RJ's in the ICU, I call the phone number, and the voice on the other end of the phone tells me, "ICU is covered, intensive brain-injury rehab is covered, skilled nursing facility . . ." And they list off all these great benefits.

And I remember thinking, *Thank God I don't have to worry about insurance. I've done everything right. I'm the vice president of a company.*

When RJ was discharged from ICU, he was transferred to the rehab facility, and shortly after he got there, they called me on the phone and they said, "Your insurance company called and said RJ's benefits are up on Friday."

I said, "No, no, no, no, he's got many more benefits," but of course I just had a voice on the other end of the phone, I didn't have the Summary Plan Description, and the facility had a different voice on the end of the phone.

So I went over there, and I said, "Where am I supposed to take him? He's in a coma."

They said, "Well, there's always foster care."

So Emma and I took RJ home. We made a hospital room in his bedroom. He had a PEG tube in his stomach, and that's how we pumped in nutrition.

They taught us how to do physical therapy. Emma was fifteen, and she said, "Mom, I will help you take care of RJ in any way I can, as long as it doesn't involve the Speedo zone." So when he needed to be changed, because of course he was in diapers, she would bring me a bucket of warm water and washcloths and put them by his door, and I would take them inside, close the door, and clean him up.

Coming out of a coma is nothing like what you see in the movies. It's a long, slow, painstaking process. It took RJ months to learn how to hold up his head in a seated position. We put him in his wheelchair, and his friends would come by every day after school. The girls took to showing up in short skirts and fishnet stockings. They would walk in front of the wheelchair (and RJ would lift up his head).

Months had passed, and I still couldn't get the Summary Plan Description. I kept calling them, and they'd be on the phone, and they'd be telling me my benefits, and I'd say, "You're giving me information that you're looking at. Give me, like, a screen grab of the computer screen that you're looking at." But they wouldn't do it.

I realised this is not a bureaucratic mix-up, this is intentional, and this is illegal. It turns out that this is a violation of a law called ERISA – the Employee Retirement Income Security Act of 1974.

So I called an ERISA lawyer and told him the situation, and he said, "I can help you, but you're going to have to give me a retainer of thirty thousand dollars."

I said, "Let me be clear. I'm a single parent. I have paid to set up a hospital room in my house. I pay a nurse to sit with my son, so that I can go to my job, so that I stay employed, so I can keep this insurance. I don't have thirty thousand dollars."

And he said, "I'm sorry, I can't help you."

At this point I was completely exhausted, and I was very concerned about getting fired, because I'd taken so much time off. So I applied for and was granted FMLA leave – the Family Medical Leave Act says that you can take twelve weeks of unpaid leave to care for a sick family member and they have to keep your job for you.

Shortly into my FMLA leave, I was fired.

These things are illegal, but you can't call the police on a corporation. And I couldn't afford an attorney.

When RJ turned eighteen, he was able to go on Medicaid, and I made the decision to put him into a nursing home. I found a facility that specialised in patients with TBIs. They had a much younger population – a lot of young men who had been in motorcycle accidents. All their patients were on Medicaid, so they didn't have much money. But they took really good care of RJ, and he continued to make slow progress.

He could do thumbs-up for yes, thumbs-down for no. We were visiting him, and Emma was teasing him, and he flipped her off, and I got really excited, 'cause that's like some manual dexterity happening there, right? And then he turned to me and he put his hand down, because, brain injury notwithstanding, he was not about to flip off his mother.

Before RJ's accident I had to drag him to Mass on Sundays, but after the accident he loved to go to church.

I'd say, "Do you want to go to Mass today?" He'd put his thumbs up.

He learned how to be able to put money in the collection plate again. And when he learned how to swallow – because apparently swallowing is incredibly complex; that took like a year to come back – he could take Communion, and you could see that it provided him so much solace.

In August of 2005 RJ got very sick, and we thought it was the flu. He still had his PEG tube in his stomach, and it had fallen out. That happens, and when it falls out, you put it back in. And you're supposed to X-ray to make sure you have it in the right place. Well, this facility couldn't afford an X-ray machine, so they guessed, and they guessed wrong.

His food had been going into his abdominal cavity, and he had sepsis. At the hospital the surgeon took me aside, and she said, "I can operate on RJ, and I might save his life, but he's going to go back into a deep coma, and he will never come out. Or you can let him go. You have to decide."

So I went down the hall, and I called his father, who was still in Europe, and I said, "What should I do?"

He said, "You're caring for him, it's your choice."

So I went into RJ's room, and RJ was completely aware of what was happening, and he was afraid. His eyes were open really wide.

And I said, "Honey, you're very sick, and they can't fix you. So you're gonna go to God." I tried to think of who he knew that had already died, but he was nineteen.

So I thought of my dad, who died before RJ was born, and I said, "RJ, you're gonna go to God, but my dad is there, and he's gonna come and find you, and I will be there soon."

It took RJ three days to die. It took him three days to come into the world, and three days to leave it.

People ask us how we cope. Emma has been an EMT, a volunteer firefighter. She works in an emergency room that is a trauma center, and she's applying to nursing school.

My friends saw what happened, and they started a nonprofit to help people who are fighting with their insurance company for covered benefits, even if they don't have enough money for a retainer. I'm the chair of the board, we have ERISA lawyers, and they're very good at what they do.

RJ would be twenty-seven years old. I still have that strong maternal love for him. The challenge now is to channel it, so it doesn't become corrosive. So that I don't say things to myself like, *Why didn't you keep him at home? Or, If you had made more money, you could've afforded to put him in a private nursing home, and then he never would've died.*

Most days I wake up, and the world is so diminished without him in it, it's like there's been a total eclipse of the sun. Only I'm the only one who can see it, and I know the light is never coming back.

But there are days where I wonder if RJ's existence isn't part of a larger narrative arc than I can understand. If maybe this slice in time was how RJ had to work out his destiny, and maybe my job was to walk with him.

Between the time of RJ's accident and his death, he wasn't able to speak; he was only able to say a handful of words. And the word he said most was "Mom."

And there are times now where I feel RJ. I feel that he *is*. And in those moments I know it's his turn, for his love to carry me.

STEPHANIE PEIROLO chairs the board of directors of the Health Care Rights Initiative, a nonprofit organisation providing advocacy and navigation services for patients and caregivers. She works in Seattle as a business consultant and is the author of the novel *Radio Silence* (2010). She's a graduate of Stanford University and has an MA in transformational leadership from Seattle University. Her daughter Emma is now a registered nurse who works in emergency medicine at a trauma center.

THIS STORY WAS TOLD ON DECEMBER 3, 2013, AT THE **NEPTUNE THEATRE, SEATTLE**. THE THEME OF THE EVENING WAS *TAKE ME OUT*. **DIRECTOR: MAGGIE CINO.**

An Icy Cold Patch

Magda Szubanski

Reclaiming Fear

So, you may or may not know that for a while I was the very public face of Jenny Craig weight loss. I lost a lot of weight, which was great. But then I started to put the weight back on, which wasn't so great.

And I got a call from the publicist, and she said, "Darling, I've had a phone call, and the paparazzi have got some shots of you on Bondi Beach in your bathers."

Now, I'm not an especially vain woman, but there are not too many women I know who would feel completely comfortable with having candid, unflattering pictures of themselves in their wet, clinging bathers splashed across every news stand in the country. And for just a moment, I felt so vulnerable that I wanted to cry.

Because I knew what was in store. I was about to be Kirstie Alley'd. I was going to be publicly shamed for my failure to keep the weight off. And that was not a prospect that I relished.

But there was a deeper and a far more disturbing fear. I felt as though a cold hand had reached deep into the depths of my soul, and was rattling the cage of a long-buried fear that I had completely forgotten I had. And that fear was a fear of the mob – that somehow I would do something unwittingly, and that people would turn into an unreasoning, nasty, irrational mob that would attack me.

It must seem strange to hear me say that, because I've been famous in this country for a very long time. And I have a great relationship with the public – people are very nice to me. In fact, one of the nice things that people say is, "Magda, you're so brave with the comedy characters that you portray in your performance. You're so *brave*."

I think often when they're saying that, what they're saying is, "You're so brave because you're prepared to let yourself look unattractive on national television." And I can't really relate to that because, to be honest, willingness to look unattractive has never, ever entered into my calculus of what it means to be brave.

I can't really relate to that word, *brave*. I can't really claim it, and that's because of my name.

You know me as Magda Szubanski. But the way my father would have said the name is *Magda Szubanski* [pronounces name with a thick Polish accent]. Because I'm half-Polish. And that Polishness completely determines how I feel about that word, brave.

When my father died, Mrs Pietcek came up to me at the funeral, and said, "Magda, you must understand. Only the bravest of the brave were asked to do what your father did in the war."

In 1939, when my father was 15, Hitler invaded Poland, and the world as my father knew it ceased to exist. His world of boating, and skiing trips to Zakopane, and nights at the theatre, was over, replaced by six years of brutal Nazi occupation.

And in 1943, in possibly the darkest hour of that occupation, my father, who was only 19, was recruited to become an assassin in a top-secret counterintelligence unit. The chief job of that unit was to protect the high command of the Polish resistance. And the way that they did that was to assassinate collaborators.

Just to make it very clear, my father was on the good side, fighting the Nazis. But the way that he was doing that was by killing his own people. And the crimes that these people, these Polish collaborators, had committed was that they were telling secrets of the resistance to the Germans.

Some of them were telling the Gestapo where Jewish people were hiding. It's important to know that Poland, under the Nazi regime, was the only country where the penalty for hiding a Jew was the death sentence. In fact, just even knowing of the existence of a Jew and not reporting it would likely get you killed.

And my father's parents, my grandparents, hid many Jewish people during the war. Of course I didn't know that when I was a little kid. Nor did I know that my father was an assassin. I just thought he was an ordinary dad out there mowing the lawn in his terry towelling hat.

And if you'd known my dad, you wouldn't have picked it either, because he was a very warm, affectionate kind of guy. But there were hints. It was like swimming in a warm river, and suddenly you would hit an icy cold patch that would just make your heart stop.

I didn't really know an awful lot about the war as a kid, and what I did know was from TV and movies. Of course in those movies, it was always about American soldiers, occasionally British, very rarely French. But I never, ever saw any Polish people. And so I kind of came to the conclusion that my father must have been fairly peripheral to the war, and maybe he wasn't really there in a big way, in the thick of it.

Until one day when I was about eight or nine, and I was sitting with my family in the lounge room of our home in North Crowden. We were watching a documentary, and it was about the Holocaust.

This was *nothing* like the war I'd seen in the movies. And as I saw those images of ordinary people, not soldiers – women, children, old people, little kids pleading for their lives, gaunt eyes staring from behind barbed wire, piles of naked bodies being bulldozed into pits – I was *beside myself*, utterly beside myself with grief and despair and a kind of helpless rage. But also a kind of incomprehension. I couldn't understand what could happen that could make people do that to one another.

And just at that moment, my father looked at the television screen and he said, "Ah, that's the street where we used to live before it was rezoned as part of the Warsaw Ghetto." Suddenly I realised that that horror wasn't out there – it was right here in our lounge room.

I looked at my father, I suppose for guidance and validation and comfort. But he was completely unaffected, completely impassive. And I felt then that there was a huge gulf that separated us.

As I grew older, I realised that the crucial difference was that he had been right there in the thick of it. And that immediate threat of the Nazis – of death, of torture, of being sent to a concentration camp – meant that he had had to perform a kind of emergency emotional triage, and he had jettisoned absolutely every single feeling that didn't support his survival.

But I *hadn't* been there. And without that urgent imperative to disassociate, I had the luxury of having a normal human response to this horror.

And I was terrified.

When I looked at my father, I saw his fearlessness, and it was reassuring. But I saw something else that eviscerated me – I saw his discomfort with my feelings. I saw his subtle, almost imperceptible, but unmistakable complete contempt for my fear.

In that moment, I vowed I would never feel fear again.

So began a kind of lifeline master class in the art of disassociation, as taught to me by my father, the assassin. But of course I hadn't conquered the fear, all I'd really done was to drive it into the deepest, darkest corner of my unconscious. So that as I grew up and matured, the fear didn't – it remained the fear of a nine-year-old girl, petrified.

So now, when the publicist was waiting for my response, in an instant, my world has changed. What had started out as an innocent swim on Bondi Beach had become a moment of reckoning, and now the paparazzi had me in their sights.

That fear came screaming out of my unconscious, in my face, and I was reduced to being that nine-year-old girl again. I felt as though every irrational fear that I had about human nature, about what humans are capable of, was about to come true.

The publicist said, "So, darling, what do you want me to do?" And I could feel my world crumbling. I could feel the ground giving way beneath my feet.

But just as I was about to fall, something happened, and it was something I didn't see coming. Something completely unexpected. And a voice that I didn't know I have came out of me.

And I said, "Fuck them. Do your worst. Do your worst, paparazzi. You are not gonna shame me off the beach. I'm gonna go down to Bondi, and I'm gonna be a fat middle-aged lady, along with the supermodels and the muscle men. I'm gonna wear my wet, clingy bathers, and there's not a freaking thing you can do about it."

So they published the photos. But because I'd refused to participate in the same game, the photos were unflattering, but the headlines said, "Magda Sports Her New

Beach Body." It was quite crazy, but nothing terrible happened, and the Australian public were lovely to me.

But this isn't about me saying, "Aww, gee, look, I was brave like my father would have wanted me to be."

I'm the second generation. I have the luxury and the very great privilege of being able to feel the normal feelings that my father, poor bugger, couldn't feel.

And finally, I was able to forgive myself for feeling that fear.

MAGDA SZUBANSKI is best known fo her roles as Mrs Hoggett in the Academy Award winning film *Babe* and its sequel *Babe: Pig In The City*, and as Sharon Strzelecki in the hit TV series and now feature film *Kath & Kimderella*. She has co-written and performed in some of Australia's most successful TV comedy shows, including *Fast Forward*, *D-Generation* and *Full Frontal*; co-wrote and produced the series *Something Stupid* and *Big Girl's Blouse*, and wrote, produced and starred in the series *Dogwoman*. Magda teamed up with the *Babe* creators again to voice *Happy Feet* and its sequel. Her other film credits include *Santa's Apprentice*, *The Crocodile Hunter: Collision Course*, *The Golden Compass*, *Dr Plonk* and *Bran Nu Dae*. Her first book, *Reckoning* (2015), won the ABIA Book of the Year. In addition to this, she has won NSW Premier's Literary Award, six other major awards, and was shortlisted for several more including the National Biography Award.

....

THIS STORY WAS TOLD ON AUGUST 22 2013 AT THE MELBOURNE WRITER'S FESTIVAL AT **THE TOWN HALL, MELBOURNE**, AUSTRALIA. THE THEME OF THE EVENING WAS *GUTS: STORIES OF MOXIE AND MIGHT*. **DIRECTOR: SARAH AUSTIN JENNESS**.

Adam Mansbach

<><><><><><><><><><><><><><><><><><><><><><><><><><><><><><><><><><><><>

Go the %&# to Sleep

It's November 2011, and I am the most controversial parent in America by virtue of a short, obscene, fake children's book by the name of *Go the Fuck to Sleep*.

It's fourteen stanzas long – about four hundred words, many of them repeated more than once – and I wrote it in thirty-nine minutes with no pants on.

Now, I'm a literary novelist by trade, so the manner in which this particular creation of mine ascended into the zeitgeist was perplexing to say the least. All I was trying to do in this book was simply capture the interior monologue of a parent attempting to put a small child to bed.

My daughter, Vivien – my beautiful, brilliant, amazing daughter, Vivien – was two and a half at the time, and sleeping was not high on her list of priorities. I would sometimes be in her room for two, two and a half hours.

This gets tedious after a while.

And I just wanted to capture the paradox that on one hand you can love a kid to death, and on the other hand be so desperate to get out of that room after the first hour that, you know, if Don Corleone walked in the room and was like, "I'll put the child to bed, but you may have to do a service for me one day, and this day may never come, . . ." you'd be like, "Whatever, Don Corleone, just take this baby. We'll work the details out later."

So I read the book for the first time in public at a museum in Philadelphia, in late April, six months before the book was supposed to be published. It was part of an evening of ten-minute performances. There were about fifty of them, and I went on last, after a ninety-four-year-old tap dancer. And you really never want to follow a ninety-four-year-old, you know what I mean? Not on the highway, not onstage – just never.

I get up there, and I read the book to two hundred people, and the response is good, but I don't think much of it.

I go home, I go to sleep, and when I wake up the next morning, *Go the Fuck to Sleep* is ranked 125th on Amazon.

Now, as a literary writer, I didn't even know they made numbers that low. And by the end of the week, the book has shot up to number one.

I don't want to get overly technical here, but the book *does not exist*. And is *not going to exist* for some months. So we very quickly rush it toward production, with the hope of getting it out into the world by Father's Day.

Meanwhile, however, a PDF of the book leaks and starts ricocheting around the Internet, and lands in hundreds of thousands of people's mailboxes.

We had put this PDF together because we wanted to send it to booksellers. We thought it might be something of an uphill battle getting them to stock, much less support, a book called *Go the Fuck to Sleep*.

So hundreds of thousands of people are getting the book for free, and we're panicking. We're thinking that we're not gonna sell a single book.

Luckily for us, it's bad form to show up at a baby shower with a low-resolution, stapled-together PDF that you printed out off the Internet and be like, "Here, we love you so much, it's such a wonderful time in your life."

But things start going crazy. I notice that a woman in Australia has posted the entire book as a Facebook album, and all this traffic is going to her Facebook page.

So I write her an email, and I'm like, "Thank you for your enthusiasm, but the book hasn't come out yet. We'd like to sell a couple of books when it does eventually get published. So please take this down."

And she said, "I'll take it down if you want, but I want *you* to know that seven hundred people have contacted me since yesterday asking where they can buy the book, and I'm sending them to Amazon."

I'm like, "Please. Ignore my previous email."

So we weather the storm, and the book comes out, and it debuts at number one on the *New York Times* Best Seller list. Samuel Jackson reads the audio book, probably his best work since *Pulp Fiction*.

And all of this craziness is just unending. There's a group called Family First New Zealand that wants to ban the book. Their press release was amazing. I have it framed in my office. It said, "While this book may be harmless, and even amusing, in the hands of normal, well-adjusted parents, it could pose a real danger to children in the hands of maladjusted, dysfunctional parents."

The same, of course, could be said of, like, a spoon. They didn't really catch much momentum on the boycott.

But the weirdest thing of all for me is that I'm thrown into a crisis, because suddenly – and inexplicably – I'm being positioned as a parenting expert. I'm getting emails from people thanking me for saving their marriages, and from therapists saying they bought the book in bulk and handed it out to their freaked-out young-parent clients. And also from people who are furious and irate and saying things like, "I would never read this book to a child."

It would take a very specific blend of literacy and illiteracy to mistakenly read this book to a child. I mean, it does say "Fuck" on the cover.

At the time the publishing industry is in free fall, my visiting professorship has just ended, and I'm on my way back to California and my mortgage. So I feel like I have to ride the gravy train, and if I'm gonna be a fake parenting expert and feed my family, that was fine with me. I'd do it.

But because all of the publicity and the rigmarole around this book, I'm actually not spending much time at all with *my* child. So not only do I feel like I'm not a parenting expert, I feel like I might not even be a decent parent. I'm on the road all the time. When I *am* home, I'm on the phone eight, ten hours a day, answering the same five questions from media around the world.

So that was my state of mind when I was asked to host a fund-raiser for Boston Children's Hospital that was being held in Los Angeles, counterintuitively. They offered to fly me and my family to Los Angeles for the weekend, and put us up in a hotel where John Wayne had once kept a cow. They were gonna give away copies of the book, and all I had to do was shake hands and sign books and imbibe alcoholic beverages.

It should tell you something about where I was at, that an evening spent hobnobbing with rich, drunken Los Angelenos sounded like a vacation. So I say, "Cool," and we go to L.A.

I get to the fund-raiser, at which point I find out that I am cohosting this event with another controversial luminary of parenting, Dr Richard Ferber. For those who don't know, Dr Ferber is the author of a book called *The Ferber Method,* which is a sleep-training concept.

I haven't read the book, but I'll try to summarise it for you. In essence, Dr Ferber's method stipulates that if your child is crying, you ignore that child. You let them "cry it out," thus teaching them to self-soothe. And also that the world is a cold, horrible place, filled with people who only pretend to love them.

By contrast, what we were practicing with Vivien is called "attachment parenting." Attachment parenting dictates than when your child makes a peep, a whimper, the slightest sound, you rush into their room, grab them, cradle them in your arms, and tell them that you love them.

Thus ensuring that the child will sleep in *your* bed until she leaves for college. Or in some cases, grad school.

So I wasn't really sure how this fund-raiser was gonna go. But I meet Dr Ferber, and he's a nice, avuncular guy. We have a nice chat. And then the fund-raiser commences, and I begin to drink.

Dr Ferber's role, however, is a little more involved than mine. At a moment when inebriation has settled heavily on the crowd, Dr Ferber pulls down a screen and begins to give a lengthy, highly detailed slide show about how to put a baby to sleep.

The problem is that he and I are probably the only people here who've ever put a baby to sleep, because the rest of these people have nannies who do that. So nobody's really interested.

The highlight of the slide show comes when a picture of me from *Go the Fuck to Sleep* flashes on the screen.

It's me sneaking out of a child's room, and Dr Ferber's like, "This, right here, this is what you should *never do*. This is completely wrong." I'm like, *Dr Ferber just threw me under the sleep-training bus*. Everybody turns to look at me, and I just keep drinking.

I go back to my hotel room, and I wake up the next morning, and I find in my inbox an email from Dr Richard

Ferber. The subject heading of the email is "Why didn't you tell me that I know you?"

I'm like, *Dr Ferber has lost his mind.*

Then I opened the email, and my mind is blown, because it turns out that unbeknownst to me, I went to summer camp with Dr Ferber's son, the unforgettably named Thad Ferber. He and I were friends and camp-mates, until I got kicked out of the camp. He lived two towns over from me, which at thirteen means you only see that dude like once a year.

But in 1990 the play date I had with Thad Ferber consisted of a trip to Tower Records on Newbury Street in Boston to buy rap records. I was a deejay and an emcee, and this is what I did.

We get to Tower Records and find that the rap section is being guarded by a life-size cardboard cutout of MC Hammer, who was himself a very controversial figure in 1990 – not considered to be the most authentic or talented dude by hard-core hip-hoppers like myself.

So naturally I rip the head off of the cardboard cutout and stuff it into my jacket – not in an act of theft, as much as decapitation. And as I attempt to sneak out of Tower Records, Thad Ferber and I are accosted and captured by Tower Records security. Thad Ferber – guilty only by association – and I are taken down into the dungeon, deep in the bowels of Tower Records, where we are seated, informed that the cardboard cutout of MC Hammer is worth five thousand dollars, which seems spurious in retrospect, and told that we will be released only into police or parental custody.

Now, this was not my first rodeo. I got in trouble all the time. This was like a regular Tuesday for me. So I gave the Tower Records police a phone number that I had memorised for occasions such as this, one that I knew just rang and rang and rang, and nobody ever picked up, and there was no answering machine. This was an incredibly important phone number for me to have at thirteen.

And it would have worked. They would have tried it three times, gotten bored, and let us go.

Thad Ferber, however, had never been to the rodeo. So he gave them him his actual phone number, and in short order Dr Richard Ferber shows up at Tower Records. I am released into his custody, somehow, and he drives me home.

Oh, and Thad Ferber and I are banned for life from Tower Records. Which turned out to be their life, not mine, because they're defunct now.

All this came flooding back to me as I read the email. And it was a great weight off my shoulders, because clearly, even the great and powerful Dr Richard Ferber is not so infallible as a parent, in that he had let his kid hang out with me.

I start to think that maybe all of the worrying I've been doing is unnecessary. Maybe I am as much of and as little of a parenting expert as anybody else who's ever had a child.

Maybe I'm not actually faking this. Or maybe we're *all* faking this equally. And maybe I do know a couple of things. Like keep your sense of humour at all costs. Or embrace the absurdity of the situations in which you find yourself.

Or even, realise that there are worse things than spending two hours trapped in a room with the person you love most in the world.

I mean, you could be in the basement of a Tower Records.

Or listening to a slide show by Dr Ferber.

So with a sense of profound relief, I packed up my family. And for what felt like the first time in a very, very long time, we went home.

ADAM MANSBACH is a novelist, screenwriter, cultural critic and humourist. He is the author of the *New York Times* bestseller *Go the Fuck to Sleep* (2011), and its sequel, *You Have to Fucking Eat* (2011). His novels include *Rage Is Back* (2013), *Angry Black White Boy* (2005) and *The End of the Jews* (2009), winner of the California Book Award, as well as the thrillers *The Dead Run* (2013) and *The Devil's Bag Man* (2015), and several middle-grade titles. He also wrote "Wake the Fuck Up," a 2012 campaign video starring Samuel L. Jackson, and the screenplay for the motion picture *Barry (2016)*, about Barack Obama's first year in New York City.

THIS STORY WAS TOLD ON SEPTEMBER 21, 2015, AT THE **BOULDER THEATER, BOULDER, COLOURADO**. THE THEME OF THE EVENING WAS *HIGH ANXIETY*. **DIRECTOR: SARAH AUSTIN JENNESS**.

Karen Gearon

∞∞∞∞∞∞∞∞∞∞∞∞∞∞∞∞∞∞∞∞∞∞∞∞∞∞∞∞∞∞∞∞∞∞∞∞∞∞

The Dunnes Stores Strikers

I'm 20 years of age. I'm the shop steward in Dunnes Stores Henry Street in Dublin, and I receive an instruction from our trade union called a "mandate" that we're no longer to handle South African produce because of Apartheid.

We knew very little about South Africa. We didn't know how to *pronounce or spell* Apartheid. But we followed the union instructions. We went around the store to find out what was South African. It was mainly Outspan oranges and grapefruits. And we informed management that we were going to follow this instruction.

We were immediately put on cash registers, and I remember sitting there, myself, Mary Manning and Liz Deacey, and this woman coming up with two Outspan grapefruit in her basket. And we looked at each other, and we prayed that she wasn't going to come to one of us.

But she did. She came to Mary Manning, and Mary Manning refused to handle South African produce and was suspended.

We came out and went on strike. And I remember well, that that was the first day, the 19th of July, 1984, at a quarter past 12 on a Thursday, that the Dunnes Stores anti-Apartheid strike started.

As I said, we knew very little about South Africa. We knew there was discrimination, but we didn't know what sort of discrimination it was. And we were a few days on the picket line, and a man called Nimrod Sejake came onto the line, and he started telling us about what Apartheid was all about. He was an exile from South Africa, and he'd been living in Ireland for about 15 years.

He told us what it was like to be a black person living in South Africa. You couldn't sit on the same seat as a white person, you couldn't use the same toilet. You had to be out of the cities and the towns that white people lived in by a certain time, and you had to have a passbook to leave your township.

He explained what Apartheid was like in one of the best ways that I've heard it described:

It was like a pint of Guinness. The majority of the people living in South Africa were black, and the minority were white. And like a pint of Guinness, the white sat on top of the black.

Nimrod and what he was telling us about South Africa changed everything for us personally. It was no longer a union instruction. We were never, ever going to handle South African goods until Apartheid had gone, and freedom for everybody in South Africa had been achieved.

The strike went on, and our union official told us, "May take a coupla weeks."

We were *six months* on strike when we got an invitation to meet Bishop Desmond Tutu. He was coming from America, going over to Oslo to pick up a Nobel Peace Prize, and he said, "I'd like to meet the Dunnes Stores strikers in London."

So we took the ferry over to London to meet Bishop Desmond Tutu, who was about to collect the Nobel Peace Prize. It was the first time that we really had any media interest, and the cameras are there. This small man came into the room, and people that know me know I'm not a very huggy person. So the first thing he did was come and hug us, and I was like, *Oh God*.

Then he told us and the media how proud he was of us, and how brave we were. And for somebody like that to say that, it just brought more passion to us than we ever had before. He told us that he would go back to South Africa, and he would tell the ordinary workers – the ordinary black workers in South Africa – that they weren't on their own, that there were people from other countries that cared enough to do something about Apartheid.

That was in December of '84. We went through a long winter. The first anniversary of the strike happened, and we were getting very little support from the government, or from a lot of Irish people, or the trade union movement, but we stuck to our guns.

And then Bishop Desmond Tutu asked us to come to South Africa to see for ourselves what Apartheid was all about.

Well, we had no money to go because we had earned, when we were working, about 85 pounds a week, and we were now on 21 pounds a week. The union would only give us 1,000 pounds, and the trip was going to cost about 8,000. So one night in Dublin city, we got as many supporters as we could together, and we went around to every pub in Dublin city raising funds for that trip.

We raised *7,000* pounds, *in 1985*, to go on that trip to South Africa. That was the support we got from ordinary, working-class people in Dublin.

The trip was organised, and we headed over to Heathrow, and were about to board the British Airways plane at Heathrow to go to South Africa, when we were stopped and held for a number of hours there. They wouldn't let us on the plane because the South African authorities said they wouldn't allow the plane to land with us on board.

Eventually, through negotiations, we boarded the plane (only to be told afterwards that the captain had told all the passengers that we were the reason the plane had been delayed for so long.) We were all separated, we weren't allowed to sit together. So you can imagine the atmosphere. We were quite terrified.

Remember, we were only 20. The youngest of us was 17, the oldest was 24. We arrived in what was then called Jan Smuts Airport, and when we arrived, on each side of the tarmac, there were soldiers. We thought this was the norm.

We got our passports checked, and soldiers came and asked us were we the group from Ireland? We said we were. Immediately there were about 40 armed soldiers around us with machine guns.

We were escorted upstairs and held under armed guard for eight hours. We did not know what was going to happen to us, because we had heard stories of people disappearing once they got to South Africa.

Eventually we were informed that we were going to be sent back on the same plane, but while we were there for eight hours we couldn't even go to the bathroom alone. Two women soldiers would come in with us, and the door would have to stay open.

When we eventually got back on the plane, we were disappointed that we were leaving, but were relieved that we were safe.

Going up the steps of the plane, I'll never forget, when I got to the top of the stairs, I turned around, and I put my fist up, and I said, "We will be back when South Africa's free!"

And Sandra, one of the strikers, pushed me in and said, "Get the . . . into the plane."

We arrived back at Heathrow. We had left on a Monday at 12 noon, and this was now Wednesday at seven in the morning, and none of our families knew where we were at all. So you can imagine the worry.

When we arrived we were told by the captain that all passengers must remain seated, that the police were boarding the plane.

We looked at each other and said, "Oh God, here we go again, we're going to be thrown out of Britain as well."

But we weren't. We were escorted into a press conference.

Eleven workers – ten young women and one young man – and we were in a press conference with all of the media from the UK and Ireland.

There was a headline that ran that said: "The most dangerous people in the world." And that was us, the Dunnes Stores strikers!

When we got back from South Africa and London, a mass picket was organised. Now, up to that moment, as I said, there was very little support for the strike. There was a lot of lip service paid, but not real support.

On that day, the Saturday, there were nearly 7,000 people on that picket line. You couldn't walk up or down Henry Street for the amount of people that were out there supporting us. (So thank you to the South African Apartheid government for kicking us out.)

The strike continued, and then in October of 1985 the most amazing thing happened. We were invited over to address the United Nations in New York. Can you imagine? We were shop workers, and the UN wanted us to talk to them. So I went over, and a colleague, Michelle Gavin, came over with me.

I got up to do my speech, and I was terrified in South Africa, but I think I was even more terrified in New York, because there were all these people in suits and, you know, what would I say to posh people, rich people, people that were really important, not just Dunnes' little workers from Dublin in Ireland?

But I did my speech, and it was the first time ever recorded in the UN's history where there was actually standing applause, because we were just ordinary, every-day people standing up for what was right. And that made a difference to everybody that was sitting in that room that day.

When we first started the strike, there were two anti-Apartheid movements, one in Cork and one in Dublin. By the time the strike ended – which lasted two years and nine months – there were more than thirty-six anti-Apartheid groups, and there were Dunnes Stores support groups that formed anti-Apartheid groups after that. So the momentum was really good. The Irish government introduced a boycott of South Africa on the first of January, 1987. We were the first Western country to actually put a boycott of South African produce in place. And that was a direct result of the work of us, the Dunnes Stores strikers.

We eventually went back to work. Then we all kind of drifted apart, and tried to go back to some sort of normal life. Then all of a sudden – we couldn't believe it – Nelson Mandela was released from prison! Did we ever think we'd see the day? And then we found out he was coming to Ireland, and he wanted to meet the Dunnes Stores strikers. The person that we had idolised for so many years, and we had lost so much, but we had gained so much too because we had so much passion about what he represented.

When we met him, I looked up at him, and he's a very tall man. I thought, *Oh my God, you are the person I've always wanted to meet, and now I'm standing here*. It was totally surreal.

He shook hands with us and said, "You are so brave."

He gave us his medal of bravery. Nelson Mandela, us. I just couldn't believe it. And when he said we were so brave, all of the bad feeling, all of the hurt that we went through in those bad winters, just totally fell away because he acknowledged what we did, and we didn't care about anybody else.

I wasn't at home the night Nelson Mandela died. I was actually in the pub, and my mom rang me to tell me he had died. It was heartbreaking.

The following morning we got a call to go up to Dublin to sign the book of condolence. I'm living in Kerry and when I got in my car, I was going down the drive, and I got a another phone call.

"Bring your passport just in case."

I thought, *Yeah, right*.

But I arrive, we sign the book of condolences, and within an hour, we're told we're going to the funeral of Nelson Mandela in South Africa.

All of us.

When we arrive in Johannesburg, we're scared, right? We're so nervous. But everything goes well, and we're going through arrivals, and we see an Irish flag. And it's the Irish Embassy coming to collect us, the Dunnes Stores strikers, to bring us to our hotel. And then we're invited to the Irish Embassy in Pretoria to have dinner that evening with the President of Ireland, Michael D. Higgins, with our deputy leader and with the ambassador.

We're all there, and we're back in South Africa.

And South Africa is free.

KAREN GEARON was the shop steward of the Dunnes Stores Anti-Apartheid Strike, which started on 19 July 1984 and lasted two years and nine months. Karen returned to Dunnes after the strike ended but was dismissed thirteen months later; she went on to win an unfair dismissal case. After the case, Karen found it very hard to get employment in Dublin so moved to Kerry where she has lived for the past 26 years and works in the community development sector.

THIS STORY WAS TOLD ON SEPTEMBER 5, 2014, AT **THE FREEMASON'S HALL, DUBLIN**. THE THEME OF THE EVENING WAS *DON'T LOOK BACK*. **DIRECTOR: CATHERINE BURNS**.

Cole Kazdin

<><><><><><><><><><><><><><><><><><><><><><><><><><><><><><><><><>

Déjà Vu (Again)

I wanted a fresh start. I was living in New York. My boyfriend, Adam, had just broken up with me and moved across the country to Los Angeles. He was a good guy – it was just one of those "going nowhere for three years" relationships.

Neither of us had done anything horrible, like have an affair. We just weren't a good fit.

Which my mother used to tell me on the phone the whole three years. Very gently. Like, "You're both such nice people. Maybe you're just not a good fit."

But Adam and I were both just passive enough to keep it going. If things got bad, and one of us might begin to muster the courage to pull the plug, then it would be one of our birthdays. Or we'd get really great concert tickets. And that would keep the relationship going for a few more months. And months turned into years.

In three years Adam never told me he loved me. And I think I loved him, but I wasn't going to say it first. (Because I'm so mature.)

Then one night Adam took me out to this beautiful dinner. He told me he cared about me very deeply. And that he never wanted to marry me.

It was essentially a reverse proposal.

And that was it. He broke up with me, he moved to Los Angeles, it was over. And it was so painful for me.

I remember just wanting to forget him – forget the past three years and just wake up one morning and start fresh.

I got my wish.

I woke up in an ambulance, wearing a cheerleading outfit (which, if you're over thirty and it's not Halloween, raises questions, you know?).

There were EMTs all around me, and then I was on a gurney. Then I was being placed into a CT scanner, and then I was in this hospital room with all these concerned strangers gathered around me. But they weren't strangers. I just couldn't identify them.

What I didn't know was that earlier that day there'd been an accident. I'd been filming this television pilot. It was a movie spoof show. The pilot was a parody of *Bring It On,* the cheerleading movie. We were asked to do a stunt that we never rehearsed.

The stunt was I was to be thrown high up in the air and *caught.*

I was thrown high up in the air . . . but I landed on my back and my head.

I suffered a massive concussion and a slipped disk in my back. I could barely walk, and I had no idea who I was.

Diagnosis: amnesia.

So I also didn't know that my boyfriend had dumped me a few weeks before and moved to Los Angeles. I didn't know anything.

In the hospital someone put a phone up to my ear and told me it was my mother. I heard this frantic female voice on the other end of the line, and it meant nothing. A friend knew where I lived, took me home, dug the keys out of my purse, got me into my apartment, and put me into bed.

I wanted to call my dad. I remember having that thought.

My friend said, "Why don't you rest? We can call him later."

But I wanted to call my dad, and I needed help, because I didn't know the number.

Again my friend kind of put me off. "Why don't you rest? We'll call later. Sleep a couple of hours."

I started getting frustrated. "Why aren't you helping me? I want to *call my dad!*"

My friend was looking at me like I was out of my mind.

Finally he said, "Don't you remember? You just called your dad. You've talked to him three times. We've done this *three times.* So you can call him, but it'll be the fourth time. And I'm just worried we're starting to freak him out."

This whole conversation, by the way, is happening with me still wearing the cheerleading outfit. This little white pleated skirt and matching top. Because when the hospital discharges you, it's like prison – they give you the clothes you showed up in, which for me was the costume from the pilot.

I had both short- and long-term amnesia. So I knew some things: I knew how to speak and I knew how to read. But I didn't know the big stuff, like who I was.

I also couldn't retain anything. So if someone left the room and came back ten minutes later, we had to start over.

I was living quite literally moment to moment.

A cat walks into the bedroom. *Why is there a cat in here?* People tell me it's my cat.

Everyone that came and went, they were just strangers to me from a past I didn't even know existed.

They tried to help. I remember my best friend, Amy, stormed into the bedroom, screaming, "She's a vegetarian! Don't let her eat any meat!!"

143

That sounded familiar, but it didn't mean anything. I mean, I could have been gnawing on a veal shank. But it sounded important, and I didn't want to forget it, so I wrote it down. There was a pad of Post-it notes on a table next to my bed.

I wrote, *"You are a vegetarian."*

Someone had called Adam, and he flew in from L.A. right away and was at my bedside with tears in his eyes.

In fact, the first night he slept in my bed with me, which I remember was kind of weird and, I thought, presumptuous because, like, *Who is this guy in my bed?* He said he was my boyfriend, but he could have been the mailman. I don't know – I've got amnesia.

The next day Adam showed me pictures of us together, to see if maybe that would jog my memory (and maybe even to make a case for the fact that we were a couple). Pictures of a recent trip I had taken to L.A.: Adam and Cole at the beach, Adam and Cole in front of Mann's Chinese Theatre, Adam and Cole in the Ferris wheel on the Santa Monica Pier.

I was in the pictures but I remembered none of it.

I wrote down everything. I was terrified of forgetting. Every piece of information was precious. Anytime someone told me something, or on the rare occasions when something might come back on its own, I wrote it down.

"You are a vegetarian."

"We are at war with Iraq."

"Kristen is your friend who is slutty."

One afternoon I was in a cab, coming home from physical therapy, going over the Queensboro Bridge. I noticed the hole in the skyline where the Twin Towers used to be. My accident happened in November of 2001, and this was a month or so after that.

I thought, *That's funny* . . .

I wrote it down on a Post-it: *"Twin Towers gone."*

Adam was the Wonderful Boyfriend. This accident was the best thing that could ever have happened to our relationship. He moved into my apartment. He took me to my weekly neurologist appointments and almost-daily physical therapy.

He doled out my medications at night and then held me when I woke screaming in the middle of the night from the nightmares that those medications gave me. Or from the sheer disorientation of not knowing who or where I was.

A girl from yoga visited. *I do yoga? What else do I do?* I was on this detective mission to find out who I was.

I found journals written in my handwriting, in another language. Adam told me it was Portuguese from when I lived in Brazil. *I lived in Brazil?*

Cool. What else?

Do I paint?

Can I cook?

Am I an asshole?

(I mean, what if I'm an asshole?)

I overheard doctors saying things like, "We don't know how long she's going to be like this" and "We're not sure if she'll ever fully recover." And they're talking about me. I mean, I'm sitting right there in the room.

The only thing I could be sure of was this growing pile of Post-it notes on my bedside table. I thought the bigger that pile got, the more of a person I became.

But it still wasn't me. It was just information, filling an empty space.

Then one afternoon I was in a cab coming home from physical therapy, going over the Queensboro Bridge again. I started to cry. I had no idea why. But I couldn't stop.

And it was right as we passed the hole in the skyline where the Twin Towers used to be. When it first happened, there was that really chilling empty space, like ghosts of buildings.

I felt flooded. I mean, I wailed. And I couldn't figure it out. And then it came to me: I was *remembering*. But it wasn't a fact or a thing – it was a *feeling*. It was the first time since the accident that I felt real.

That night Adam was tucking me into bed. He had just given me my medications, and he was writing it down on a Post-it note, for when in five minutes I asked if it was time for my medications, as I did every night.

I watched this man taking such wonderful care of me, and I was overcome with emotion.

I said, "I love you."

And he said nothing.

So I said it again (because I had amnesia and I could get away with that).

"I love you."

Again nothing. I didn't understand.

And then I remembered. The breakup and all the pain that went with it. His move to L.A. Then a post-9/11 reconciliation. September 11 happened, and we were going to give it one more try.

I went out to L.A. to visit him. We went to the beach, and we went to Mann's Chinese Theatre, and we rode the Ferris wheel at the Santa Monica Pier.

I thought of everything he was doing for me. If this wasn't love, what was?

Why was he even here? And I think the answer is, he's a good, good man, and he cared for me very deeply. But he was a Giuliani boyfriend. Good in crisis.

Maybe he loved me and just couldn't say the words. I'll never know. I mean, I think I loved him, and I wanted to hear it. But maybe I just wanted to say, "Thank you," and I couldn't differentiate.

It took about six months for me to recover. My memory just came back slowly over time. And then I must have been fully healed, because a few months after that, Adam and I broke up again. Only this time I knew it was coming because we'd done it before.

I wanted this fresh start. And I got it. I lost myself completely, and then got myself back, almost as if following a script, replaying my entire history with Adam. Nothing had changed.

But this time, that was comforting. Because if nothing changed, it meant I knew who I was. That I was a real person.

And that even without my memory, I was still me.

COLE KAZDIN is a writer, performer and four-time Emmy-winning TV news producer living in Los Angeles. She is a regular contributor for VICE and has written for the *New York Times, Salon* and *Cosmopolitan*. She has produced television for HBO Documentaries, ABC Network News and Discovery. She tells stories across the country with The Moth MainStage and performs all over Los Angeles, where she is a proud three-time Moth GrandSLAM champion. She has lectured at universities and teaches writing and storytelling around the country. **www.colekazdin.com.**

THIS STORY WAS TOLD ON AUGUST 27 2014 AT THE **BYHAM THEATER, PITTSBURGH.** THE THEME OF THE EVENING WAS *DON'T LOOK BACK.* **DIRECTOR: CATHERINE BURNS.**

Samuel James

Jenny

I was twelve years old, and I was in my third foster home. And my very *first* foster father had just called.

He called to say that he was very sorry to hear about my mother. But what *he* didn't know was that nobody had told me she was dead.

I was in foster homes because my parents drank. They weren't bad people; I always felt loved. But when they weren't drinking, they were better parents. And they were drinking more and more frequently.

Eventually people started to notice. I never noticed, because I didn't have another childhood to compare it to. So when I got taken out of my home, I was very confused and upset.

When I found out that she had died, I just got empty – hollowed out. And then when no one else called to say that she had died, I started to get really angry.

You know, like, burn-the-world angry.

And being a kid, a black kid, in foster homes in Maine, and burn-the-world angry, there's not a lot of foster homes that wanna hang on to you for very long.

I started going through 'em pretty quick. I learned the magic number was five. If you get to five foster homes, you're marked. You're trouble.

So you can't get placement, and you are homeless. And then you go into shelters. You can only stay in a shelter for thirty days, and then you're on to the next, and on to the next.

This is affectionately called the "shelter shuffle."

The education you get in the shelter is nothing to mention. When I was a little boy, I remember my father telling me that, because I am black, I will have to be twice as smart as the smartest white man in the room to get recognised half as much.

So education was always a very important thing to me. I knew I had to straighten out. When I was fourteen, and I got my seventh foster home, I knew I had to hang on to this for dear life, no matter the cost.

I get to my seventh foster home. The caseworker drops me off. I bring all my stuff into the room, my room, which was in the basement (they're almost always in the basement).

And I'm really nervous, because I don't wanna mess this up. So I go up onto the porch, and I light a cigarette.

The foster father comes out, and then it hits me that maybe this man, that the state has put in charge of me, might have something to say about this. But he doesn't. Instead he leans on the railing with me and lights his own cigarette.

I think, *This is beautiful. This is just me and him, watching the sun set over the pines. Beautiful, beautiful.*

He turns to me, and he says, "Yep. I never had no problem with coloureds."

And I think, *Well, with an attitude like that, how could you?*

So this man, it turns out, wasn't the prince you might think. There was another foster child there, and he was twelve years old, and he had foetal alcohol syndrome, and this man liked to torture him. The man also had a dog who was old and dying, and he liked to kick the dog.

It wasn't going well, and it becomes this frustration where this is your life, and you can't do anything about it. I can't help the kid. I can't help the dog. I can't help myself.

It's like you're starving to death, and there's one source of food, and it's this apple down between these rocks. You can reach your hand in and grab it, but you can't pull it out while holding it. And this is your life.

But on the bus to school, there was this cute little brunette named Jenny, sitting by herself, nose in a book. And that was usually what *I* would do. So one day I asked her if she wanted to be loners together.

She laughed. And I have to tell you that it is so great to have somebody in your life who laughs.

So I'm talking to her on the bus every day, and pretty soon we're talking every night on the phone. And that's going really well, but back at the foster home, things are getting worse and worse and worse. There's this family get-together, and during dinner the foster father blows up at me, and he calls me a black bastard in front of everybody in the room.

It wasn't the first time I'd heard a racial slur out of his mouth. But it wasn't that. It was the rage in his voice. And the fact that there was a roomful of people, and when I looked at every pair of eyes in the room, they all just went to the floor.

I was abandoned, and completely alone, and nobody had my back. This was when the panic set in. Where it was finally too hard to stay. I had to go.

So the next morning my caseworker drops me off at the shelter. And at this point I'm completely accepting of this, because I'm not gonna get an eighth foster home. It's very clear I'm not gonna make it three more years at this place, so this is the best I'm gonna do.

But I take my allotted phone time at night, and I still call Jenny. I don't tell her where I am, because I just lost my one chance to go to college. And because I move so much, I've lost every friend I've ever had, including her.

She just doesn't know it yet.

And as long as I can keep her on the phone, she won't.

But eventually, it slips out. And I can't remember what she said. I just remember getting empty again and hanging up. I wait the next week to call her, and almost immediately she hands the phone to her father.

Now, at this point I've had a lot of conversations in my life about "Don't call the house again," "Don't come by here," "You're a bad influence." But that's not the conversation I have. What he says to me is, "Would you like to come live with us?"

When I tell you that, you need to understand that my relationship with Jenny had been only on the phone or on the bus. She'd never been to my house. I'd never been to hers. And her father, who I'm talking to right now, had never even met me.

He'd never seen my face. The first contact we're having is *right now,* on the phone.

So when he asked me if I wanna do this, my visceral gut reaction is, *Hell no.* Because I have actual blood relatives that did not take me in when I went into foster care. No family had ever done me any good.

But my father raised me from a very young age to know it's okay to be scared but not to ever be stupid.

So I said, "Yes."

My caseworker drops me off at Jenny's, and it is a huge, beautiful place. Everybody there has huge, beautiful smiles. Her father, her mother. Her four siblings.

A bigger bunch of overachievers in your life you have never seen. None of them had seen an A-minus, ever.

And this was the time when I realised that, for the first time in my life, I am in way over my head. Because prior to this, everything had been about survival. But this was gonna have to be about betterment, and achievement.

While this is all happening, my father is trying to prove to the state that he's got his act together, and eventually we get to a place where we get a supervised visit.

Now, supervised visit means this: it's him and me and a caseworker in a very stale, fluorescently lit office. And I am petrified, because I've always lived by these little credos that my father has taught me.

But there's a part of me that thinks, *Uh, I might have made this up just to get through. Maybe he's the drunk jerk that they think he is. But I need him to be the man that I think he is.*

I get in there. And he's the man I think he is.

So eventually we get a visit where he gets to come to Jenny's. And he comes, and they are naturally protective of me and a little trepidatious about this.

They have an old piano, and I mention, "My father plays the piano."

What I don't say is that my father is a world-class jazz pianist. So when he sits down to play the piano, the only thing more beautiful than the sound coming out, is the sound of all of the family's jaws hitting the floor at once.

And in what was a really *surreal* moment for them, he becomes *real* to them as well. And they begin to champion me and him getting together, and after a while I go back to live with him.

Eventually I go to college. And the other day, I was talking to Jenny about this very thing, and I told her that the thing that sticks with me about it is that I was a really angry kid. I wasn't a good kid. These people took me in.

And by no means did I pay them back with kindness when I was there. I was still very, very angry.

And it hangs on me that I didn't treat them as well as they treated me.

Jenny said, "I don't remember you being a bad kid. I think you're being too hard on yourself."

And I can't tell if she's right, and I am being too hard on myself, or if she's just as kind as somebody raised by her parents should be.

SAMUEL JAMES is a world-touring musician and the creator of *Kitty Critic*, a music/comedy web series in which musicians perform live for their fans' cats. James was born last in a long line of performers, including dancers, storytellers, choir singers, porch-stomping guitar thumpers and a session jazz pianist, all dating back to the 1800s.
www.therealsamueljames.com and **www.kittycriticmusic.com**.

THIS STORY WAS TOLD ON JUNE 5, 2014, AT **THE STATE THEATRE, PORTLAND**, MAINE. THE THEME OF THE EVENING WAS *LEAP OF FAITH*. **DIRECTOR: MEG BOWLES.**

Josh Bond

◇◇

Call Me Charlie

I managed a hotel in an apartment building in Santa Monica for about seven years. I lived in the apartment building, and I had an office in the hotel across the street. Super-easy commute. It's particularly great when you live in L.A.

You meet a lot of interesting people when you manage an apartment building. For example, there was a retired couple who lived in the apartment next to mine – the Gaskos. The first time I met the husband, I was in my apartment playing guitar and trying to write a song.

There's a knock on the door, and I open it to find a seventy-year-old man holding a black case. He tells me that he heard me playing music, and he liked it, which was good, and he thought I could use this black Stetson cowboy hat.

Really nice gesture. I thank him, and he says his name is Charlie.

So fast-forward five years, and I'm taking a nap on my couch. I'd been working for two weeks straight, no days off, on call every night. But this particular Wednesday, I was taking off work early, and I was going to see this band, My Morning Jacket, in Hollywood. I was meeting a friend. All planned out.

At 2:00 p.m. the phone rings, and my co-worker is at the hotel with the FBI.

Before I know it, I'm on the phone with an FBI agent, and he says, "I need to talk to you about a tenant in your apartment building."

I'm on my couch, so I say, "Can we do this tomorrow?" He says no.

"Where are you? Come here now."

So I get to my office, and I have a seat, and there's a large man wearing a Hawaiian shirt and jeans.

He closes the door and throws a manila folder down on the desk. He opens it and points to a sheet of paper. Across the top is "Wanted" and, underneath, a photo of a man and a woman, with names.

He asks if these people live in the apartment next to mine. And at first glance, I know the woman is my neighbour, Carol Gasko. Yes, I know these guys, these are my neighbours.

And while I've never heard the name "Catherine Greig," the name "James J. 'Whitey' Bulger" is very familiar. I had heard this name many times when I was in college at Boston University.

But I didn't really know anything about him. He was a Jimmy Hoffa–type guy to me, like, "Oh, this guy's missing, he's never gonna be found." It was almost like a joke.

So I'm standing there, and the FBI agent says, "What do you think?"

I say, "What does my face tell you?"

He says, "I need percentages."

I say, "Ninety-nine point five, a hundred percent."

So he gets on his radio, and while this is happening, it is almost like in a movie after an explosion where the sound just disappears, and you're trying to process something that you're not familiar with. You don't know what's going on, and you don't know what's about to happen.

This is an old man who bought me a bike light one time because he was worried about me riding my bike at night without one. And now I'm discovering he's a notorious fugitive.

Another agent quickly appears, and he says, "We need the keys to his apartment, and if you don't give them to us, we'll bust his door down."

I say, "Okay, here are the keys."

He leaves, and then the other agent, Hawaiian Shirt, says, "Look, this guy's pretty high on the most-wanted list. We could use your help apprehending him."

My first response is, "I just gave you the keys to his apartment and told you he lives there. So I'm not really sure what else I can do."

He says, "Well, we can't just go to his apartment. We have to make sure he's in there. If it's just her, it doesn't really work for us. So why don't you go knock on the door and see if he's there?"

In the previous months, Carol had been telling people in the building, "Charlie has dementia, he has heart problems."

They'd put notes on their door during the day that said, *"Don't knock on the door."* I knew from talking to him over the years that he slept during the day.

I explain this to the agent, and without skipping a beat he moves on, and he says, "Well, what are you doing tonight?"

I say, "I'm going to a concert."

He says, "You might want to cancel those plans."

So I call my buddy and tell him, "Look, I don't think I'm going to make the show tonight, and I can't tell you why."

As the original shock is dissipating, I realise I'm going to be with these guys until they have him in cuffs.

Then things really kick in. They place an agent in the hotel at a window that has a good view of the Gaskos' balcony. Then the agent wants to go to my apartment. I take him through a back alley and some side streets, so we aren't walking in front of the apartment building in clear view of Charlie and Carol. We're stopping at cars, and he's talking on the radio, and there are agents everywhere. I'm starting to think this is a pretty big deal. It must be. There are this many people staked out in the neighbourhood?

The FBI agent says, "They just closed their blinds. Did you tip 'em off?"

"I've been with you the whole time, no, *of course not.*"

We get to my apartment, and I draw them a floor plan of the Gaskos' place. We're throwing ideas back and forth about how to get this guy out of his apartment.

My living-room wall shares a wall with Charlie's bedroom, so I'm like, "Uh, you know this guy can hear everything we're saying? Like, he's repeated conversations I've had at night with my friends, asking me why we don't curse or fight as much as he and his friends did in his younger days."

We go into my bedroom, and we come up with an idea. We're going to break into his storage locker in the garage. We go down to the garage, and the FBI agent goes to get his car, and he has some bolt cutters in there.

I'm suddenly just pumped up. I'm involved in something. It's like a movie. I'm having fun, almost, at this point. The adrenaline is helping me forget about my relationship to these people over the years. I mean, this is the same man who bought me a Christmas present every year for the four years I'd lived there.

Once the lock is broken, we go back to my apartment, and the agent's telling me, "Okay, this is what's gonna happen. I'm gonna go down, we're gonna get everything set, I'm gonna call you, and you knock on his door and bring him down."

And I'm like, "No, I'm going to go to the hotel, I'm going to *call* him, and I'm going to tell him to meet me there. Then you guys take care of your business."

I'm in my office, and I'm thinking about this guy, my neighbour, who looked after an old woman on the first floor. Who one year, when I didn't write a thank-you note for a Christmas present he gave me, gave me a box of stationery. I'm thinking, *What did this guy actually DO?*

So I go to Wikipedia, and I'm reading about murders and extortion and gambling.

I get to the bottom, and in one of his last public sightings with one of his Mafia buddies there's a quote from him: "When I go down, I'm going out with guns blazing."

I start to rethink my involvement in the day's events.

Conveniently, my phone rings, and it's the FBI, and they say, "Make the call."

I start to waver: "Look, man, I just read something about this guy . . . and I don't know about this."

He says, "No, no, no, he'll never know, he'll never know." Which is obviously *not true.*

But I am this close to getting to my concert, so I say, "All right, I'll make the call."

I call the Gaskos from the hotel, and there is no answer. I am relieved. I am so happy that they didn't answer the phone.

I call the agent back, and I say, "Hey, man, sorry, they didn't answer. Going to have to do something else."

He says, "Are you *sure* you don't want to knock on the door?"

And I'm like, "Look, man, curtains closed, guns blazing. What if he comes to the door with a gun?"

He says, "Just be like, 'Hey, man, what's going on?'"

I'm thinking to myself, *Uh, he will shoot me before I finish that one statement.*

I tell him I'm not going to do that. But while this is going on, Carol calls back. And so I get on the phone, and I explain to her that the storage unit's been broken into. I can either call the police, or Charlie can meet me in the garage and we'll look at it.

So she discusses this with him, and she says, "He'll be down in five minutes."

"All right, great."

Hang up, call the FBI. "He's on his way. Do your thing."

Then I walk outside, and I'm standing in the courtyard of the hotel, and Carol walks out on her balcony, which is directly across the street. She looks at me, and then she quickly looks down to the garage, and then she looks back at me. I don't know if she knew, but she looks worried.

She walks back in, and then I get a call from the FBI, and they say, "We got him, go to your concert."

So I go change clothes, and the adrenaline, and the rush. As soon as I open the door, it's like a slow-motion shot of Suburbans and vans and FBI agents everywhere. And my neighbour, Charlie Gasko, standing there in cuffs, surrounded by agents, laughing and telling stories.

He almost looks relieved.

I'm staring at this, and as I pass him, I see Carol standing there a few feet away in cuffs. And the magnitude of everything that has happened starts to sink in a little bit.

She looks at me, and she says, "Hi, Josh," and I can't speak.

I just meekly waved, and walked to my car, and got on the highway, and called my brother, and said, "You'll never guess what happened to me today."

"What?"

"I helped the FBI arrest the most wanted man in the country."

So a couple of months later, my family's a little worried about me, and my friends are taking bets on how much longer I have to live. I get home one day, and there's a letter in the mail from the Plymouth Correctional Facility. I open it, and I see the same familiar cursive writing, and the same "shoot the shit" dialogue tone that I knew from four years living next to Charlie Gasko.

But in this letter he's reintroducing himself as Jim Bulger. And so I wrote him back, and I said, "Look, you know I had something to do with the day of the arrest, and my family's a little worried. So, uh, you know, just a little note of 'everything's good' would be nice."

He wrote back and said, "Look, they had me with or without your help; no worries."

So that made my mom feel better, definitely.

New neighbours eventually moved in, and they seemed like nice people.

But what do I know?

JOSH BOND is a resident of Santa Monica, California, where he manages commercial and residential real estate. He also writes original music and performs solo and with his band, For the Kings. Born and raised in the Mississippi Delta, he attended college at Boston University, where he received a bachelor's degree in film production.

....

THIS STORY WAS TOLD ON MARCH 21, 2015, AT **THE MUSIC HALL,** **PORTSMOUTH, NEW HAMPSHIRE**. THE THEME OF THE EVENING WAS *BAIT AND SWITCH*. **DIRECTOR: SARAH AUSTIN JENNESS.**

Sara Barron

∞∞∞∞∞∞∞∞∞∞∞∞∞∞∞∞∞∞∞∞∞∞∞∞∞∞∞∞∞∞∞∞∞∞∞∞

Modern Family

Six months ago I married a man named Mike. And my marriage to Mike made me a stepmother. To a dog.

Now, what I mean when I say this is not just that Mike had a dog, and now that we're married, we co-own his dog together. (Although to some extent, that is true.)

What I mean more specifically is that Mike shares custody of a dog with his ex-girlfriend. And as I am now his wife, I *also* share custody of a dog with his ex-girlfriend.

I found out about this dog-share situation very early in the relationship. The first time I went over to his apartment, there was a dog there. And she was like, "Woof. Woof."

So I was like, "Oh, my God, are you a cutie? Are you a little cutie?!"

To be clear: I'm not a dog person.

I'm also not *not* a dog person. It's just that prior to co-owning one myself, I was unfamiliar with the unconditional love of an animal. So to me it always seemed like a lot of poop, and not much in the way of conversation, and I just wasn't that interested.

However, if I was interested in a man who *owned* a dog, I would do a full song and dance *about* the dog, to lock the business down.

I'd be like, "Ah, blah, blah, blah. Yay! Your dog!"

I always felt it was this very weird, sort of surreal audition for my maternal instinct.

So I was like, "Ah, blah, blah, yay! Mike! Your dog!"

Then one week later, I'm back at the apartment, but this time, no dog.

I'm like, "Mike, where's the dog?"

And Mike says, "Oh, well, the funny thing, actually . . . is that I share custody. Of the dog. With my ex."

And I said, "That is *super funny* . . . and also so surprising, really, because I didn't even know there *was* an ex, because I did NOT stalk both of you on Facebook!"

And he's like, "You're being sarcastic."

And I'm like, "Yes, I'm being sarcastic."

Then he says, "Okay, but what I'm trying to get at here, in a nonsarcastic way, is, like genuinely, how do you feel about the whole situation?"

And I said, "Well . . . I don't know."

Because I didn't. There *was* part of me that kind of thought, *Oh, okay. This is what cool, hip people do!*

But then the other part of me was like, *This shit sounds dysfunctional. What?!*

It really was both those things, and this next part is cheesy, and I apologise in advance for that. But the thing was, I was smitten with Mike (it was early days), and so I did what you do when you're smitten, which is you just act agreeable. You're not actually even *acting* agreeable, because you're so genuinely smitten you *feel* so agreeable. So you're like, "Sure! I'll go along with whatever." And then it's, like, *Roll of the dice as to whether or not I'm going to resent you for this later on.*

A few quick words on the dog. She's a miniature schnauzer, and she is pretty cute, actually. Her name is Wilma. A few quick words on the ex. She is a human woman. She's also pretty cute, actually, and her name is

Kelly. Mike and Kelly were together for ten years, which is a long time. Never married, no kids. Mike was the one to end it. And two months after Mike ended it – which is not a long time – Mike met me.

And one month *after* Mike met me – which, again, is *not* a long time – Kelly found out about us. She found out that we were dating, which was horrible, and which happened because Mike and I had gone to dinner with this good friend of mine . . . and she'd loved him, and he'd loved her, and she'd loved us together, and it was one of those rare and impossibly good social evenings out.

And then – because those kinds of things don't actually exist these days if you don't take a photo and then put them up on Facebook, I awoke the following morning to discover, to my profound dismay, that my friend had put a photograph of Mike and me together up on Facebook.

And not only that, she tagged us in it.

And not only *that,* she'd used the caption "Lovebirds."

A few quick words on me. Prior to meeting Mike, I was single, which I know is a given. But the reason I want to make a point of saying that is, it's not *just* that I was single – it's that I *self-identified* as single.

By this I mean that I'd been single a lot. I'd been on so many dates with so many men who were like, "Sara, I think you're great, but the thing is . . ." Et cetera.

So when suddenly *I* was the one with the guy and a fellow member of my sisterhood was in pain, in part because of me, I made a promise, not dissimilar from the Girl Scout promise:

On my honour I will try to serve the sisterhood of single women by being kind and understanding to this one woman who just went through a breakup.

And of course, keeping this promise should have been effortless. But the thing was, okay, it was *not* effortless.

And the reason why, at least in part, was because I was not prepared – and that was on me – but I was not prepared for the amount of ... let us say *involvement* that Kelly seemed to want in Mike's current life. I'm talking in addition to any and all kinds of dog-related things, right?

So there's a lot of calling. There's a lot of texting. There is a lot of activity on the old Facebook page. A lot of "We really need to catch up over coffee. We really need to catch up over dinner."

And the best part of me understood that all that stuff, every single inch of it, was about a woman who was in pain, right? She's going through a breakup. These things take time, and she'd *had no time.*

But the worst part of me ... which is, basically, me ... just desperately wanted for her to go away. And that made me feel bad about myself. So I did what we do with feelings that make us feel bad about ourselves: I just shoved them all the way down and pretended they weren't there.

What could possibly go wrong?

So that was my mode of operation for a long time. That was how I led my life for about a year.

Then, around the one-year mark, something seemingly insignificant but actually quite significant happened. And that is that Mike had a mole removed – stay with me – from his upper, upper, upper inner thigh.

He had done this because I'd asked him to. Because he comes from a long line of people who are like, *If you don't go to the doctor, then the problem isn't there!* Whereas *I* come from a long line of people who are like, *If you don't go to the doctor, you're gonna DIE!* And I'd had my eye on this mole, okay? It was dangerously textural. So I was like, *IT NEEDS TO GO.*

So eventually Mike does as I've requested and gets said mole removed, and I was truly grateful and relieved.

The day following the mole removal, he posts this very tiny, intentionally funny thing about it on Facebook.

And Kelly, as is her way, leaves a comment. Which read as follows:

"What? No! You are at least one percent less yourself without that mole. I shall mourn its passing."

And I read that particular comment, and I thought about it for a second. And I don't know what the technical medical term is for what happened next, but speaking as a layperson, I can tell you:

I went apeshit.

It was as though every little *Uh, are you kidding me?* that I'd been suppressing for a year exploded into the big, great *ARE YOU FUCKING KIDDING ME?!* of my life.

I lost my mind. I screamed, I pounded my fists against the wall. I was saying things out loud to myself, like, "You know what, Kelly? Just go ahead and write 'Mike and I are so close I know what he LOOKS LIKE NAKED' on Facebook. Seriously! Just do it. Because it would at least be more honest and direct if you did."

I was angry for a multitude of reasons:

1. I'd been repressing my natural feelings for a year, and that's gonna do it to you.

2. Kelly wasn't going anywhere. Because of Wilma, Kelly was around, and she was gonna stay around, and I felt powerless as a result.

3. I'd been reminded, as I so often was, of the length and intimacy of Mike and Kelly's relationship. It was like, *Oh, right, yes, of COURSE she knows that mole, because THEY SHARED A BED TOGETHER FOR TEN YEARS!* It was such an overwhelming length of time.

And 4. Because that mole was some precancerous shit.

It was the mole, but it was everything.

And so because if you cannot run away from the wave, you must then dive into the wave, I did the only thing I knew how to do.

I went back onto Facebook. I went back to Kelly's comment, and clicked on Kelly's profile.

I clicked on the message button on Kelly's profile.

And then I wrote the following: "Kelly, in light of our particular relationship, let me get straight to the point. I was thinking maybe we should meet up for a drink. I think it might be helpful for the both of us. But let me know what you think. All best, Sara."

And Kelly wrote back: "Sara, I read your message and had two prevailing thoughts. The first was, thank you. The second was, fuck off. But the thing is, the part of me that thinks thank you is the part I like the best. So yeah, let's go for a drink."

Three nights later Kelly and I met up for a drink.

Personally, I prepared for what I now call the "X Games of Emotions" with a manicure and full facial threading, because I had to, like, *beautify*. Do you know what I mean? Because I was so nervous about the whole thing from the get-go, and what made it worse was that the subway broke down on the way there, and so I had to literally run the last fifteen minutes. And I don't know when last *you* combined a bit of sweating with a full facial threading, but it stings, okay? So I just remember walking into this bar and being like, *My face is on fire! My face is on fire!!* Then Kelly walked in, and she looked perfect, and *that* made me more nervous.

So then, as my conversational entrée, I said, "Hi, you look like all the photos of you that I've stalked on Facebook." But she didn't laugh. Not that she should have, but it was initially just a total mess.

But then eventually I stopped sweating. And we both had a drink. And then we both had a couple *more* drinks. And then it was less of a mess. Because the thing was, we had both showed up to the X Games of Emotion, and that helped build this base level of respect that allowed us to talk honestly. Kelly talked about how so many of her actions towards Mike just felt to her like this fight for a friendship *with* Mike.

I talked about how I'd made the promise of the sister-hood of single girls to her, but that I found it hard to keep. And we talked together about what it was that we both represented to the other person – which, of course, is that you can build a life with someone . . . and that person can make a choice to leave.

So that all took about an hour, but we wound up out together for another five.

And here's how. It was sort of like once all that baggage was off me and on the table, I realised that I actually liked her. I thought she was much more self-aware in person than she seemed online. She was funny, she was warm, and I really appreciated that she was open to talking all this stuff out in the attempt at defusing it.

Because believe me, we defused it. We talked, we got drunk, we laughed, and we defused it. And by the time I got home, it was 3:00 a.m., and Mike was like, *"Oh, my God! I was worried she killed you."*

And I was like, "Who? My girl Kelly? No waaay, man, No WAY! We defused that shit. We defused it, and I liked her, and she liked me, and I understand why you were with her, and it's possible that I'm drunk, and I just feel so good."

I'd've loved if this story could end with me being like, "And from that day forward, we became the best of friends!" But unfortunately that feeling of "My girl Kelly!"

was not sustainable, because even if you like a person *in* person, you're mostly *not* in person. And if they tend to text your husband a bit more often than you'd like, you can still get . . . *annoyed.*

Several months ago I took Wilma the dog for a walk, and on the way we met this other miniature schnauzer, and I got to talking with the owner, like you do.

She said, "Oh! Your dog's so cute!"

And I was like, "Oh! Thank you! Your dog's so cute!"

And she said, "How old is she?"

And I said, "Oh, she's five. How old is *he*?"

And she's like, "Oh! Well, *this* little sweetheart is eighteen. . . . Ma'am . . . ma'am . . . are you okay?"

And I am. I'm great.

I've still got thirteen years to work out all my problems.

SARA BARRON is the author of the story collections, *The Harm in Asking: My Clumsy Encounters with the Human Race* (2014) and *People Are Unappealing* (2009). Her work has also appeared in *Vanity Fair*, on Showtime's *This American Life* and at the HBO Comedy Festival. You can find her on Twitter **@sarabarron** and at **www.sarabarron.com**.

THIS STORY WAS TOLD ON MARCH 19, 2014, AT **THE PLAYERS, NEW YORK CITY**. THE THEME OF THE EVENING WAS *THIS MORTAL COIL: STORIES OF FLESH AND BONE*. **DIRECTOR: JENIFER HIXSON**.

Grace Rushes In

Tomi Reichental

◇◇

The Shower

I'm in Bergen-Belsen concentration camp. I don't even know what a concentration camp is. I'm only nine years old, and I see barbed wire and a watchtower. So I know I'm not free.

Not long before, I was in my village, called Merašice in Slovakia, where I could still play. In summer I used to run barefoot. In winter we used to toboggan. So my village was, for me, sort of a paradise.

But now I found myself a little prisoner. I'm confused. I'm starving. I'm cold. And I'm very, very miserable.

It was the sixteenth of October, 1944, when we were betrayed, arrested by the Gestapo, and deported to this hell on earth, Bergen-Belsen.

I remember this one particular day when we children began to understand what was happening around us, and learn what the adults already knew.

We had been in Bergen-Belsen perhaps two weeks. There was a routine. Every morning we had to go to a roll call. We had to stand in the freezing cold outside for an hour to wait for our supervisors. They were young women SS guards.

But this particular day, they were accompanied by a group of armed soldiers.

I could hear whispers around: *Something is wrong. Why these soldiers?*

They called our number, and we had to say, *"Ja."* After the roll call, we were told to go to the hut and bring our blankets and towels out, because we were going to go to another place to have a shower.

Now, that was good news, a hot shower. For me it was great news, because then I wouldn't need to go to the washroom outside and wash myself with freezing-cold water. But there were looks around, and I thought the women seemed sort of uncomfortable. We ran in to pick up the blankets and the towels, and there was quiet activity inside the hut.

And I saw this woman sort of lean against her neighbour and say, "You think everything is okay? They are telling us the truth?" The neighbour just shrugged her shoulders and didn't say anything. But I could see she had tears in her eyes.

I wanted to ask my mother, *What's going on?*

But she was busy helping my *omama* and my cousin Chava to pick up the towels and blankets.

Auntie Margo was standing in the doorway, and she was urging us to come out quickly, because the soldiers outside were very impatient, waiting for us.

So, slowly, people were coming out, and when everybody was out, we had to be put three into a row, and then we began to march. It was very cold and eerily quiet. I felt more scared than usual, but wasn't sure why (although it did bother me that none of the adults would meet my eye). I had heard the women talking about how we would like to have a shower, and suddenly we have it, and they don't seem to feel happy about it.

I saw a woman in front of me suddenly take her wedding ring off her finger. She looked around, to see if any of the soldiers were looking at her. And then she threw the wedding ring into the ground, to the dust.

Talking to her friend, she said, "These bastards will not get my gold."

We continued to go, and in perhaps thirty minutes or so, we stopped in front of this big concrete building with a tall chimney on the roof. There were gasps around me. And one woman even shouted, sort of loudly, "Oh, my God!"

My brother and my cousin, they were puzzled, and I couldn't understand the panic around me.

Next the soldiers began to hurry us into the building. *"Schnell, schnell."*

So we were pushed in. We came to this long hallway. On the left side, we saw benches. There was a chemical smell that hung in the air, and there were metal trolleys with bars on the top with hangers on it. And on the right side, we saw these heavy metal doors.

Again the soldiers were barking orders at us. I didn't understand. They were speaking German.

But Auntie Margo conveyed the order that we have to undress and put our clothes on the trolleys and the blankets, to leave everything there.

Everybody began to undress. The soldiers were standing on the side, and they were joking and smiling, making remarks and faces.

And when we were standing there, all naked, there was this little incident where one of the soldiers, who was rather young, suddenly started walking towards us. He was looking firmly at my cousin Chava. Like my brother and myself, she didn't look very Jewish. She had long golden blonde hair dangling over her shoulders.

When my aunt saw it, she stepped in front of her daughter and stopped the soldier, and the soldier said, "What is this Aryan girl doing here?"

And my aunt retorted, rather loudly so that the SS women could hear it, "GO AWAY!"

He turned around, and he walked away, and no more was said about it.

When I was looking around, it was shocking to see the old women with their white, crinkled skin, including my grandmother. They were so pathetic standing there, innocent and naked. I felt the shame and insult. I was tainted.

We were told to move towards the doors, and everybody got a piece of soap. We entered this large room with concrete floors and pipes with showerheads crisscrossing the ceiling.

And when everybody was in, it suddenly became very silent. We didn't hear the soldiers anymore. The door was slammed behind us. We stood there, and the adults all looked up towards those showerheads.

I didn't know what was happening. I saw some of the women were crying.

It was cold. My mother took me and my brother and pressed us against her body.

I don't know how long we stood there, perhaps a few minutes or several seconds, when we heard this gurgling sound coming through the pipe. My mother squeezed us even harder. I could hear her heart beating fast, and she was breathing very hard, like she was gulping for air.

Everybody was looking towards the ceiling. We heard this noise coming nearer and nearer. And suddenly, hot water was sprouting from the showerhead.

And this was exactly what I was expecting.

But I couldn't believe what was happening around me. The women were kissing their children. They were laughing and crying at the same time. They were embracing one another.

I couldn't understand, what is all this happening around? I just wanted to wash myself with the soap and the hot water.

I didn't hear such laughter again while we were in the camp. In fact, that was the only shower that we had during our stay in the camp under the German imprisonment.

Of course, in late 1944 the adults among us already knew about Auschwitz and Birkenau. They knew about the gas chambers. But we kids, we did not know anything about it. Millions of Jews were fooled by being given soap in hand, pretending they were going to have a shower, and they ended up in gas chambers. So I can only imagine today what our mothers were thinking at the time.

Bergen-Belsen was liberated on the fifteenth of April, 1945. In a week's time, we will commemorate the seventy-year anniversary of our liberation. That day was the day that our nightmare ended.

TOMI REICHENTAL is an engineer, an author and a human-rights activist. He was the subject of the documentaries *I Was a Boy in Belsen* and *Close to Evil*, directed by Gerry Gregg. In 2012 Reichental was awarded the Order of Merit by the president of the Federal Republic of Germany, for his untiring commitment to furthering mutual understanding, reconciliation and German-Irish friendship. He has also received a Global Achievement Award and was the recipient of the 2014 International Person of the Year Award. He is the author of *I Was a Boy in Belsen* (2011) and is currently working on a second book.

THIS STORY WAS TOLD ON APRIL 9, 2015, AT THE **LIBERTY HALL THEATRE, DUBLIN**. THE THEME OF THE EVENING WAS *THE TIES THAT BIND*. **DIRECTOR: MEG BOWLES**.

Josh Broder

Cut

It's the late 1980s, and I'm in my early thirties. I'm a lead actor in a hot downtown New York theater company. In those ice-cold rehearsal halls and those dank basement theaters, I am all-powerful.

I trust my instincts. I make big choices. I surprise the hell out of my audience. Coming to our shows is like coming to a wild party, and to some extent, *I am the party*.

But downtown theater is a very small world. A corporate friend of mine told me that he liked to impress first dates by bringing them to our shows, "Because you guys are so funny, you're so smart, and no one has ever heard of you." Now, when your claim to fame is "no one's ever heard of you," there are financial implications. In a good week, my company can pay me a hundred twenty-five dollars. And even a quarter century ago, in New York City that's abject poverty. And abject poverty is wearing thin.

Two o'clock in the morning, end of a fifteen-hour tech-rehearsal day, the thought that I could get into a taxi for the short ride over the Brooklyn Bridge to my house? That's ten dollars. It's not in the equation. It's down into the subway and hope for the best, which sucks.

I don't want to give up the fun. I don't want to give up the party. But I need some money. And that means film or television. I'm not looking to be a star. I just wanna be able to take a taxi every once in a while.

And it's not just money in terms of a paycheck. Experimental theater, it exists outside the laws of supply and demand.

There's only supply.

There's no demand.

And for whatever reason, I want to test myself out in the marketplace. I want to see if my work has value. I want to see if I can even do what I know how to do when money is on the line.

But it's a long way from an illegal firetrap theater to Hollywood.

But then the film director Jonathan Demme becomes a fan of my company. Now, I love Demme's movies. I've been into Demme all the way back to *Melvin and Howard.* I would *love* to be in a Jonathan Demme movie.

And this could also be a gateway opportunity. He put a downtown friend of mine in *Married to the Mob.* The guy got a great agent. Three months later he's on *Miami Vice,* getting eaten by crocodiles.

And sure enough, when Demme starts casting his next movie, he puts a couple of guys from my company in it.

But not me.

Well, it's crunch time, so I get up the nerve and I ask Jonathan Demme for a part in his next movie. True to his generous nature, Jonathan comes through.

But the seeds of doubt have been planted. I mean, downtown, I am the party. Here I wasn't even invited to the party. I'm pretty much crashing the party.

But, you know, screw it. I got a part. I'm thrilled. I start reading the script.

What is this? Jonathan Demme's doing a horror movie about a serial killer? What is this thing? I look at the cover. *The Silence of the Lambs.* What do I know? It could be good.

What's my part? I keep reading. Okay, I play an EMT. And, whoa, I get killed in the back of my ambulance by Anthony Hopkins as Hannibal Lecter.

If I can pull this off, it's gonna be great.

If.

Fly out to the location. Pittsburgh. Take a taxi to a very nice hotel.

Intimate dinner that night at the house they've rented for Jonathan Demme, his wife (the artist Joanne Howard), his producing partner, cinematographer, me. And Anthony Hopkins, who I end up seated next to.

From his questions you can tell the guy knows nothing about Jonathan Demme. This was supposed to be just a couple weeks' work in a busy year.

He tells me that only a fool would try to judge a film by the dailies. "But I must say, they're looking awfully good, and I've never had so much fun on a set."

Well, I haven't even seen the set, but so far I'm having a great time.

And I keep telling myself that pulling off a conversation with Anthony Hopkins isn't the same thing as pulling off a scene with Anthony Hopkins, but so far I'm doing great.

They're filming at night, and the first couple of nights I'm really an overpaid extra. I'm riding shotgun in my ambulance and hurrying the gurney inside.

Then comes the night of my first real scene. Not my scene with Hopkins, but the first scene where I speak.

My crew of extras huddles around this apparently injured cop while I shout orders and the camera whirls around us. I feel loose, focused, committed to the imaginary circumstances. It turns out to be easy to pretend when they make it so real. The guy looks like hell. His face is shredded to bits.

Take one, I rock.

Take two, even better.

Take three, trust my instincts, make the big choice. I throw in an R-rated improvisation: "Buzz, I need the fucking oxygen!"

Cut, print, wrap for the night.

Demme gives me a big bear hug. Shredded-Face Guy high-fives me. The crew, wrapping up, has adopted my profane improvisation: "Jill, I need the fucking gaffer's tape!" This is like downtown, only with a fat paycheck and all the food you can eat. I am the party.

Flash forward a couple nights. My last night on the set. My big scene with Hopkins. Now, spoiler alert – are you ready? It's not a cop in the back of the ambulance. It's Hannibal Lecter, wearing the uniform and face of the cop that he's killed.

Now, I say it's my big scene. But to the crew, my scene is the thing to get out of the way. The real business of the night is the stunt driving with the ambulance. That's gonna take some time.

There's only one interstate that tunnels through the mountains and into downtown Pittsburgh. And they have closed that interstate at the mouth of the Fort Pitt Tunnel.

We have from the end of rush hour in the evening to the beginning of rush hour in the morning to get my scene out of the way, do the stunt driving, get packed, and get out of the way so Pittsburgh can get to work in the morning.

I feel ready. Ready to end on a high note.

Setting up takes hours longer than it should. It's almost midnight before they even start to think about my scene, and that's when someone realises that my speech – a few sentences of medical lingo shouted into a radio microphone while Hannibal Lecter rises behind me – is short.

But the shot, the movement of the camera/Anthony Hopkins' business is *long*. They need more words for me to say. And all eyes turn to a guy on the periphery of the set. He's a local guy with a medical background. He's rented them the ambulance for the night. I see his face light up. This is his chance to write a line for a Hollywood movie. Now he's the party, and I know I'm not gonna have any fun at all.

Guy scribbles out three pages of tongue-twisting medical gibberish: *"Postdictal with lactated Ringer's running on a double IV, viscous evisceration."* On and on and on. And I'm handed these three pages, and I'm told to memorise them, fast.

And I do. But practicing in my trailer, I can speak them with all the élan of a bar mitzvah boy who's blown off his Hebrew studies till the morning of the big day.

We haven't shot a single frame, and I am screwed. Dead man walking from my trailer to the ambulance, my new friends on the crew shout encouragement. "One take, Josh! One fucking take! Clock is ticking!"

There's a midwinter thaw, and the temperature's spiked to nearly seventy. The evaporating snow has condensed into a thick fog.

I climb into the back of the ambulance and drop down on the bench. With the film lights, it's at least ninety degrees in here. Equally humid.

Hopkins is escorted in and laid out on the gurney. Silicone mask in place, they start ladling chopped-up *SpaghettiOs* viscera onto his face.

This hellhole instantly takes on the ripe stench of an elementary-school cafeteria.

Take one, ACTION! It's a disaster. I get the words out, barely, but worse, you can see my eyes scanning the scribbled pages that I'm visualising in front of me.

Cut, reset!

It takes twenty of the night's precious minutes to redo Hopkins's makeup. I'm starting to panic. I've got to get out of this ambulance. I've got to breathe. I've got to go back to Manhattan, where I belong. But every escape route is blocked. Hopkins and the makeup guys, the camera, the lights. I cower in there like a cornered animal.

Everyone but me is ready for take two.

Demme calls in, "Just drive the speech, Josh. Just spit out the words." I try to spit out the words, but mostly I just spit.

Cut, reset!

My heart is pounding, and my brain starts to take up its rhythm: *You blew it, you'll blow it, you blew it, you'll blow it.* And I do.

In place for take four, Hopkins asks, "Might I speak to Jonathan a moment?"

Demme squeezes his head painfully between the camera and the doorframe.

"Are we gonna be much longer at this? I'm feeling a bit claustrophobic, and this goo is making me nauseous."

Anthony Hopkins is unhappy. When take four still shows room for improvement, Demme goes into crisis-intervention mode, chopping out big chunks of my speech, while the cinematographer unhappily dumbs down this pivotal shot that pays off the entire escape sequence.

But the problem with taking out chunks of a speech I barely know is it only muddles me more.

Take five is my worst yet.

Take six – cut!

Take seven – cut!

Take eight – cut!

Waiting for take nine, I start thinking about the Pittsburgh commuter. I have no idea what time it is. Is he awake? Is he headed for his car? Is he headed for my tunnel?

Take nine, action!

And something in me snaps. Midway through the speech, I'm shocked to suddenly hear myself wail, "Jonathan!"

Now, of all the highly successful people I know, Jonathan Demme is far and away the kindest. But now I've forced him to try out tough love.

"Keep rolling! Just do it, Josh!"

[*BAM!*] He slams the high side of the van, hard.

And it works.

Take nine, continued, goes a little bit better.

Take ten, even better.

For take eleven, they reinstitute my full speech, and the full complex shot, and my brain resets to accommodate the new information.

Take eleven, action, and I am *in role*. Medical language I've used for years fires from my lips as I stare out through a windshield I can't actually see. Instinct tells me that something is amiss with my patient, and I whip around to find him sitting up . . . with a new face. No lacerations, but drenched in blood. He holds a knife to my throat.

We stare at each other. No one says, "Cut." I can hear the camera motor still whirring.

No words, but I look him a question: *What's happening?*

Hannibal Lecter looks me an answer: *I'm gonna eat you.*

Do you have to?

Oh, yes.

A great wave of sorrow washes over me, and Hannibal Lecter laps it up.

I'm acting. With Anthony Hopkins.

Outside the van, on a small monitor, Jonathan Demme watches with pleasure. For these few moments, we three are the party.

JOSH BRODER worked as an actor and director for over twenty years. Now he makes his living as a writer and an executive coach. That coaching often focuses on "narrative leadership" – that is, leadership via personal storytelling. He made his New York acting debut at the Public Theater and toured Siberia for two months before the collapse of the Soviet Union. Favourite roles include Abbie Hoffman and Pretty Boy Floyd. Josh is the co-author of two screenplays, one based on his gig in an ill-fated passion-play tour of the Bible Belt, the second a biopic of a great American charlatan. His has written for the *Washington Post* and *Travel + Leisure* magazine, among other outlets. Josh lives in Brooklyn with his wife, Karen, and their son, Luca. **www.joshbroder.net**

THIS STORY WAS TOLD ON AUGUST 23, 2012, AT THE **NEW HAZLETT THEATER, PITTSBURGH**. THE THEME OF THE EVENING WAS *WHAT LIES BENEATH: STORIES OF STEELY RESERVE*. **DIRECTOR: KATE TELLERS**.

Auburn Sandstrom

◇◇

A Phone Call

The year is 1992, Ann Arbor, Michigan. I'm curled up in a foetal position on a filthy carpet in a very cluttered apartment. I'm in horrible withdrawal from a drug that I've been addicted to for several years now.

In my hand I have a little piece of paper. It's dilapidated because I've been folding it and unfolding it, to the point that it's almost falling apart. But you can still make out the phone number on it.

I am in a state of bald terror. If you've ever had an anxiety attack, that's what this felt like.

I'd been having a nonstop anxiety attack for the last five years. And I'd never been in a darker or more desperate place than I was that night. My husband was out running the streets, trying to get ahold of some of the stuff that we needed, but I knew if he succeeded, he was not going to share.

And if I could, I would jump out of my own skin and run screaming into the streets to get what I need. But right behind me, sleeping in the bedroom, is my baby boy.

Now, I wasn't going to get a Mother of the Year award in 1992. In fact, at the age of twenty-nine, I was failing at a lot of things.

I had started out fairly auspiciously. I was raised in comfort and privilege. I was that girl who had the opera lessons, spoke fluent French and had her expensive undergraduate college paid for. I was that person who, when my checking account ran out, would say something to my parents and two hundred dollars would magically appear.

I know, when the revolution comes, kill me first, right?

So I had the year abroad. I had the master's degree. I was, you know, *pedigreed*.

But in my twenties, I ended up in Ann Arbor, Michigan, and I started noticing things like poverty and racism and unconscionable injustice. And that people like me were mostly causing it. It was a huge revelation for me.

I came to the conclusion that the thing I needed to do with my privilege and all the comfort that I'd had all my life was to destroy it.

Rip it in half. Spit on it. Piss on it. Set it on fire.

And you know, every time I've come to a major faulty conclusion in life, the man comes right after who will help me live it out. And this was no different.

Man, he was beautiful – a radical revolutionary, fine-ass poet from Detroit.

I was twenty-four, he's forty, and I was smitten, in love. It was so exciting – who he was, how he talked, the way he looked at the world. And it was beautiful for a while, until he introduced me to one of his old activist friends, who introduced us to the drug I was now addicted to.

I had tried to change my affiliations and transform myself. I had wanted to shed my class. I would have shed my race if I could have.

But instead of transformation, you have me going ninety miles an hour down I-94 with my poet, in a car full of alcohol and illegal drugs. The baby's in a car seat (it's probably not a regulation car seat). He's covered in candy and chocolate, because you have to keep the baby entertained while you're taking care of your business, getting yourself some relief.

This particular night it was bad, because if we were to have been pulled over, we were both on parole. So we would've both been locked up, and our child would have been taken from us.

Underneath my withdrawal and terrible anxiety was a sure knowledge that I was leading the life that was going to lead to me losing the most precious thing I'd ever had in my life, which was that baby boy.

I was so desperate at that moment, that I became willing to punch the numbers into the phone.

The phone number was something my mother had sent me. Now, mind you, I hadn't been speaking to my parents or anybody else for three, four, five years.

But she'd managed to get this number to me by mail, and she said, "Look, this is a Christian counsellor, and since you can't talk to anybody else, maybe sometime you could call this person."

Now, I think it goes without saying that I wasn't hanging real tight with that sort of thing in those days. But I was so anxious and in such a desperate state. I was emaciated, covered in bruises.

I punched in the numbers. I heard the phone pick up.

I heard a man say, "Hello."

And I said, "Hi, I got this number from my mother. Uh, do you think you could maybe talk to me?"

I heard him shuffling around in the bed, you know? You could tell he was pulling some sheets around himself and sitting up. I heard a little radio in the background, and he snapped it off, and he became very present.

He said, "Yes, yes, yes. What's going on?"

I hadn't told anybody, including myself, the truth, for a long, long time. And I told him I wasn't feeling so good, and that I was scared, and that things had gotten pretty bad in my marriage.

Before long I started telling him other truths, like I might have a drug problem, and I really, really love my husband, and I wouldn't want you to say anything bad about him, but he has hit me a few times. And there was a time when he pushed my child and me out into the cold and slammed the door behind us.

And then there was a time when we were going sixty miles an hour down the highway, and he tried to push us out of the moving vehicle.

I started telling those truths. And this man didn't judge me. He just sat with me, and was present, and listened, and had such a kindness and such a gentleness.

"Tell me more. . . . Oh, that must hurt. . . . Oh."

And do you know, I'd made that call at two in the morning. And he stayed up with me the whole night, just talking, just listening, just being there until the sun rose.

By then I was feeling calm. The raw panic had passed. I was feeling okay.

I was feeling like, *I can splash my face with water today, and I can probably do this day.*

I wouldn't have cared if the guy was like a Hare Krishna or a Buddhist – it didn't matter to me what his faith was.

I was very grateful to him, and so I said, "Hey, you know, I really appreciate you and what you've done for me tonight. Aren't you supposed to be telling me to read some Bible verses or something? Because that'd be cool, I'll do it, you know. It's all right."

He laughed and said, "Well, I'm glad this was helpful to you."

And we talked some more, and I brought it up again.

I said, "No, really. You're very, very good at this. I mean, you've seriously done a big thing for me. How long have you been a Christian counsellor?"

There's a long pause. I hear him shifting. "Auburn, please don't hang up," he says. "I've been trying not to bring this up."

"What?" I ask.

"You won't hang up?"

"No."

"I'm so afraid to tell you this. But the number you called . . ." He pauses again. "You got the wrong number."

Well, I didn't hang up on him, and we did talk a little longer. I never would get his name or call him back.

But the next day I felt this kind of joy, like I was shining. I think I've heard them call it "the peace that passes understanding." I had gotten to see that there was this completely random love in the universe. That it could be unconditional. And that some of it was for me.

And I can't tell you that I got my life totally together that day. But it became possible to get some help and get the hell out. And it also became possible as a teetotal, semi-sane, single parent to raise up that precious, chocolate-covered baby boy into a magnificent young scholar and athlete, who graduated from Princeton University in 2013 with honours.

This is what I know. In the deepest, blackest night of despair, if you can get just one pinhole of light . . . all of grace rushes in.

AUBURN SANDSTROM is a senior lecturer in college writing at the University of Akron. She won the Ohio Arts Council Award for fiction, a Citation for Teaching Excellence in Creative Writing from the University of Michigan and a Cowden Award for fiction. She is a career college writing instructor with a Master's in Fine Arts (fiction). A longtime advocate for urban students, she is currently pursuing a PhD in urban education policy at Cleveland State University.

THIS STORY WAS TOLD ON NOVEMBER 21, 2015, AT **THE ACADEMY OF MUSIC THEATRE, NORTHAMPTON, MASSACHUSETTS**. THE THEME OF THE EVENING WAS *LOST AND FOUND*. **DIRECTOR: JENIFER HIXSON**.

Mary-Claire King

◇◇◇

Who Can You Trust?

The week of April Fools' Day of 1981 began badly. That Sunday night my husband told me he was leaving me. He had fallen in love with one of his graduate students, and they were headed back to the tropics the next day.

I was completely devastated. It was totally unexpected. Thirty-three years later, I still don't know what to say about it. I was just beside myself.

He gave me a new vacuum cleaner to soften the blow.

It was the middle of spring quarter at Berkeley, so the next morning I had my class, as usual. And I had to either teach it or explain why not.

It was far easier to teach, so I dropped off our daughter, Emily – who was five and three-quarters at the time – at kindergarten, along with her faithful Aussie, her Australian shepherd, who went everywhere with her. I headed down to school and taught my class.

As I was leaving, my department chairman caught up with me. He said, "Come into my office."

I said, "Fine." (I had hoped to escape.)

I went into his office, and he said, "I wanted to tell you, I've just learned you've been awarded tenure."

And of course I burst into tears.

Now, this department chairman, bless him, was a gentleman a full generation older than me. He had three grown sons. He had no daughters. He had certainly never had a young woman assistant professor in his charge before.

And he took my shoulders, and he stepped back, and he said, "No one's ever reacted like that before."

He said, "Sit down, sit down. What's the matter?"

I said, "It's not the tenure. It's that my husband told me last night he was leaving me."

He looked at me, opened the drawer of his desk, pulled out a huge bottle of Jack Daniel's, poured me a half a glass of it, and said, "Drink this. You'll feel better." It was nine thirty Monday morning.

So I did – and I did. I made it through the day, got sober, and around three thirty headed back up the hill to pick up Emily from school. She hopped in the car with Ernie, her dog, and we drove home.

We got home, walked up the stairs, opened the house . . . and it was absolute chaos.

Someone had broken in. Everything was completely trashed. In retrospect what must have happened was that my then husband had often worked at home, and whoever had been casing the neighbourhood must have left our house aside because he was often there. But that day, of course, he hadn't been there, so we were vulnerable, and we were robbed.

So I called 911, and a young Berkeley police officer came up and went through the house. Of course, I had no idea what had been taken and what hadn't, because my husband had taken many things with him on Sunday night. I wasn't sure what should still be there or not.

I explained that to Officer Rodriguez, and he said, "As you figure it out, make a list."

Then he went upstairs with Emily. They opened the door of her room, and it was eighteen inches deep of just chaos. The bed had been pulled apart, curtains pulled down, drawers all dumped out.

Emily – five and three-quarters – looked at Officer Rodriguez and said, "I can't tell if the burglars were in here or not."

And Officer Rodriguez, to his eternal credit, did not crack a smile. He handed her his card and said, "Young lady, if you discover that anything is missing, please give me a call."

So now it's Monday night. I was scheduled later that week to give a presentation in Washington, D.C., to the National Institutes of Health. The way this worked in those days was, if you were a young professor, applying for the first time for a large grant, you were quite frequently asked to come to the NIH and give what was called a "reverse site visit." You'd explain what you planned to do, and then it would be decided if you were going to be granted quite a substantial amount of money over five years.

It was terribly important. I had not done this before. It was brand-new. It was going to be my first large grant on my own. The plan had been for Emily to stay with her dad and for my mom to come out, arriving the next day – Tuesday – to help out. That had seemed, at the time, like a great plan.

My mom, who was living in Chicago, obviously didn't know anything about the events of the previous twenty-four hours, so I thought, *I'll just wait and explain it to her when she gets here.* It seemed far better than calling her at what, by now, was quite late in Chicago because of all the business with the burglary and the police and all that.

So the next day, we picked up my mom at San Francisco Airport, and driving back to Berkeley, I explained to her what happened on Sunday.

She was very, very upset.

She said, "I can't believe you've let this family come apart. I can't believe this child will grow up without a father" (which was never true and has never been true since).

"How could you do this? How could you not put your family first?" Emily was sitting there in the car.

And, "I just cannot imagine," she said. "I'm going to go talk to Rob."

I said, "He's back in Costa Rica."

"This just can't be," and she became more and more upset. By the time we got home to Berkeley, she was extremely agitated. Emily was terrified. It was clearly not going to work for her to care for Emily.

After a couple of hours, my mom said, "I'm going home. I just can't imagine that this has happened. You must stay here and take care of your child. How can you even think of running off to the East Coast at a time like this?"

To put it into context now, years later, my father had died not long before, after my mom had nursed him for more than twenty years. Just two months after this visit, my mother was diagnosed with epilepsy. So, in context, her reaction was not as irrational as it seemed in that moment, but at the time, of course, it was devastating.

So I said, "Okay. You're right. I'll arrange for you to have a ticket to go home tomorrow. We'll take you out to the airport, and I'll cancel the trip."

I called my mentor, who had been my postdoc adviser at UC San Francisco until just a couple of years before.

He was already in Washington, D.C., by happenstance at an oncology meeting, and I said, "I'm not going to be able to come," and I explained briefly what had happened.

Of course, he knew me well. And he just listened to all this.

He had grown daughters and said, "Look, come."

I said, "I can't."

He said, "Bring Emily. Emily and I know each other. I'll sit with her while you're giving your presentation." He had grandchildren of his own.

He said, "It will be fine."

I said, "She doesn't have a ticket."

He said, "As soon as we hang up the phone, I'm going to call the airline and get her a ticket. Pick up the ticket at the airport tomorrow when you take your mom back. It'll be on the same flight as yours. Everything will be fine."

I said, "You sure?"

And he said, "Yes. I have to call the airline now. Good night," and he hung up.

(In those days it was very easy to rearrange tickets.)

I arranged for my mother to have a ticket to go back to Chicago. Her flight was at ten o'clock in the morning. So we left Berkeley in plenty of time, in principle, to get to San Francisco Airport. But it was one of those days where the Bay Bridge was just totally jammed up. It was a horrible drive across. What should have been a drive of forty-five minutes took an hour and forty-five minutes.

When we finally arrived, my mom's flight was about to leave in fifteen minutes, Emily's and my flight was going to leave in forty-five minutes, and in front of the counter to pick up tickets was a long, long line. And, of course, we had our suitcases. My mom was carrying hers, and she was already fairly frail.

So Emily and my mother and I were standing in the line, and I said, "Mom, can you make it down to your plane on your own?" Bear in mind, there were no checkpoints in those days, but there were, of course, very long corridors.

She said, "No."

So I said to Emily, "I'm going to need to go with Grand-mom down to her plane."

And my mother shrieked, "You can't leave that child here alone!" (Fair enough.)

Suddenly this unmistakable voice above and behind me said, "Emily and I will be fine."

I turned around to the man standing behind us, and I said, "Thank you."

My mother looked at me and said, "You can't leave Emily with a total stranger."

And I said, "Mom, if you can't trust Joe DiMaggio, who can you trust?"

Joe DiMaggio, who just like us was standing there, waiting in line – looked at me, looked at my mother, and gave Emily a huge grin. And then he put out his hand and said, "Hi, Emily, I'm Joe."

Emily shook his hand, and she said, "Hello, Joe, I'm Emily."

And I said, "Mom, let's go."

So my mother and I headed down the hall. We got to the plane, and my mother got on fine. It was probably twenty, twenty-five minutes by the time I got back, and by that time Emily and Joe were all the way up at the front chatting with each other by the counter.

Joe DiMaggio had wrangled Emily's ticket for her. She was holding it. He was clearly waiting to go to his plane until I got back.

I looked at him, and I said, "Thank you very much."

And he said, "My pleasure."

He headed off down the hall. He turned right. He gave me this huge salute and wave and a tremendous grin and went off to his own plane.

Emily and I went to Washington, DC. The interview went fine.

I got the grant, and that was the beginning of the work that now, thirty-three years later, has become the story of inherited breast cancer and the beginning of the project that became BRCA1.

DR MARY-CLAIRE KING is American Cancer Society Professor at the University of Washington in Seattle. She was the first to show that breast cancer is inherited in some families, as the result of mutations in the gene that she named BRCA1. Her research interests include the genetic bases of schizophrenia, the genetic causes of congenital Mendelian disorders, and human genetic diversity and evolution. She pioneered the use of DNA sequencing for human-rights investigations, developing the approach of sequencing mitochondrial DNA preserved in human remains, then applying this method to the identification of kidnapped children in Argentina and subsequently to cases of human-rights violations on six continents. In 2016, she was awarded the National Medal of Science by President Obama.

....

THIS STORY WAS TOLD ON MAY 29, 2014, AT **THE PLAYERS, NEW YORK CITY**. THE THEME OF THE EVENING WAS *MERCURY RISING: THE MOTH AT THE WORLD SCIENCE FESTIVAL*. **DIRECTOR: CATHERINE BURNS**.

Dori Samadzai Bonner

<><><><><><><><><><><><><><><><><><><><><><><><><><><><><><><><><><><>

A New Home

I grew up in Afghanistan during the Russian occupation, and as a child remember my dad being gone a lot. The subject of my dad's whereabouts was somewhat taboo in my household, because my mom told us we were never to ask about him, so we never did. And sometimes I wondered if he cared about me.

Growing up during the war was very difficult, because we had bomb explosions and missile attacks on a daily basis. By the time I was ten, these explosions were getting closer and closer to the city of Kabul, where we used to live. In fact, there's a distinct whistling sound that the missile makes right before hitting its target, and sometimes the explosions would be so close you could hear that.

In the meantime there was a rumour about a regime change, which was devastating news for my dad, who was a high-ranking officer working for the current regime. Historically, the newer regime takes over by violently dismantling the old regime. My parents were desperate to try to get out of the country, but they couldn't, because the government put a lockdown on everybody's visas; they needed everyone to stay and fight the war for them.

The only way to get out of the country was on forged papers. In the early 1990s, after a daring escape in the middle of the night, my parents and brother and I migrated to the US on forged papers and asked for political asylum. This meant that we could stay here temporarily while they reviewed our case. They gave us a work permit, and driver's license and Social Security card.

So all of us started working. We had family in California who helped us get settled. Fast-forward five years, our lives were so normal that the biggest thing on my mind at that time was how I could get my mom to extend my curfew and let me stay out late.

Then one day I'm at my first job at the Men's Warehouse, and my dad calls me. I could hear by the excitement in his voice that there was something going on at home.

He tells me, "You need to come home right away, because there's a letter from immigration."

I speak the best English in my household, so he wanted me to come home and translate.

(And for those of you who've been lucky enough not to be familiar with the immigration system, they don't send you regular updates, like, "Hey, still thinking about you all, haven't forgotten about you.")

I rush home, and I find my dad in his security-guard uniform. My mom and my brother are home, 'cause my dad called them too.

I'm sitting at the dining-room table, and all three of them are kinda hovered over me, and rushing me. "Come on, come on, read it. What does it say, what does it say?"

So I read just the highlights really quickly. It says our appointment has been moved up to next week, and that we need to bring all of our legal documents, and our family photos, and things that are important.

We start jumping up and down, thinking, *This is it. This is the appointment that we've been waiting for.*

The day of our appointment, we drive about forty-five minutes to downtown Los Angeles, and we go into a big government building. Upstairs, there's an immigration officer waiting for us, and he guides us into this room.

The moment that the doors opened up, all of us looked at each other. We felt like we were in the wrong place. The people that were sitting there were visibly upset. Some of them were still crying. We were told, "Just sit down until you hear your last name."

After a while my dad asked me to go and ask the security guard how long this appointment was going to take, and what were we here for.

So I go up, and I ask an immigration officer, "Hey, can you tell me how long this appointment might take? Because my dad needs to get back to work."

He says, "Your dad will get back to work, all right, just not in this country."

And my heart just dropped. Going back was not an option, because we're now considered traitors, and would be arrested as soon as we got off the plane.

I sat down and hesitantly told my dad this, and my dad lost all the colour in his face.

Suddenly my dad is hunched over, and he's holding his chest. He's visibly in some kind of pain.

So I get up, and I go up to the same officer, and I ask him if I can use the phone. He says no. Then I ask him if I could use the bathroom, and he lets me. I open up these big doors, and I'm rushing. There's a long hallway, and I'm looking to the left, I'm looking to the right, looking for a telephone. Finally I spot it at the end of the hall, and I grab the phone, and I dial our attorney's number.

Now, I was extremely upset with our attorney, because we couldn't afford even our own meals sometimes, but the thing we always wanted to be sure we had money for was an attorney. And so for her not to be here was really upsetting to me.

This girl answers the phone – she sounds like she's about eighteen years old, like my age at that time. I am asking her to put our attorney on the phone, and she keeps refusing.

I tell her it's an emergency – "PLEASE PUT JODY ON THE PHONE!" – and as soon as I hear Jody's voice, I completely break down. I explain to her that something is wrong with my dad and they won't let us get help for him.

She tells me to just sit tight and she is going to see what she can do. So we're sitting there, and my dad continues to be in pain.

After about forty-five minutes, a man walks in and says our last name, and all four of us get up, and we're following him. We're not sure where, but we're following him. We end up going into this office, which was so small that only my dad and I could fit in it.

There's a man in there who's working at his desk. He doesn't even acknowledge that we're standing there. He doesn't speak one word to us. He just hands over this paper that said our visa had been extended for three months, so that we could go get my dad some medical help.

The next three months are the worst time of my life by far, because we're fearing deportation every single day.

Whenever we would see the mailman show up and put mail in our mailbox, it was a moment of dread – none of us wanted to go and check our mailbox. And my dad's behavior was so completely over the top.

He moved out of my mom's bedroom and into the living room. Our blinds were closed, whether it was day or nighttime, and he slept with a pair of clothes right next to him. Whenever he heard footsteps, he would jump off the couch and look through the blinds to see who it was.

At the end of a few months, we finally go to our final appointment. We walk in with our attorney, and I notice that it's a different judge who is sitting there. It's an older gentleman, and he looks really intense. He won't even smile. The judge carries on with our attorney for a little bit and then turns his attention to my dad. After some basic questions, he gets right into it and starts asking my dad if he has a translator, and my dad says, "My daughter will translate for us."

I was pretty intimidated.

The judge tells me, "Young lady, whatever I say to you, you translate exactly what I say, nothing more, nothing less. And whatever your dad says, you tell me exactly what he says, nothing more, nothing less."

I agree. He asks my dad questions, really demeaning questions, like, "Do I understand correctly that you came here on forged papers?"

And my dad starts to say, "Well, yes, but . . ." And then my dad goes into this long explanation.

But the judge cuts my dad off and says, "I just want to hear yes or no. I don't care about the explanation."

And so the conversation goes on like this, back and forth, and it's not going well at all.

Finally he tells my dad, "You know, we here in the United States do not give citizenship to people that break the law. We can't, and I won't."

And as soon as I translate this to my dad, I put my head down, and I just start praying.

When I open my eyes, I see my dad rising out of his seat. He starts unbuckling his belt, at which point I'm thinking he's completely losing his mind. I'm not sure what he's doing.

But he lifts up his shirt on the right side and, in his native language, looks at the judge and says, "This is what the communists did to me."

He's pointing to a five-inch knife scar.

Then he pushes down his pants in the back and turns around a little bit, and again says, "This is what the communists did to me," pointing at three gunshot wounds.

And he takes off his shoes, and takes off his socks, and says, "This is what the communists did to me."

He's pointing at his toenails, which they had tried to pull out with pliers.

I remember thinking, *I know I'm hearing what I'm hearing.* But everything wasn't registering, because I am translating these horrible things and also learning for the first time about my dad's whereabouts. All those times years ago that I didn't know where he was, wondering if he cared about me, he was in prison being tortured.

And in that moment I have never felt more sorrow.

He continues to tell the judge, "It's easy for you to judge me. You sit in that seat and you wear that robe. But if you came on this side, and you looked at me – one man to another – you will see that everything I did, I did to save my children. I had no other choice.

"And you might deny it right now, but had it been you, I know you would have done the same thing. If you have to show the American public that you didn't take it easy on us, I understand. Send me back. I volunteer. But please let my children stay. Please give my children a new home."

And then he puts his head down and starts crying like a baby. The judge leaves. We're on a break.

The judge comes back after an hour, and as soon as he enters the room, I notice that he doesn't have his robe on. He goes up to his chamber and grabs something and starts walking back towards us.

We're pretty nervous. The entire time his eyes are on my dad. He goes past me and stops right next to my dad.

My dad looks up at him, and the judge says, "Mr Samadzai, let me see your hand."

My dad shows him his hand, and the judge puts a stamp in my dad's hand and says, "Mr Samadzai, I would like you to be the one to stamp your children's papers."

Together they stamp our papers, and when they move their hands, it reads, "Asylum granted."

He then flips the page to my parents' papers and stamps it with the same stamp.

Then he looks down at my dad, and puts his hand on his shoulder, and says, "Welcome to America."

It took us eighteen years from the day that we arrived here for me to be granted an American citizenship. On January 29, 2009, I was sworn in as an American citizen, and I pledged allegiance to my new homeland.

And it is through my children, my two-year-old son and my unborn child in my womb, that I will make sure that this gratitude that overflows in my heart every single day will continue to live on long after I am gone.

May God always bless our America.

DORI SAMADZAI BONNER is a writer and essayist. On August 31, 2010, based on her passion for tennis and her life struggles in Afghanistan, Dori was honoured at the US Open tennis tournament's opening-night ceremony. She has been featured on Bloomberg News and on National Public Radio. Dori and her husband have two boys. However, it is her love for her newfound homeland that she prides herself upon above all.

THIS STORY WAS TOLD ON NOVEMBER 12, 2014, IN THE GREAT HALL AT **COOPER UNION, NEW YORK CITY**. THE THEME OF THE EVENING WAS *NOW YOU SEE IT: STORIES OF ILLUMINATION*. **DIRECTOR: MAGGIE CINO**.

Simon Bill

❬❬❬

The 1796 British Light Cavalry Sabre

This is something that happened a bit more than three years ago. I was sitting at home in my big Victorian house in Sheffield. It was a warm night, and the windows were open. I was at home with my ten year old daughter, who was asleep. It was late at night, and I was thinking of going to bed myself.

I'd been hearing percussive sounds coming from outside. They sounded close, but I put it down to that thing that hot weather does where far away things sound close.

I was about to go to bed, when I heard that unmistakable sound of somebody booting a door – my back door. And I looked out the bedroom window, which is over the back door to the kitchen, and there's a man booting the door repeatedly.

So I said "Oy!"

And he said "What?"

And I said "Well, fuck off."

And he said "Come down and make me, you cunt."

So I knew at this stage I was gonna have trouble with this man.

I ran downstairs, went to the living room, where I got the phone, the landline. Picked it up, dialed 999 and raced into the kitchen, near the door that he was going to come through, and made the 999 call while I was looking at him through the window of the back door, repeatedly ramming the door.

For some reason they always pick very slow-speaking people to answer 999 calls.

So it was,

".... which

... service

.... do

... you

... require?"

The call proceeded, and I was about to give my address, when the frame of the door splintered completely, and I thought, *Right, it's in the next one*.

So I said to the operator, "Too late, he's in."

I dropped the phone on the kitchen table, and I thought, *I need something*, so I ran to the cupboard under the stairs, where we keep garden tools and stuff, and I looked at the shovels and the spades and the rake. The spade could've been very handy, because a spade makes a reasonable weapon if you hit someone on the head with it.

But I used to collect Victorian swords. I'd lost interest in it as a hobby, and I'd sold most of them. But I still had the 1796 British light cavalry sabre, which is a fearsome looking thing, and I thought, *even if I don't use it, from a psychological perspective, it's what I need right now*.

The 1796 British light cavalry has a broad, very wide, curved blade. It looks awesome. So I grabbed it, and I rushed back into the kitchen.

The other thing about it is that in movies when people draw swords, they go "*schwing*," and real swords mostly don't, but this one does, because it has a steel scabbard.

So as I'm entering the kitchen, I'm drawing the sword and it goes "schwing!" And at that instant we enter the kitchen from both directions simultaneously, me and the burglar. He walks through the door, and this guy is off his nut. His eyes are bulging, his eyes are blue and red because the whites of his eyes are completely bloodshot.

And he's got a kind of cudgel or club. It's a thing the size and the shape of a baseball bat that he's holding, ready to hit someone with it. So he's ready and I'm ready. And he looks up, and I see him register the sabre, and he bolts.

I think, *Brilliant, it's worked perfectly.*

What I want to do at this stage is lock the back door, but I can't because it's in bits. So I need to make sure he's off the property. I run out into the back garden, and at this point he changes his mind about being frightened of the sword, and decides he isn't frightened at all anymore, and he runs at me, and starts trying to hit me with this length of timber, his club.

And there then ensued quite a long fight. It was a fight in which he was trying to hurt me, and for all sorts of reasons which I'll go into in a second, I was trying *not* to hurt him, but *look as if I was going to*, because I needed to get him off the property.

So why wasn't I trying to actually hurt him, since he was obviously so intent on hurting me? Well, there is the moral thing, but also it was because my daughter was asleep upstairs, and I thought she's got to have heard this – the sound of a man booting a door in, it was loud – and I had this mental image of her coming downstairs, and if I had hit him with the sabre, of her coming out and saying "Daddy...?" and seeing me standing over this twitching corpse of a burglar with blood everywhere.

I thought, *That can't happen.* I had to get him off the premises. So there was this long, long fight during which he was swinging at me with his club, and I was ducking and blocking, and I was swinging at him with the sword, and he was backing off, as you would when a chunky piece of metal keeps going "shwee" by your face a lot.

So we back across the garden, and around the side of the house, where he'd got the club. See, I'd been collecting some wood for the stove, and I had some lengths of thick timber. The sounds I'd been hearing earlier in the night were of him snapping the end off a nine-foot length to make something more handy to use as a weapon.

The house is on a dual carriageway, but there's no one around, it's dead quiet, so it's just two men swinging at each other with primitive weapons.

We go a ways up the dual carriageway and this has been going on for about a minute, which when you're really fighting like crazy, is a frickin' long time. And I reach a point where I'm out of ideas, and I've got no energy left.

I thought, *Any second now he's going to realise I'm not trying to hurt him, and then what am I gonna do?*

But at that point he gave up, and suddenly he disappeared – I can't emphasise too much how quickly this man was moving. I don't know what he was on, but it was helping him move around very quickly. And he was just gone, *POOF*, like that, like a spot on the horizon, like a genie evaporating.

I turned and started walking back to the house, and I was thinking about how I was going to explain to my daughter Evlyn what Daddy was doing outside in the garden with a sword, and why he looked shattered.

I was developing my strategy, thinking, *I can leave the sword by the door, don't need to take it in. . .*

And I then heard very fast footsteps behind me.

He'd run away very quickly, and he'd come back even quicker. I turned, and he was almost on me with his arms raised above his head, about to hit me with the club.

I took the blow, and we hit each other simultaneously – I turned and swung the sword across my body, catching him on the chest at the same time as his club caught my forearm. The sword actually is blunt – if it had been sharp, it would've been much, much more messy. I think I broke the skin, but he was not that badly injured.

Then he kept running. He bolted up the dual carriageway, and he was really gone this time.

I got back in the house. Evlyn had slept through the whole thing.

So I made another 999 phone call, and the police turned up incredibly quickly.

I said "That was quick," and they said "No, we were responding to your earlier call."

I hadn't hung up the phone when I called the first time, and apparently you can find out where a phone call is coming from.

They said "Yeah, we heard a lot of it over the phone, we heard this fight, you know, *Crash! Bang! Wallop!*"

They were so tooled up, they had guns and armour and riot shields and stuff. And they'd turned up, and as luck would have it, the burglar had been running up the dual carriageway, and he ran into this convoy of police vans full of heavily armed police. They caught him there and then – they actually had him in the van. Obviously he was arrested, very much, and he was remanded in custody.

It took a long time for it to come to court. It came in December, and I was very glad I didn't have to go to court because he fessed up last minute and said, "Yeah, I did do it."

He got three and a half years for aggravated burglary.

But that's not quite the end of it. This story got into the *Guardian* magazine in a column called "Experience" which features people writing about real-life experiences. And this article had a huge response online. There were 15,000 shares, and hundreds and hundreds of comments. Most of them were, you know, nice comments, of people saying things like "I'm glad you're okay" and "that sounds horrible."

But some of them were actually reviews – *negative* reviews of my performance dealing with a violent intruder. A lot of these hostile reviews came from the United States, especially Texas. I had no idea that people in Texas read the *Guardian*, but some do. And where they felt I'd gone wrong here is I didn't kill him.

I didn't enter into a debate, because you can't really have a conversation online about serious matters. So I thought of answering online, but I didn't. I haven't actually spoken to any of those people.

But what I would like to say to them if I got a chance to do it in a sensible context is, if it does ever happen to you that you have a violent intruder – and I know most of you are thinking, *I hope I never have a violent intruder, please.* But some people really seem to *want* a violent intruder, I guess because they think they're going to be like Bruce Willis in the *Die Hard* movies. If it does happen (and statistically it almost certainly won't) the first thing you think of doing should *not* be that you start shooting guns in the house, because it's just going to go badly wrong from there on.

I only told my daughter about it this year. It was three years on now, and enough time had elapsed, and she was old enough.

She went "Really?!"

She was quite surprised that she'd slept through a thing that was that big in her own house.

The burglar will be getting out anytime now. But I'm okay, my daughter's okay, and even though I don't love the guy, I sort of hope the burglar's okay now too.

SIMON BILL is an artist and writer. His novel *Artist in Residence*, about a dissolute painter who discovers redemption and success as artist in residence at a neurology clinic, was published in 2016. His most recent solo exhibition, at the BALTIC Centre for Contemporary Art, featured his characteristic oval paintings, identical in size and shape but wildly diverse in style, subject matter and media. His interests include European swords and the neuropsychology of visual perception. Bill is currently a Fellow of the Instituto Gulbenkian de Ciencia.

THIS STORY WAS TOLD ON SEPTEMBER 26, 2016, AT THE **UNION CHAPEL, LONDON**. THE THEME OF THE EVENING WAS *YOU ARE HERE*. **DIRECTOR: CATHERINE BURNS**.

Peter Pringle

<><><><><><><><><><><><><><><><><><><><><><><><><><><><>

As If I Was Not There

It was the week before Christmas, and I was sitting in the death cell in Portlaoise Prison in County Laois, Ireland. Some weeks previously I had been wrongly convicted and sentenced to death by the Special Criminal Court for a murder I did not commit. The Special Criminal Court is a non-jury court.

I sat in that death cell, which was a very dismal place. The windows had been blocked off. There was no natural light and a bank of fluorescent lights overhead, which were never turned off day or night and which after a little while began to burn my eyes. I was forced to be always in the presence of at least two jailers, and they would sit quite close to me.

One day I heard them having a conversation. They were discussing what role they might have to play in my hanging. One said to the other, "Seamus, were you told also that two of us would have to participate in his execution?" (This was said as if I didn't exist, as if I wasn't a human being.)

And Seamus said, "Yes, that's right. What do you think we're going to have to do?"

The third guy, Eddie, said, "Well, whatever we have to do, they're going to have to pay us extra money, because that is not our usual job, and so we're going to have to get a bonus for doing this work."

They went on to discuss what role they might have to play, and they came to the conclusion that at my execution two jailers would be positioned underneath the gallows. When my body came down through the trapdoor, each jailer would have to pull on one of my legs to ensure that my neck was broken quickly.

It was as if I was not there. It was as if they weren't speaking about *me*. And I was very angry and upset and disturbed by this, but it illustrates the inhumanity of the death penalty. It even affects the jailers. They're not allowed to speak to the condemned prisoner, because it wouldn't do them any good to learn to like the prisoner or to respect the prisoner. Because how can you cold-bloodedly help to kill somebody that you like or respect?

Now, this was in the year 1980, and it was twenty-six years since this state had executed anybody. And there was a body of opinion which said that it was unlikely they would carry it out. But when I heard these jailers discussing my execution, and the fact that the authorities had told them there would be a role for them in it, there was no doubt in my mind that I was facing death. I tried as best as I could to distance myself from that, and to curb my anger.

Christmas passed in a lonely, dismal way without any contact with the outside world, and without any contact with my loved ones. Shortly after Christmas, as the post was being delivered to the prisoners, a jailer came and handed me a postcard. And this postcard was extraordinary.

It was written by a woman whom I did not know, and she told in the postcard how the day after Christmas she was walking on the shore at Greystones, south of Dublin, grieving for her brother, whose name was Peter. He had been a seaman and had lost his life in an accident at sea.

And she remembered that there was another Peter who was facing death. You see, I had been a fisherman, and I had spent a long time at sea. She remembered that there was another seaman named Peter, and she thought she would write to me to wish me well, and to pray that I would not be executed.

When I got that card, it just lifted my heart. That lady, whom I didn't know, restored my humanity to me and lifted my spirits. And while I knew that I was facing death, and I knew with certainty that the worst thing that they could do to me would be to kill me – until such time as they did that, I was my own person.

While they could imprison me physically, they could not imprison my mind or my heart or my spirit. And so it was within those realms of myself that I determined that I would live. Within that death cell, in that small space around myself, I had my own sanctuary. I learned to almost totally ignore what was around me.

Sometime later, almost six months later – and eleven days before my execution date – my sentence was commuted from the death sentence to forty years' penal servitude without remission, and I was placed back out into the general prison population. This was done because an execution was not in the political interest of the government at that time.

Now, I knew I couldn't possibly face forty years there, and, inspired by getting off death row, I determined to try to prove my innocence. I studied law in the prison, and I took my own case. With the help of a human-rights lawyer named Greg O'Neill, we took the case to the Court of Criminal Appeal.

While there were a number of grounds upon which my conviction could have been overturned, in May of 1995 my conviction was overturned because of conflicting testimony of police, and I was released from the Special Criminal Court.

It was almost surreal, and when I stepped outside the court, I was faced with a huge crowd of media people with their cameras and their microphones. They were all shoving them in my face, and throwing questions at me, and wanting me to do things like give a clenched-fist salute and all that nonsense.

I didn't have a moment to myself. And then my lawyer took me, and we went to the television station, and we had an interview for the news. Afterwards my friends had organised a party, and everybody was drinking and happy and enjoying themselves and talking to me and clapping my back.

But I wasn't really in it. I hadn't had time to assimilate my liberty.

That night I stayed with a friend in the suburbs of Dublin. The following morning I woke up early, and I went downstairs. The rest of the household was still asleep, and I went out to the backyard.

They had a lovely backyard. It was stretched way back from the house. And I walked down the back garden, and the sun was shining, and I felt so good. I began to breathe in the fresh air and the colours and the greenery and hear the birds singing.

Down at the bottom of the garden, there was an old, old apple tree. I went up to this apple tree, and I put my hand out, and I touched the bark of the tree, which was gnarled.

I was thinking about this tree, which had been growing there for countless years, season in and season out. Every year producing its fruit, shedding its leaves, producing new leaves, and just carrying on its business in nature, oblivious of the big city around it.

Oblivious of the hatred and the anger and the injustice and the wars, the depredation and the hunger and everything that goes on. Just simply being in nature.

And I put my arms around that tree, and I wept.

PETER PRINGLE won his freedom in 1995. He has since established the Sunny Center, with his wife, Sunny Jacobs, where they provide respite and rehabilitation to other wrongly convicted people once they are released. Learn more at **thesunnycenter.com**. Peter is a graduate of The Moth Community Program and participated in a workshop in collaboration with the Innocence Project.

....

THIS STORY WAS TOLD ON SEPTEMBER 5, 2014, AT **THE FREEMASONS' HALL, DUBLIN**, IRELAND. THE THEME OF THE EVENING WAS *DON'T LOOK BACK*. **DIRECTORS: SARAH AUSTIN JENNESS, LARRY ROSEN**.

Melissa Lucashenko

Ruby

In 2004 a real estate agent drove me, my husband Bill, and our young daughter Ruby down a winding country road. The road was near Mullumbimby in northern New South Wales, and on either side horses and cattle grazed. The hills that surrounded this valley were cloaked in lush rainforest, home to king parrots and pademelons, and just on the other side of those hills we could hear the booming of the great Pacific Ocean on the coast at New Brighton.

It was a paradise in miniature. And for all that real estate agent knew, we were just another cashed up couple trying to make the sea change that all of Australia was dreaming of. But in truth, there was something else going on. Because this was Bundjalung jagun, this was Bundjalung country, my ancestral land, land that my grandmothers had been forced off.

And I was determined that my daughter was going to grow up on that ancestral land. I wanted her to swim in Bundjalung creeks and rivers. I wanted her to walk with us barefoot on those long north New South Wales beaches. After almost a decade of following Bill's foreign aid work around Australia and the world, I'd put my foot down; it was time, I said, for our daughter to learn how to be not just Aboriginal, but how to be Bundjalung, in our own country.

And so after some argument, debate and discussion, Bill relented. We bought 30 acres in that same valley with an old wooden farmhouse on it. We settled in, I built connections amongst my grandmother's people, wrote novels and bred Arabian horses. It was a sweet life there on that sacred land.

And Ruby thrived. She did swim in Bundjalung waters, and she did hear kurumburuhn, the magpie, singing her talga in the morning as the sun came up. Bill was less content, though, and as time went on his trips overseas grew longer and more frequent. A month in the Philippines, three months in Laos, nine months in East Timor, until finally in 2007 our marriage began to crack and then crumble.

By the time he came to me and said, "I've rented a room in a friend's house, and I'm moving out tomorrow," what I mainly felt was relief.

Now divorce hits everybody hard, but it hit 14-year-old Ruby the hardest.

I sat at my desk one morning, and I looked out on those green pastures, and I looked at those Bundjalung hills, and I knew that they were going to be lost to us again.

I thought, *What's going to become of us? What's my life with my daughter going to be like?* 'Cause I knew there was no way in hell I could afford as a single parent to stay on that land. *What am I gonna do with all these horses?* I thought. *Will I be a bag lady?*

As I was pondering these unhappy questions, the phone rang. It was Bill. "I'm on my way to Tweed Heads Hospital," he told me, "And you'd better get in a car and head up too, because Ruby has been taken to hospital after throwing up most of a bottle of Panadol on the floor of a school bus."

I put the phone down, reeling, and burst into hot tears. Life quickly became a blur of psychologists and guilt and deep recrimination between Bill and myself. Six months later Bill had relocated to Sydney, and Ruby and I found ourselves living in Logan City, just south of Brisbane, officially one of Australia's poorest urban areas.

To me this move wasn't terrifying. It was unwelcome, but I knew how to do it. I had the skillset, because I'd grown up as one of seven children in a working-class Brisbane family. Having spent a lot of my childhood in Logan, I knew how not to make eye contact with strangers in the street, lest you be asked that unanswerable question, "What the fuck you lookin' at?"

And I knew what life was like in a suburb where the majority of people were ordinary, decent Australians, but a significant minority were prepared to sell their children's Ritalin in order to fund a heroin habit.

I remember the first week we moved in, and pulled up to what was going to become our corner store, and for someone with a deep depressive illness, Ruby could still muster an occasional wisecrack. As we pulled up to this dingy establishment, she turned to me in the car and said, "Mum" – she quoted from the BBC comedy A League of Gentlemen – "This is a local shop."

I turned to her and said, "Yes, it is our local shop, and we're locals, so we should go in," and we were just about to do so, but were interrupted by a junkie hurtling out of the doorway to projectile vomit on the concrete footpath not three metres away. We fell about, snorting and leaking with laughter.

So it wasn't all bad. I mean make no mistake, I wanted out of there, because I had tasted that good life in Mullumbimby, and it tasted mighty sweet. I didn't expect to live in Logan City for very long. In fact, in a moment of crazed optimism, I even filled out an online application form for Millionaire Hot Seat. Yes, I thought, I'll win back that big dollar, and that will send us back to Bundjalung country.

But you have to understand, jokes aside, I was living a life where, as a single parent, I'd given away every extension cord I owned – I'd thrown out every rope. My job every morning was to get up and make a long and frightening journey downstairs to see if Ruby had hung herself during the night.

So geographic location was not my biggest priority. I drew on a lifelong study of Buddhism and I said to myself, *you're poor again, so what? Suck it up.* "It is what it is" became my mantra. I dusted off my CV, and I started working with women in prison for the first time in twenty years.

We took in a homeless girl who contributed a bit of board, and I started shopping at those cheap Asian supermarkets. We lived on rice and vegetables, bread, occasionally meat, never takeaways, and I just kept putting one foot in front of the other, saying, *Your job is simply to keep your daughter alive.*

And I told myself I could do it. But deep down, I could feel something beginning to unravel, because the truth is I wasn't sure I could do it, but at the same time I couldn't allow myself to believe that. One day not long before her fifteenth birthday, Ruby asked if she could get a mohawk haircut, and I was so happy that she'd asked for something underpinned by life – something that implied that she was willing to be around for more than another day or two – that I scraped the money together, and I took her to the hairdresser myself.

She came out an hour later with a sculpture on her head in red and green and purple and yellow. And I smiled to see my daughter. I thought, *Maybe she'll make it after all.*

It was the next day that Ruby told me that she was really happy with the haircut, but that the bug inside her head was bothering her with its efforts to get out. She scratched at her head as she told me this. I looked at her and my heart sank, because I knew this was the beginning of a journey into another level of mental illness altogether – a journey that would take us to an extended stay in the adolescent psychiatric wing of the Logan Hospital.

If I live to be a hundred, I'll never forget the first day I visited Ruby on that ward. I went to those big glass doors that hospitals have and waited to be let in, because it was a locked ward, and I went into that antiseptic smell that hospitals have.

Ruby was nowhere in sight at this point, but another Aboriginal girl was there, and ignoring the warning sounds from the staff, this girl got up and ran at me. Before I had time to move, she had flung her arms around me, and she had told the ward, "my mother's here, she's come to take me home."

And as I put my arms around this unknown girl, I felt like I was teetering on the brink of a precipice, a precipice that Ruby was in danger of falling over. It was then that I decided that, whatever it took, I would stop my daughter from becoming someone who had to hug strangers in hospital wards because there was no one else to hug.

With some pretty tightrope parenting over the next few weeks from me and from Bill, who visited periodically from Sydney, and the help of a very good young psychologist in the public health system, Ruby slowly began to improve – marginally. Her psychosis ended, and I thought, maybe we can make it after all; maybe the unraveling won't become any worse.

And then I got another phone call which left me reeling. Was I available the next week to go on Millionaire Hot Seat in Melbourne?

The following Tuesday I was sitting opposite Eddie McGuire on national TV, Ruby in the audience, foot-high mohawk and all. I answered five or six questions correctly, took a pass on one, and then came back to the hot seat, to the final question.

"What is the scientific unit for the measurement of light?" What is the scientific unit for the measurement of light ... But you see, all those months earlier when I'd filled out the application form, they'd asked for areas of strength and areas of weakness, and if I had learned anything growing up in Logan, it is you don't telegraph your punches.

Under strengths I put literature; under weaknesses I put science, but I know science. There were four multiple choice questions.

I answered "candela."

And that night in the hotel room Ruby and I danced and hugged and laughed and sang, because on the table in front of us was a cheque signed by Eddie McGuire for $50,000.

Ruby picked it up and turned to me; her hair bounced and her eyes shone, and she said, "Mum, you did it, it's our ticket home. Can you believe it?"

And I looked at her, I looked at that shining face, and I thought, *I would rip that check up and throw it in the bin if it would guarantee that smile.*

But I didn't have the words to explain that to her, so I just took the cheque off her, and I took a deep breath, and I said, "Ruby, you know what? It is what it is."

MELISSA LUCASHENKO is an award-winning Bundjalung novelist. Her most recent novel, *Mullumbimby*, was awarded the 2013 Deloitte Queensland Literary Award for Fiction, won the 2014 Victorian Premiers Prize for Indigenous Writing, and was longlisted for the Miles Franklin, Stella and Dublin IMPAC awards in 2015. Melissa is a Walkley Award winner for her non-fiction, as well as a founding member of the women's rights organisation, Sisters Inside. She is the holder of the Copyright Agency Limited Fellowship for 2016.

THIS STORY WAS TOLD ON AUGUST 22 2013 AT THE MELBOURNE WRITER'S FESTIVAL AT THE **TOWN HALL, MELBOURNE**, AUSTRALIA. **DIRECTOR: SARAH AUSTIN JENNESS**.

To Be a Boy

John Turturro

<><><><><><><><><><><><><><><><><><><><><><><><><><><><><>

Stumbling in the Dark

I am driving my silver Volvo station wagon from Brooklyn to my mother's house in Rosedale, Queens, on a hot midafternoon August day in 2003.

My mother is a widow. My father has passed away from lung cancer fifteen years before, in 1988, and she has not resumed dating. She has sworn off men in no uncertain terms. She has told me that "I am never, ever going to wash another pair of men's underwear again. I am finished with the species. I'm done."

She's somewhere around eighty years old, but I don't know for sure, because she's never told me how old she is. As a matter of fact, on my birth certificate, you can see that she has altered her age.

I'm very close with my mother. We've always had this bond, this silent love between us. I check in with her almost every evening to make sure she's okay, and to alleviate her loneliness.

As long as I can remember, I've always been my mother's protector against my father, my brother and the rest of the world, and she's also been mine.

I grew up in a very volatile house. My father was a World War II veteran. He suffered from posttraumatic stress syndrome, which wasn't really diagnosed in those days. My older brother, who also had problems, lived downstairs.

As my father got sick from cancer, he lost his booming voice. But as his voice faded away, my brother's voice in the basement rose. And I could tell that this was not a good sign for things to come.

You know, when we grow up, we all think we're gonna get married, we're gonna have our own family, and we're gonna leave the other family behind – our siblings and our parents. But it doesn't actually always occur that way. It's very hard to break those ties from the first family that formed you.

Anyway, my mother and I get in the car that day, and we're going to visit my brother Ralph, who no longer lives with my mother. He now resides at the Creedmore Psychiatric Center. It's the state mental hospital, the one that's located in Queens off Union Turnpike.

He's not too happy about living there, but that's where he's been for the last seven years. He's been diagnosed as paranoid schizophrenic, bipolar, obsessive-compulsive, borderline personality – any diagnosis that's out there, he's got it, okay?

So he's been to therapy. He's had shock treatments. He's had every combination of antipsychotic drugs and all the side effects that go with them – the weight gain, the teeth loss, the tremors, the shaking, the stiffness, the diabetes.

When he's stable, we're actually allowed to take him out on a pass, and he loves to go out on passes, because we take him shopping, and he can get something to eat, because he doesn't like the food there.

He also loves to go to the hair salon. My brother Ralph's hair is very important to him. He doesn't have many teeth, but his hair has to be done just so. If it's not just so, his emotional state plummets, and then we have to deal with that.

So we're on the way to Creedmore. He lives in Building 40, a seventeen-story building, and he's in a locked facility on the eleventh floor.

When we were kids, we used to pass Creedmore on the parkway, and it was a place where the boogeyman lived – where *all* the crazy people lived.

My father used to say, "You don't want to wind up in Creedmore."

And now it's my brother's home.

We get there, and we have to go through two sets of doors, and then we're locked in. I walk to the elevator, and I press the button, and as we're waiting for the elevator to descend to the lobby, the lights go out.

We're all looking around. We don't know what happened. It's two years after 9/11. Everyone's a little jittery. We're thinking, *Hey, maybe this could be another attack or something.* It's 2003, most people don't have cell phones. I don't have a cell phone.

About ten minutes later, they say, "It's a blackout."

It's the blackout of 2003, which affected, I think, 50 million people and knocked out Ontario and eight states here in America. But we don't know this at the time. All I know is that my brother has a pass, and he wants to go out – he's looking forward to it.

So I ask the guys, can they call upstairs and talk to the doctor? And they do, and they say I can go up there.

I say to my mother, "Listen, you wait down here."

I start walking up the eleven floors. They're very long flights. It's kind of dark.

And I'm thinking what a roller coaster mental illness is. Not just for the patient, but for everyone else involved. It's a sentence that you're given, and it's a life sentence. And there's all the things that you have to go through: the doctors, the drugs, the violent outbursts, the destruction (literally and emotionally), the police coming to your house, the shame that you live with. It just goes on and on.

It's not like those movies like *A Beautiful Mind* where someone reaches out and says, "All you need is love." You know?

Love is a given, but it's a war of attrition. It really is. It's a long, endless baseball season that never, ever ends. It goes on and on. You have to have unbelievable patience and emotional fortitude to survive. That's what wears you out.

It kills a lot of people, and that's why you see so many people out on the street, because their families flee (and I don't blame them), and they become wards of the state.

So anyway, that's what's going through my mind as I come up and knock on the door. My brother's happy to see me. I talk to the doctor. And then my brother's friend, this young, thin black man named Isaiah, who draws pictures of his life every day – he storyboards his entire existence – comes over and shows me his latest masterpiece.

And I say, "Nice, Isaiah," as I'm trying to deal with my brother and the doctor.

Isaiah whispers in my ear, "Can I come, too, with you?"

And I say, "Isaiah, listen. I'd love to take you, but it's a blackout and I'm just gonna take Ralph, okay?"

So we go down the stairs. We have to go down slowly, because my brother can't see so well. He had an altercation with a very huge patient who was an ex-prisoner from Rikers Island, and the guy savagely beat him, and now my brother's blind in one eye.

I come outside with my brother and my mom, and of course we've brought him cigarettes. Now, I'm worried about the time, because it was 4:10 when the blackout happened. By now it's around 5:00. I'm worried about the light. But my brother is in no hurry.

So I give him a cigarette. He can't have one cigarette, he has to have one after another after another, and he smokes them down to the very tiny butt end. And when you give him the pack, you have to open it just so. Everything according to his specifications, otherwise he will take the cigarettes out and break them.

And that's kind of symbolic of my relationship with him much of the time:

I buy him cigarettes; he breaks them.

I buy him a CD player; he rips off the cover.

I renovate my mother's house; he burns it down.

We get in the car. He has to sit in the backseat, so I can see him in the mirror, because it's precarious. I have to make sure I keep my eye on my brother, who can sometimes punch the window out of frustration.

And I have to figure out where am I going. It's a blackout. What are we going to do? I know he's hungry. My mother sits to my right. She's never driven, so she doesn't know that much about driving. There are no stoplights.

My mother says, "Why don't you make a left turn?" I'm in the far-right lane.

I say, "Mom, I can't go over three lanes like that," but she seems kind of oblivious.

It's getting later. We see the diner that we normally go to. We pull in. There's no one in there, but it seems open. So we get out, and we walk in. The owner is this big Greek guy with a walrus mustache. I say, "Are you serving?"

And he says, "Blackout. It's a blackout!"

My brother looks at him and goes, "I want a cheeseburger."

"No cheeseburger. Blackout. Coffee."

So my mother tries to referee the situation.

She says, "You must have a gas stove."

"Pilot light electric. Coffee. No cheeseburger."

My brother says, "What about french fries?"

"No. No. No."

My mother and my brother look at him incredulously, like, *Look at this guy, what a weakling. There's a blackout, and he folds like a cheap suit, you know?*

I'm looking at the clock. It's getting later. I get my brother back in the car after another cigarette. We're driving. Everything is closed. It's like a ghost town, because people worry when there's a blackout. They remember the blackout of 1977. The looting. The stores are closed, the restaurants are closed. Even the hair salon is closed (which is very upsetting to Ralph).

We just keep driving and driving, and I'm going, *Okay, it's gonna get darker, and we don't know where we're going.* Plus, I have my own family back in Brooklyn – my wife and two kids.

So finally I see a little pizzeria on the corner, and I pull over. It looks open. I run in there, and the guy has a wood-burning oven.

He says, "Yes, I'm open." He's an Italian guy, of course, so that's good.

We sit outside, and we order brick-oven pizza and warm soda. It takes a long time to come. And I'm looking at my mother and thinking, *Wow, she's getting older.*

And I'm looking at my brother thinking, *What's gonna happen after she's gone? Who's gonna take care of him?*

I'm the middle child, one of three boys, and I'm the responsible one, for good and for bad.

I think, *I'm gonna be alone with him one day, and it's gonna just be me and him.*

And my brother looks at me, and he's very perceptive when he's calm. He can spot a person's weakness with startling accuracy and speed. He says, "You know, you get a lot of material from me, don't you?"

I go, "Mmm-hmm. Yeah, yeah."

He goes, "Where would you be without me?"

We have the pizza. Of course Ralph wants ice cream, but it's all melted by then. So he has kind of a milk-shake ice-cream sandwich, which he's happy about, and he wolfs it down.

The sun is now setting, so I'm thinking, *We've got to get back.*

I finally get them in the car. We drive slowly. There's no streetlights, no stoplights. It's starting to get dark.

We finally make it back to this big seventeen-story, foreboding, ugly building with bars. I leave my mother in the car, and I help him in. The place is not lit, and it's not air-conditioned anymore.

I feel pulled in all these directions: my mother, my brother, my family in Brooklyn. But I go with my brother, help him up the eleven flights. It's always hard to say good-bye to him, but this day it's even harder. And so I give him a hug, I tell him I'll see him soon.

I come down, get my mother, and I drive on the parkway to her house in Rosedale, which is a long trip. I get her in the house and make sure the flashlights work. I check the refrigerator, and the food is actually still cold.

We light a candle, and we talk a little bit. And I'm thinking, *Well, this is how it was for thousands of years.* People didn't have electricity, you know? They had a little fire. They talked, and people invented stories.

I get in my car, and I make my way back to Brooklyn. And I'm thinking about the fact that we imagine that we live in the light. We imagine we can foresee what's gonna happen. We imagine we can control everything: *I'm gonna do this, and I'm gonna do that.*

But the reality is, almost all of us are just stumbling along in the dark, searching, trying to reach some kind of home, while we're juggling all these balls and hopefully on most days keeping them afloat.

JOHN TURTURRO has performed in numerous stage productions, including Yasmina Reza's *Life x 3* on Brodway, and directed *Relatively Speaking*, an evening of one-acts by Ethan Coen, Elaine May, and Woody Allen. He was nominated for SAG Awards for *Monday Night Mayhem* and *The Bronx Is Burning* and won an Emmy Award for *Monk*. His film appearances include Spike Lee's *Do the Right Thing* and *Jungle Fever*; Martin Scorsese's *The Colour of Money*; Robert Redford's *Quiz Show*; Alison Anders's *Grace of My Heart*; and Joel and Ethan Coen's *Miller's Crossing*, *The Big Lebowski* and *O Brother, Where Art Thou?* For his lead role in *Barton Fink*, Turturro won the Best Actor Award at the Cannes Film Festival. He received the Caméra d'Or Award at Cannes for his directorial debut, *Mac*.

THIS STORY WAS TOLD ON NOVEMBER 9, 2015, IN THE GREAT HALL AT **COOPER UNION, NEW YORK CITY**. THE THEME OF THE EVENING WAS *STATE OF AFFAIRS: THE MOTH MEMBERS' SHOW*. **DIRECTOR: CATHERINE BURNS**.

Tim FitzHigham

<><><><><><><><><><><><><><><><><><><><><><><><><><><><><><><><><><><><>

All at Sea

Imagine if you will, I'm out rowing in the middle of the English Channel. It's a lovely stretch of water. It's very difficult to row, however, and I'm rowing quite quickly, really, really quite quickly.

Fast.

It's the fastest I've ever rowed in my life. It's so fast that my lungs are beginning to die. And the reason for this incredible burst of speed – some would say legendary burst of speed – is that just behind me, bearing down on me, is an oil tanker.

It's five hundred metres long, and it is bearing down on me with incredible speed, which is why I am rowing faster than anyone has ever rowed in their life. I am desperately trying to get out of the way of that massive oil tanker.

Did I mention, by the way, that I am sitting rowing in a bathtub?

It's in moments like this that you question how these things happened. It started in a bathtub very like the one that I was rowing in, about eight months beforehand. I was lying in the bath, and I had this idea. I was thinking to myself, *I wonder if anyone has ever rowed the English channel in a bathtub?*

And then I started looking it up, and the more I looked it up, the more it looked like no one had ever rowed the English Channel in a bathtub.

I thought, *Someone should row the English Channel in a bathtub.* And then the more I thought about that, the more I thought, *You know what? The person that should row the English Channel in a bathtub, that should be* me.

I said this to some friends of mine. I said, "I'm going to row the English Channel in a bathtub."

And they said, "Good luck with that."

So I started to go into the preparations for this. Now the key preparation was. . . get a bathtub.

So I phoned hundreds and hundreds of bathtub companies, and nobody would get involved in what I thought was an incredible project, until finally one of them wrote back.

I got my bathroom company. And not just *any* bathroom company. I got the finest bathroom company in the entire world to give me a bathtub. Yes, that's right, ladies and gentlemen, I got a bath from Thomas Crapper and Company.

A third of a ton roll-top Victorian copper bathtub. The sort of thing that you see in a museum. A fantastically beautiful piece of bathroom kit. It goes up and has a fluted roll top. It's a gorgeous Victorian artifact.

And on that beautiful artifact, I screwed two outriggers from a rowing boat that would take the center of gravity slightly further out, which would help me to spread the weight over a wider area, so hopefully I'd be more balanced, and I wouldn't sink.

A problem began to arise. The English Channel turns out to be the busiest shipping lane in the world. There are more tankers, container ships, frigates, and just general traffic going up and down that tiny stretch of water than any other stretch of water in the entire world.

Some of these tankers, as discussed, are huge. But what I didn't realise is that they also have giant stopping distances. Some of their stopping distances are *twenty-five kilometres*. That means that by the time they have seen you and applied the brake, they have already gone through you, and somebody is calling the undertaker.

They go north to south, these tankers and container ships and frigates. And I have to go from east to west, from England to France. So I am going to be crossing the busiest motorway in the world, at right angles to the direction of traffic, riding a concrete snail.

This is problem number one. The second problem is that half of the English Channel turns out to be owned not by Great Britain, but by the French.

Now. I wrote to the French government and said, "This is what I'm going to do. I'm going to row the English Channel in a bathtub." They were kind, and they were generous, and they were helpful. They sent me tons of stuff to read, and it was like years and years of stereotypes of the French not being helpful to the British were just blown away.

And all the time they were going into the French parliament, and passing a new clause in the shipping act of France, making it illegal to row a bathtub in French water. And that, in the context of my plan, was a bit of a blow.

Now I thought to myself, *This must be an initiative test, right?* So I went to the Ministry of Transport, in Whitehall, and I said, "Now, this is what we're going to do, gentlemen. We are going to register my bath as a British ship."

And to my shock, horror, and amazement, they said, "Yeah, fair enough, Tim, that's a good plan, yeah, yeah."

They put me on the captains' register. They gave me a small ships' registration certificate. They sent me a letter that genuinely said:

"Dear Mr FitzHigham, Please find enclosed the paperwork for your newly registered British shipping vessel [bathtub]. Please keep it with you at all times and in all places, even on the high seas. To assist you in this aim, please find enclosed, we've had it laminated. We think the French are going to want to see this."

I don't think I have ever been prouder to be British than when I looked down and saw in my hand *laminated* paperwork.

There was another problem that I became aware of, and that is: I couldn't row. I also knew nothing about the sea. Nothing at all. Never been on it.

So I phoned loads of people to try to get someone to talk to me about the sea. I tried all the various organisations I could think of. Nobody had time to talk to me. I tried the Coast Guard. They seemed to be busy.

In the end, I did what anyone would do in this situation. In total desperation, I phoned the Royal Navy, and by mistake, at the switchboard, I got put through to an admiral.

Now, the only sailor who's ever existed in my entire family is a great uncle. And he said to me, a long time ago, "Tim, if ever you're talking to a member of Her Majesty's Royal Navy, always start the conversation with the question, 'How are your futtocks, old man?'"

What the heck is a futtock? I had absolutely no idea, but I thought, *Well, I'll give it a go.*

So I said, "Ah, Rear Admiral, how are your futtocks, old man?"

And he replied, "At their furthest reach, dear boy. At their *furthest reach.*"

Now I asked my great uncle about this, and he said, "Yes, Tim, that is the correct nautical response to, 'How are your futtocks, old man?'"

I said, "That's fantastic, Uncle. But what does it actually *mean?*"

He said, "Well, that's the thing, Tim. Nobody actually knows."

I thought there was something incredibly British about the fact we had both just had a conversation that neither of us had understood a single word of.

We might as well have said, "Ah, ostrich hairy gusset strap, Rear Admiral?"

"Yes, Plantagenet blue ass cheese, dear boy."

But the both of us were just too darn British-ly polite to admit to the fact that we didn't understand.

Now after this slightly weird beginning to the conversation, me and the Rear Admiral are getting on really rather well, and after a while I plucked up the courage to say, "You know this vessel that we're talking about taking across the busiest shipping lane in the world? You *do* know it's a bath?"

And then the line went dead.

And then the line crackled into life, and the voice said, "Well, same rules of navigation apply, dear boy. I'm on board."

So in one second, I suddenly had the Royal Navy backing the bath project.

Then I decided to do what any great British explorer I'd ever heard about has done in the history of Britain: I decided to write to the Queen, and tell her what I was planning to do and say, you know, "Do you mind if I have a crack at the Channel in a bathtub?"

And to my shock, horror, and amazement, she wrote back.

Should we just recap on what's going on here? I've set off to row the Channel in a bath, and I now have a letter from the Queen saying, "Not only do I not mind you rowing the Channel in a bathtub, you have my heartiest support. Good luck, and let me know how you get on."

So now, just to get back to where this story started, I'm in a third of a ton roll-top Victorian copper bathtub, there's a tanker bearing down on me. I'm rowing like no one's ever rowed in their entire life, desperately trying to get out of the way of this thing, because about two hours beforehand, I had taken what, as it transpired, was not a very good navigating decision. I had thought, *I reckon I could probably get 'round the front of that.*

So I'm rowing in front of the tanker as fast as I possibly can, and my only thought is, *I'm about to die. I'm about to get killed in the English Channel in a third of a ton roll-top copper piece of Victorian bathroom equipment.*

And a thought popped into my head, and that thought was, quite simply – *who has right of way?*

Now in my bath, I had a radio, and the sailors' almanac. And so as I was frantically trying to row with one arm, I was flipping through the sailors' almanac, desperately trying to get to the page that tells you about who has right of way in the English Channel.

I finally got to it, and it says, massive big tankers (like the one about to crash into me) have to give way to sailing ships. Sailing ships have to give way to rowing ships. Rowing ships have to give way to rowing ships of restricted maneuverability – and that's *got* to be me in a third of a ton roll-top Victorian copper bathtub.

So I grab the radio, and radioed up to the tanker captain and said, "I am in a bath! I am in a bath! Back down! Back down! I am in a bath! Over."

There was total silence, and then the captain responded, "Do you want me to scrub your back?"

Now then the weirdest thing happened, which is that the tanker *did* divert around a bathtub for the first time in the maritime history of the world, and create what the admiral later called a naval precedent in law.

He said, "This is the first time in the maritime history of the globe that a tanker has backed down to a piece of plumbing on the high seas. We are going to name that precedent in law after you, Tim. The FitzHigham Precedent."

However, the problem wasn't over yet, 'cause I carried on rowing, and then something went just a little bit awry in that the mists started to come in, and I couldn't find the support boat.

And then very quickly, as happens at sea, there was suddenly a massive storm that hit the English Channel. It's a terrifying thing to be out in any storm, but this was a Force 7. For people who don't go to sea, a Force 7 will give you waves of the height of three and a half metres.

At one point, the storm got so bad it ripped the roll-top off the Victorian copper bath – it popped out of the water. I realised it was essential ballast, and dived across the bath, pushed it back in with my shoulder, and ripped my shoulder so badly on the serrated edge of the bath that it went all floppy and stopped working.

But I thought to myself, *I can still keep rowing through this, with one arm. I am British.*

So I carried on, and survived in that horrible storm, totally on my own, having lost the support boat, rowing with one arm. And after forty minutes, they found me, because apparently for the entire forty minutes, I had been heroically rowing *in a giant circle.*

They pulled me back in, but the disaster wasn't over yet, because we were in French water. The French navy came on the radio, and they were calling me a problem. Their solution was to put explosives on my bath and blow it out of the water.

Now, I had lost a lot of blood at this stage, and I wasn't thinking very clearly. But I went on the radio, and apparently said the following, "Just to remind that the sinking of a registered British ship without the permission of the captain will be taken as an act of war. (In Dover, you could just hear the Coast Guard screaming.)

The French then went away and looked this up in the legal book, right? And they worked out that actually in law, I *was* right.

Then something very moving occurred. Boats came from all the other nations in the English Channel (mainly Holland and Belgium) to take me and the bathtub back to the UK, which proved something vital to me, and that is, it's not just Britain, but *all* the other nations in the English Channel, who hate the French.

Now I was in quite a bad way at this point. I had to go into hospital. Had to get patched back up again. But thanks to the Navy, I got another crack at rowing the English Channel in my bathtub, and I did – I made it across the English Channel in the bath.

Lots of amazing things happened as a result of the bath crossing. It raised a load of money for charity, I got made a commodore in the Royal Navy, which is the fourth-highest rank in the Royal Navy. It basically goes: first sea lord, second sea lord, Princess Anne, me.

I got my own flag. And being the navy, they had to put me in charge of a port, but they chose to put me in charge of the port of Sudbury, which is fifteen miles *inland*.

And then the weirdest thing happened. I got a letter from the Queen saying I had to go up to the palace for an audience with the Queen. I went to the palace, and normally you're not allowed to report anything you say to the Queen – there's this whole "Chatham House Rule" thing. But she has allowed me to say a couple of things that we talked about.

She said to me, "Gosh, that bathtub must have been awfully heavy. It must have weighed half a ton."

And I thought, *This is my one moment of being Bond.*

I just smoothed my hair down, looked her directly in the eye, and said, "Well, it was actually a third of a ton, ma'am, but still really rather heavy."

Then she said, "But did you not think about putting a shower curtain on it?"

And I said, "Well, I did consider it, but I couldn't decide on the colour."

And she said, "I think blue, don't you?"

But more than all of these honours, I got a phone call from my beloved sponsor, Thomas Crapper and Company, right?

They phoned me up and said, "Tim, in honour of the bath Channel crossing, we at Thomas Crapper and Company are going to release a commemorative toilet named after you." That's right, ladies and gentlemen, The FitzHigham, my family seat.

It's an amazing thing about Great Britain that I have found to be very, very true, and that is that Great Britain is a land where you can turn to the Great British public, and say, "I'm going to do something really quite hard. I'm going to run up Kilimanjaro," or "I'm going to climb Everest".

And the Great British public will look you in the eye, and they will go, "Well, it's not *that* hard."

But if you say to them, "'I'm going to do something really quite hard, like run up Kilimanjaro, or climb Everest, or row the English Channel *dressed as a dolphin*, or *carrying a fridge*, or *wrestling a weasel*,'" the Great British public will say, "This man's a hero! Get right behind him, ladies and gentlemen. Someone get the Prime Minister on the phone."

I don't know what it says about Britain as a nation, but I have broken my entire body to prove it to be true.

TIM FITZHIGHAM, FRSA, FRGS, is a multi-award winning comedian, author and adventurer. He holds the record for the longest distance travelled in a paper boat and is the only man to have successfully rowed the English Channel in a bath, an adventure recounted in greater length in his book, *All At Sea: One man, one bath tub, one bad idea* (2009). He's also run across deserts in suits of armour, climbed the world's tallest buildings from the outside, tried arrow catching, bus pulling and run across ice caps barefoot in his pants. On his Radio 4 show, *Tim FitzHigham: The Gambler*, he tries to win ancient, weird and eccentric bets. He presented Super Human Challenge for CBBC; has been in films directed by Clint Eastwood among others; and his live shows have been Critic's Choice in most British newspapers. He shares an ancient, falling apart house in East Anglia with chickens, running ducks and several geese who won't leave the library.

....

THIS STORY WAS TOLD ON APRIL 13 2015 AT THE **UNION CHAPEL, LONDON**. THE THEME OF THE EVENING WAS *HIGH ANXIETY*. **DIRECTOR: MEG BOWLES**.

Shannon Cason

◇◇◇

Downstairs Neighbours

We were coming down the steps when they were coming in. A new family was moving into our three-flat building that we lived in in Chicago. They were moving into the garden apartment, which is really small for a family.

I stopped, talked to the husband. My wife talked to the wife. And our two-year-old daughters introduced themselves on the porch. They had a two-year-old, and we had a two-year-old.

Me and the father smiled looking at our little girls. Kids introduce themselves by what they have: "This is my doll," "This is my bear."

The father said that they were moving from the shelter down the street and were happy to have a place to call home.

I told him, "I know how it is, man. If you need anything, just give a knock upstairs. Anything."

We left, and they went inside.

The very next day, I get a knock at the door. The father was asking for money for train fare to go downtown.

I told him, "No problem. I'm headed downtown to go to work. We could just walk together. I'll swipe you through, too."

We walked down the sidewalk and down the long line of three-flat buildings like ours. There's a big apartment building across the street. The neighbourhood in Uptown in Chicago is really diverse. It's Asians, Africans, Europeans, Americans, all of us.

You can get Starbucks coffee from one building and a fifth of Henny from another. There's Mexican food, Thai food, an Ethiopian restaurant, or you can get some Flamin' Hot Cheetos, all on the way to the train. We live in the Starbucks area.

We're walking on past this big church with a shelter in the basement, and then it's the corner store. Guys hang out at the corner store. There's been some shootings at the corner.

I ignore the guys at the corner. They sell drugs on the corner. There's gangs in Chicago, if you haven't heard. I'm from Detroit, so I'm not clueless, but I know if you're not from a certain area, it's best just to keep your eyes open and go unseen. They ignore me, I got nothing to do with what they're doing. None of my business.

So I'm a little concerned when my new neighbour knows all the guys on the corner really well. But we talk on the train, laugh. He's a good guy. His name is Jessie.

Another night I get another knock on the door. This time it's the mother from downstairs. It's after midnight. My wife works late, she isn't home. The mother's asking to borrow twenty dollars for baby diapers.

First, it's after midnight. The baby should be sleeping. The store's closed. The other thing, did she forget that we have a baby, too? So when I give her a couple of diapers to make it through the night, she looks disappointed, which makes me suspicious.

Another night my wife also wasn't home. Knock at the door, and the mother, she just hands her daughter over to me. She's in a panic, in a fluster, and says she has to go across town for an emergency.

I'm holding her daughter, and she doesn't even wait for an answer. She just leaves. I look from the window, and I see her get in the car with a man who isn't Jessie.

I knew it was drugs. I'm going to be real wit'cha, I knew it was crack. You know, you ain't that wide awake that late at night, unless it's drugs, or the pursuit of some drugs.

The thing is, I have a heart towards people with addictions, because I got some of my own. It's not drugs, but I'm no stranger to community rooms and church basements.

In the morning my wife cooked breakfast for us, and the girls played in the living room. My daughter, Zoe, brought every toy she ever got into the living room to play. (You know, kids are show-offs.)

I said, "Zoe, which toy you going to give Ashley to have?"

Zoe gave me that look like, *What?*

But Zoe is generous. She gave her a doll that was better than I expected. It was this little plush doll with a bonnet and pigtails.

My wife called Ashley's mom, and told her that we'll keep her an extra day, and that night I put them under the Dora the Explorer covers and tucked them in.

One day I'm coming home from the train from work, and I pass by the corner, and the corners are empty. It's kind of nice, like a regular neighbourhood. I pass by the church with the shelter, the big apartment building across the street.

I get to my house, and all the guys from the corner are sitting on my porch, smoking with Jessie.

I just stood there for a second.

I can't ignore it now.

The thing is, I came up in a rougher neighbourhood than this Uptown neighbourhood in Chicago. You know, this is a pretty nice neighbourhood to me. I work hard so my family can have a different experience than I had around drugs and violence. I want better for my family.

It's at a distance I can ignore at the corner, but not on my porch. But I don't say anything. I just go inside.

They were smoking in the garden apartment, and it was coming into our place, and my wife isn't as passive as me. She don't really play that.

She went downstairs and banged on the door like the police and told them, "Y'all got to stop smoking down here. My daughter's coughing."

So they just went out to the porch. I went downstairs to talk to Jessie.

I'm like, "How many people you got living down here now?" He said it was just them, but the guys from the corner will come in and out. They hard to get rid of. They like roaches.

I told him, "Man, I'm going to tell you, y'all going have some problems, because my wife – she hates roaches."

Cindy had seen one of the guys from the corner selling drugs in front of our place. And she yelled out the window, "If I see it again, I'm calling the police!"

She told me when I got home. I'm like, "Baby, you can't go yelling out the window to a bunch of drug dealers and gang members that you're going to call the police. If they get caught, who they gonna point to? You smarter than that."

But she was just frustrated.

Cindy saw some guys selling drugs again, and she told me she's going to call the police.

I stopped her.

You don't call the police. I have this programming in my mind. I grew up in Detroit in the crack era, the eighties. You don't call the police.

First, there's a distrust that the police will actually do something to help the situation. Another thing is the threat of retaliation from the person you're telling on.

Snitches get stitches.

But I think about that little girl, and all those men coming in and out of that tiny apartment – the dazed look on her face when I see her, and how when she stayed with us, she didn't want to go home. I've got to confront this stupid way of thinking. I can't just ignore it.

One night another knock at the door. My wife wasn't home. I'm a little frustrated now. I'm thinking it's the mother or the father downstairs, and I opened the door mad, but it's the police.

I could see them all in this little foyer, with vests and badges, and they tell me to go back inside and lock the door. One of the officers I see has a battering ram. I go back inside.

I hear them bust down the door: BOOM! I can hear scuffling and wrestling down below. The police are yelling and cussing. I go in to check on my daughter, and she is still asleep. She didn't know anything was happening.

I can hear the guys from the corner screaming at the police, and then it just goes silent. I look from the window, and I see that the police are carting everybody up from the basement to a wagon, all the guys from the corner, then the family, Jessie, his wife and their daughter.

One of the officers has Ashley in his arms. She's in her pink pyjamas against his dark blues and blacks, and she has that little doll that Zoe gave her.

I want to go out there and tell the officer, "Hey, I can just keep her until everything is taken care of."

But I don't want to go out and have the officers think I'm a part of everything else that's happening.

We all look the same to the police.

My wife's not home. I go out, get arrested, and then my daughter's in some officer's arms. I think the best thing is to stay where I am. It's none of my business.

The next week corners are empty. No smoke in our apartment, nobody on our porch. About a week after that, same guys on the corner. They don't say anything to me. They ignore me, and I ignore them. We live in two different worlds. But I don't know if that's really true.

I get to my place, and I hear the landlord downstairs. I go down there to check on him, see if he going to discount my rent for all the stuff we've been putting up with. And I'm surprised to see the family, Jessie, his wife, and Ashley. Our daughters play on the porch while me and Jessie talk.

Jessie says, "You didn't have to call the police." I tell him I didn't.

And I didn't. I don't call the police. I can't be a part of putting more black men in prison.

I looked at him, and I said, "But I should have done something, because you need help." And he's nodding.

He said they have to leave. They hadn't paid rent for like a year.

I asked him what he was going to do. He didn't know. He asked if we could keep Ashley just till he got himself together.

I wanted to say yeah, but we struggling to make it ourselves. We can't just take their little girl. It don't work like that.

We looked at our daughters playing on the porch. And I looked him in the eyes, and I said, "Take care of that little girl. And if you need anything, give me a call. Anything."

SHANNON CASON is a writer and storyteller. He is a GrandSLAM champion, a MainStage storyteller and a host with The Moth. Shannon also hosts his own storytelling podcast with WBEZ Chicago, called *Homemade Stories,* where he shares interesting stories from his life and some of his fiction, too. He is a husband, the father of two beautiful girls, and lives in Detroit. **shannoncason.com**.

THIS STORY WAS TOLD ON MAY 6, 2016, AT **OZ ARTS IN NASHVILLE**. THE THEME OF THE EVENING WAS *FISH OUT OF WATER*. **DIRECTOR: MEG BOWLES**.

Suki Kim

◇◇◇◇◇◇◇◇◇◇◇◇◇◇◇◇◇◇◇◇◇◇◇◇◇◇◇◇◇◇◇◇◇◇◇◇◇◇◇

Undercover in North Korea with Its Future Leaders

I was packing my suitcase when there was a knock at the door. I knew who was there, so I ignored it and kept packing. But she kept knocking, so finally I gave up, and opened the door.

She was one of the evangelical Christians that I had been working with for the past six months.

She said, "He's dead." For the moment I was confused. I thought she meant God.

This was Christmastime, and there had been a lot of these Bible-study meetings lately, which is why I didn't want to open the door. It was exhausting, pretending to be one of them for months. And this was my last day teaching. I just wanted to get out of there.

Then she pointed at the ceiling and, now whispering, said, "*He* died."

Then I knew she meant the other god in that world, Kim Jong-il, the then Great Leader of North Korea.

So the place was Pyongyang. The time was December 2011. I had been teaching at an all-male university in Pyongyang founded and operated by a group of evangelical Christians from around the world.

Now, religion is not allowed in North Korea, and proselytising is a capital crime. However, this group of evangelical Christians had struck a deal with the North Korean regime – an unofficial one – to fund the education of the sons of the elite in exchange for access.

They promised to not proselytise, but they were getting a footing in a country of 25 million devout followers of the Great Leader. If he were to fall, then they would need another god to replace him.

To be allowed there, I pretended to be one of them. But I only got away with it because the *real* missionaries were pretending to *not* be missionaries.

Why did I go to such an extreme to be there? Writing about North Korea with any depth or meaning is impossible unless you are embedded there. A full immersion was the only way. I had been going to North Korea since 2002, returning there repeatedly, but all I ever got was propaganda. And if I were to just write whatever they showed me, then I would be the regime's publicist.

The only other way to get to the reality of North Korea is through the defectors who flee North Korea. They tell their stories to journalists, often years later. And I feel bad for saying this, but I have travelled to all the surrounding regions and talked to many defectors, and it was always difficult to tell how much of these stories to believe. Because the worse the story, the more reward there is for them, and verification is nearly impossible.

But this was also personal. I was born and raised in South Korea into a family that was torn apart by the Korean War. In 1950, when North Korea bombed South Korea, my grandmother was living in Seoul, and she packed up her five children, including my mother (who was then four years old), to flee.

All the southbound trains were jam-packed, so the family secured seats in the back of a truck.

When the truck was about to pull off, somebody shouted, "Young men should give up seats for women and children!"

My grandmother's first child, my uncle (who was then seventeen) got up and said, "I'll get a ride, and I'll join you in the next town." He never arrived.

Later the neighbours reported seeing him with his hands tied, being dragged away by North Korean soldiers.

In 1953, after millions of Koreans died and families got separated, an armistice was signed, and the Korean War paused. Along the 38th parallel, which is an artificial division originally created by the United States with the help of the Allies, the five thousand year old kingdom of Korea was split in half.

From that point on, like millions of mothers on both sides of Korea, my grandmother waited for her son to come home.

Over seventy years have passed, and that border – which Koreans thought was temporary – is still there. Even though I moved to America when I was thirteen years old, this family history haunted me. Later, as a writer, I became obsessed with North Korea and finding out the truth of what was really going on there.

So I went undercover as a teacher and a missionary.

When I got there in 2011, they were preparing for Year 100. The North Korean calendar system begins at the birth of the original Great Leader. To celebrate the occasion, the regime had shut down all universities and put the university students to work in construction sites, supposedly to build Great Leader monuments.

In actuality, however, the then Great Leader was dying, and his young son was about to take over. They scattered all the youth to prevent any possible revolt. Outside, this was the time of the Arab Spring, and they didn't want a North Korean Spring.

The only ones who did not get sent to the construction fields were my elite students. But the campus was a five-star prison. The students were never allowed out. The teachers were only allowed out in group outings with minders to visit Great Leader monuments. Every conversation was overheard, every room was bugged. Every class was recorded, every lesson plan had to be preapproved.

I ate every meal with the students, and they never veered from the script. They went everywhere on campus in pairs and groups, and watched each other.

In order to get to know them better, I assigned letter and essay writing. Although many of them were computer majors, they didn't know of the existence of the Internet. Although many were science majors, they didn't know when a man first walked on the moon.

The vacuum of knowledge about anything other than their Great Leader was shocking, but I was under a strict set of rules to never tell them anything about the outside world.

One night at dinner, a student said he listened to rock and roll on his birthday (usually they all said they only listened to songs about the Great Leader). When he blurted this out, he looked around to check who might have heard him, and he froze. And the fear that I saw on his face was so palpable that I knew that whatever punishment that would result from this slip was something beyond my imagination, so I changed the subject.

What really disturbed me was that I had been waiting for that slip in order to understand their world better. But when that slip happened, I became so nervous and worried for him that I began to question what it was that I was doing there. Then I began to notice something strange about my students. They lied very often and very easily. Their lies came in different tiers.

Sometimes they lied to protect their system. There was a building on campus called Kim Il-Sung–ism Study Hall, where they went to study Great Leader-ism every day, and they had to guard this building 24/7. So I would see them guarding the building all night, but if I asked them, "How was your night?" they'd say they slept well and felt really rested.

Sometimes they would just regurgitate lies that they had been told. For example, they'd say that the scientists in their country could change blood types from A to B.

Sometimes they lied for no apparent reason, as if the line between truth and lies just wasn't clear to them. They would tell me that they should have cheated better than they did, or they'd say a hacker in their country gets rewarded if he hacks really, really well.

Initially I was upset and repulsed by these rampant lies, but as I spent months with them in that locked compound, I began to understand their predicament, and I felt such empathy. They were so easy to love, but impossible to trust. They were sincere, but they lied.

But if all they've ever known were lies, then how can you expect them to be any other way? It's as if their great humanity was in constant conflict with the inhumanity of their system.

But then *I* was there, pretending to be something *I'm* not, in order to get to the truth of the place. In that world, lies were necessary for survival.

Then one day a student asked me about the National Assembly. There was no way I could explain Congress without bringing up democracy and the outside world.

And I was nervous that other students at the table were watching this conversation, so I answered as honestly as I could and as vaguely as I could.

That night I couldn't fall asleep. I was afraid that the student was trying to trick me into saying something so he could report on me.

I was, in fact, writing a book in secret. I had pages and pages of notes hidden on USB sticks, which I kept on my body at all times. I thought, *If those were discovered, would I disappear the way my uncle had, and would my mother then have to repeat the life that my grandmother lived through?*

Being in North Korea, if you tap into the fear that's beneath the propaganda, is bone-chillingly depressing. That night I felt more alone and more afraid than ever. But the next day I ran into a friend of the student, and he said, "He thinks like you." Then I realised the student was not making reports on me. The student was in fact *genuinely* curious.

Now, this was even worse. I was now afraid of the consequences of that curiosity that I might have inspired. My role there was to plant a seed of doubt, but then what would happen to the student that I might have reached? Would he then be punished for questioning the regime? Or would he be doomed to a life of unhappiness? I was no longer sure if our truth, the truth of the outside world, would in fact help them.

I adored my students. I called them my "gentlemen," and they opened up to me little by little, through the letters that I assigned. And in those letters they talked about missing their mothers and their girlfriends, and also being fed up with the sameness of everything.

Because their lives were only about the Great Leader, the only break they ever got was playing group sports.

Some evenings I would watch them play soccer and basketball, and I would marvel at their beauty, such exuberant energy and joy and grace of their youth. I wanted to tell them about this incredible world outside, filled with the infinite possibilities that they so deserved.

But all I was capable of doing was to observe that, while their body bounced, their mind remained stuck in that timeless vacuum of their Great Leader.

On my last day, Kim Jong-il's death was announced to the world. Everything came to a sudden end, and I saw my students from a distance as they were hauled away to a special meeting.

Their faces looked at me, but their eyes didn't see me. It was as if their souls had been sucked out of them. They had just lost their god, their parent and the reason for everything in their world.

I never got to say good-bye to them.

The horror of North Korea is beyond famine and gulags. To survive there, real human beings have to not only believe in the lies of the Great Leader but also perpetuate them, which is a mental torture. It's a world where all citizens are complicit in the deprivation of their own humanity.

Towards the end of my stay, a student said to me, "Our circumstances are different, but we always think of you as the same as us. We really want you to know that we truly think of you as being the same."

But are we really the same? Maybe we were at some point, but there have been three generations of the Great Leader, and for seventy years the world has sat back and just watched. To me that silence is indefensible.

Lies run so deep there because the center is rotten, and that rottenness is irrevocable. What would happen to my students, my young gentlemen, as they become the soldiers and slaves of their Great Leader, Kim Jong-un?

If my uncle had managed to survive, would he be the same boy that had jumped off that truck?

SUKI KIM is a novelist and investigative journalist. Born and raised in South Korea, she is the only writer ever to live undercover in North Korea, and has travelled to North Korea since 2002, witnessing the country during events surrounding Kim Jong-il's sixtieth birthday celebration and his death in 2011. Her book, *Without You, There Is No Us: Undercover Among the Sons of North Korea's Elite* (2014), became a *New York Times* bestseller. Her first novel, *The Interpreter* (2004) was a finalist for a PEN Hemingway Prize, and her nonfiction has appeared in the *New York Times, Harper's,* the *New York Review of Books* and the *New Republic,* where she is a contributing editor. Kim's 2015 TED Talk has drawn millions of viewers online. **www.sukikim.com**

....

THIS STORY WAS TOLD ON SEPTEMBER 6, 2015, AT THE **SYDNEY OPERA HOUSE,** AUSTRALIA. THE THEME OF THE EVENING WAS *THE RAZOR'S EDGE: THE MOTH AT THE FESTIVAL OF DANGEROUS IDEAS.* **DIRECTOR: CATHERINE BURNS.**

George Dawes Green

◇◇

Coming of Age in a Mausoleum

When I was fifteen years old, I lived for a while in a mausoleum. It was a very short while, less than a week. But it was actually an ecstatic time, a summer of honeysuckle and fireflies and stars, and the deep education that I got, being alive in there.

I was desperately in love with a girl who was dead, and with a man who was living but psychotic. And it was the happiest time of my life.

This is how I came to be there. I had come there from a place where I felt dead, which is my hometown of Brunswick, Georgia. Everything was grey. The skies were grey, the Spanish moss was grey. That part of coastal Georgia, everything is covered in Spanish moss. *The people* are covered in Spanish moss. It's hot, and it's slow.

And the cicadas sing *that one note*. All the time. That one note. Constantly.

It was like being buried alive.

I was lonely, and my parents were drunks. I'd wait for them to go to sleep, and then I'd turn on the light, and stay up the whole night reading – about exploration, mostly, arctic exploration, or searching for the source of the Nile, or really anything that was about getting as far away from Glynn County, Georgia, as one could get.

And of course, because I stayed up all night, mornings were torture to me. Glynn Academy was torture to me. My grades went into a death spiral, down through the thirties to the twenties to the teens. And I actually kind of longed for the perfection of absolute zero, but I didn't have the stick-to-it-iveness.

So I dropped out of high school when I was fifteen, and I hitchhiked north. I got a job in New York City as a messenger, and I got to wear this really sharp tie and jacket. I loved being a civilian – I sneered at all yellow school buses.

For a while I lived in some flops around Manhattan. Then one Saturday I went on a drug run with a friend of mine on a road trip up to New Rochelle, New York, which is a little suburb.

But anyway, we wound up hanging out at this divey apartment full of drug dealers and derelicts. At one point I went back to the bathroom, and I saw in a back room a man sitting at an upright piano and singing an operatic aria about a dying king cobra. It was this writhing, beautiful, heartbreaking song. And I was mesmerised.

He turned around after the song, and he looked at me and said, "Do you play chess?"

His name was John Orlando. He was about thirty. If you can imagine, he kind of looked like a slender Alfred Hitchcock.

We wound up playing chess for a week, and John's strategy for chess was to gather all of his pieces into a kind of fortress in the rear of the board, on the left side, which he called "the west." From there he would send his knights out on these long, gallant expeditions, from which they'd never return.

It would take me hours to pick my way in there and find his king and kill it. And the whole time, John would be laughing hysterically. Afterwards, I could never really see the point of competitive chess. I just wanted to play what John called "chivalric chess."

But why was this original man living in this flophouse with drug dealers? Well, the rent was very cheap, and it was split eight ways. And when I moved in, it was split nine ways.

I used to commute to my job down in New York City and then come back on the train to this drug den every night. I didn't do . . . *all* that many drugs. But I did happily help to sort and clean, and it was an utterly depraved life for a fifteen-year-old.

There was a girl my age who used to come by. She was this beautiful redhead and just exploding into her sexuality. Of course she came by for the older guys – she didn't even notice me. But I was painfully in love with her, and just the smell of her would cripple me.

Downstairs lived this little old lady Irene, who used to worry about me and tell me that I had to go home. She would bake me lasagna. I would tell her that I really had no home, because my parents were drunks. I loved her. I loved talking to her.

And I loved John Orlando, who was unbalanced, and who would sit up at that piano all day long working on that opera about the Bronx Zoo, where he had once worked. He was making all of the zookeepers and all of the animals sing these arias.

I think this opera was driving him insane, because one day I remember walking up from the train station, and John was coming toward me, and he had on this fedora.

He didn't really see me, and he sort of walked almost past me, and then he stopped and said, "Mr Glow, there's a four-ply fozy flying out of here at five o'clock. Get a line on it."

And then he just walked away.

I was in love with him. I mean, I'm not gay, but this was a physical love. When I was around him, I couldn't breathe. I felt like he was the world.

I loved him the way that a worm loves its apple.

And I think he loved me, too, because the drug dealers were always trying to throw me out.

They were always saying, "John, this punk kid, he's fifteen years old, he's gonna draw unwanted attention."

And John would say to them, "No, George stays. I don't know if you've noticed, but George has one amazing thing about him. It's that he doesn't buy into anything. He just floats through life. I want to see what he's going to buy into. He stays."

So they threw us *both* out.

And then we had nowhere to go. We were homeless, and I wasn't going to get paid for a week, and John never had any money. But he said that there were these mausoleums in the back of the local graveyard that were in disrepair. So we packed up some blankets and some pillows and some wine, and we went and broke into one of these mausoleums.

It had two marble shelves on either side, and under one was the mortal remains of some man, and under the other was his wife. John and I sort of made our beds on these marble shelves, and we felt so safe there. The caretaker was old and never came around at night. And the police never would go into that graveyard at all.

We wandered around and got to know our neighbours. There was a dead nineteen-year-old girl buried there. She died in 1928, and her name was Hazel Ash.

Her inscription read:

SHE LIVED FOR POETRY.

I immediately forgot the sexy redheaded girl, and when we went back to the mausoleum, I said to John, "We have to write poems for Hazel Ash tonight."

He wrote these horrible, disgusting, obscene verses. I had to tell him to shut up. He just laughed at me, and his laugh echoed in that mausoleum.

People ask me if it was spooky in there, and, you know, it really wasn't spooky to me. I will say that if you don't like spiders, you would not have liked living there. And I will also say it was clammy and grey and lifeless, and I probably would have been scared out of my wits if John Orlando hadn't been with me.

But he was with me every second, because he wouldn't spend a moment in that graveyard alone. So if I went out at night to take a leak, he would come shuffling out after me, and sort of stand behind me. And in the morning, when I got up bright and early and put on my jacket and tie and went to my job, he went out of the graveyard with me. And then when I came back on the train that night and walked up to the graveyard, he was waiting there by the fence.

We'd always be hungry. We were hungry to the point that we had to do something. John had a friend, and we walked to the friend's house. And as we walked, we made up a poem about John's friend. When we got to his house, we recited the poem to the man, who in exchange gave us supper and a few dollars.

Later, when John and I were walking home to the graveyard, John said to me, "Now you're a professional writer."

I said, "Oh, come on, John. He just gave us dinner and five bucks."

John said, "That's what the hooker said. You're a pro."

And I was so proud. I had a little piece of pie that I saved for Hazel Ash, and I put it on her gravestone.

Then John and I went into the mausoleum, and he sang his songs of the elephants all night. Every now and then, he would let out these amazing farts that he called "El Destructos," and we would have to evacuate the mausoleum.

Then the sprinklers came on in the middle of the night, and we ran around buck naked under the sprinklers. And I was so happy that my scalp ached.

John saw this, and he said, "You know, you're buying into this, aren't you?"

I said, "Into what?"

He said, "Living in a graveyard."

And I laughed, but I wasn't buying into that. I was buying into being with somebody who turned every moment of his life into art.

Then, a few days later, I was on my way home from work, coming up the graveyard lawn, and I saw that our mausoleum's door had a brand-new lock.

I immediately turned and ran.

I went to Irene's house, and she said to me, "So now you have to go home."

I said, "I can't go home until we find John."

So I went looking for John every day. About two weeks went by, and then one Sunday morning someone came to get us and said that John was at the chapel on Mayflower Avenue and that he was singing songs about zoo life in the middle of the Mass.

I ran as fast as I could, and when I got there, they were putting John into a police car and taking him to the mental hospital (from where I don't think he ever came out, as far as I know).

But as he got into the car, he saw me. And he tipped his fedora and said, "Mr Glow. I got to go."

And then so did I. I had to go home.

GEORGE DAWES GREEN, founder of The Moth, is an internationally celebrated author whose critically acclaimed novels include *The Caveman's Valentine* (1994), *The Juror* (1995) and *Ravens* (2009).

THIS STORY WAS TOLD ON JULY 24, 2014, AT **GREEN-WOOD CEMETERY, BROOKLYN**, NEW YORK. THE THEME OF THE EVENING WAS *SOMETHING IS ETERNAL*. **DIRECTOR: CATHERINE BURNS.**

Christian Garland

My Grandfather's Shoes

I'm gonna let y'all know now, I'm a preacher's kid.
I grew up in the church. I swear I have only missed, like,
two Sundays out of my whole sixteen years of life.

My grandfather, he was a minister. And he was my best
friend. He was the person I could talk to about anything
and everything.

I'm sixteen now, but when I was ten, I wanted to be the
kid who had anything anybody else had. I was the friend
that, like, if you got the new video game – I had *that* video
game but also another one . . . that was just about to come
out . . . that you ain't know about.

So one day my friend came outside. He had these ugly,
ugly sneakers on.

I was like, "Yo, bro, I got those, man! That ain't nothing . . .
I already got those."

He was like, "A'ight . . . prove it!"

I didn't have them.

So my grandfather, being a minister, he gets the money
out of the collection plate. And I knew where he put the
money.

So I went upstairs, and I took the money. I did. It was
like two hundred dollars. And I went on Third Avenue in
the Bronx, and I bought the sneakers, and I went home.

I walk in, and my grandfather, he's going off. He found out the money was missing.

He was screaming at my uncle, "Why would you steal my money?!"

My uncle's like, "I didn't touch your money. I don't know what you're talking about."

I should tell y'all that all the way home walking, I was talking junk.

I'm with my cousin, and I'm like, "Yeah, when my grandpa asks me where I got the sneakers from . . . I'm gonna lie. I'm gonna say I got 'em from you."

And he's like, "Ain't gonna work."

So I walk in, and my grandpa's going off . . . and I froze. I was like, *Oh . . . he mad.*

And he said, "Christian! Come here!"

I was like, "Huh?"

He said, "Where'd you get those sneakers?"

And I was like, "Funny story . . . uh . . . I went in your briefcase and got the money . . . yeah . . ."

He said, "How much money did you take?"

I said, "About two hundred dollars."

"WHAT?!"

"About two hundred dollars."

"Boy, are you *crazy*?! Boy!"

And then he said some very hard words. He said, "I will never be able to trust you again, but one day you are going to repay me for the money you took. I don't know how, I don't know when. But you are going to repay me."

I cried. It was terrible.

Fast-forward a couple of years. I'm a drummer. I played the drums on the radio for Al Sharpton. And he paid me good. And have you ever had that thing where you start thinking about something and your mind goes [*claps loudly*].

That's when I was like, *I remember Grandpa said I'm gonna repay him.*

So I didn't get McDonald's for two weeks in a row. And with that, plus my money from drumming, I got the money to pay him back. I put it in an envelope, and I took my grandpa out to dinner at his favourite place: Crown Donut on 161st Street.

At first he was sceptical that I was taking him out.

He said, "You got somebody pregnant?"

I was only thirteen, I don't know what he was talking about. I was like, "No, *of course not*! Don't be *absurd.*"

So we got our food, and I had on a coat – it was cold; it was early November. And so I took the money out of my side pocket and put it on the table.

I was like, "It's all there."

And he looked, and he said, "What's this?"

I said, "You said you didn't know how, but I was gonna repay you. And I just repaid you."

And we started crying and hugging.

He said, "Aw, I love you."

"I love you, too, Grandpa."

And I'm just glad that I got the chance to fulfill what my grandfather said, and pay him back and earn his trust back, because he said, "You know what? You surprised me. I'm proud of you. I trust you again."

And that was the last thing he ever told me, because two weeks after that he died.

I found out he didn't get to spend the money.

And I was mad at my grandma, because I knew she had the money. I didn't know what she did with it.

And so a couple of days go by; we made funeral arrangements, I still didn't know where the money went.

But I went to go view the body, and my grandma, she stopped me, she said, "Chris?"

I said, "Yes, ma'am."

She said, "You see that suit and them shoes he's got on?"

I said, "Yes, ma'am."

She said, "Your money paid for that."

And the expression on my face was like, *What?!*

I was so proud that, number one: I got my trust back from my grandpa, and number two, he was stuntin' in the suit and shoes *I* bought him.

CHRISTIAN GARLAND participated in the Moth High School StorySLAM at DreamYard Preparatory School in the Bronx and told his story in the inaugural New York City High School GrandSLAM. These days he's finishing up high school and writing/playing music. Someday he hopes to be a music producer.

....

THIS STORY WAS TOLD ON DECEMBER 16, 2013, AT THE HIGH SCHOOL GRANDSLAM AT THE **HOUSING WORKS BOOKSTORE CAFE, NEW YORK CITY**. THE THEME OF THE EVENING WAS *FACE TO FACE*. **DIRECTORS: MICAELA BLEI AND CATHERINE MCCARTHY**.

Catherine Cross

<><><><><><><><><><><><><><><><><><><><><><><><>

A Mother's Journey

It was late in the evening when my fifteen-year-old daughter came into the sewing room at home where I work. My kids would often come in and chat to me while I worked, but she was kind of hanging around, and seemed a bit uncomfortable.

I asked her was everything okay, and she said, "Yeah, fine." But I knew something was on her mind, so I stopped sewing, and I said, "Come on, out with it. What's up?"

She shrugs her shoulders, and I knew I was going to have to tease it out of her, so I keep asking, and she keeps saying, "It's nothing, Ma."

So I said to her, "You know, you can tell me anything, right?"

And she says, "No, not this."

Now I'm worried.

So eventually I hand her a piece of paper and a pen, and I say, "Do you think you could maybe write it down for me?"

She sits down, and she looks at the paper for what seems like an eternity. And when she eventually writes something on it and hands it back to me, it reads, *I'm gay*.

And I say, "God, is that all?"

I say, "That doesn't matter at all. I still love you, and I always will. It doesn't make any difference."

We hug, and she goes off, happier with herself.

But when she's gone, I think, *I don't know what you are, pet, but I don't think you're gay.* Funny really, because I always imagined she'd come out to me as being gay, but the moment she said it, I knew that wasn't it. I knew she was going to have to dig a bit deeper to figure out what was really going on.

So, she seems a bit happier over the next few weeks, but as the weeks turn into months, she's becoming more and more withdrawn, and spending too much time in her room, and not engaging with anybody.

So when she comes into the sewing room again, late one evening, I'm expecting some sort of other big bombshell to be landed on me.

We go through the whole, "What's up?" "Nothing, Ma," again, until I finally ask, "Are you trying to tell me you're not gay?"

And she says, "Yes."

"Well, what then?"

Silence.

So, I'm afraid to ask the next question, but I ask it anyway: "Is it something to do with gender? Do you want to be a boy?"

And she says, "Oh, Ma, God's made some awful mistake. I don't want to *be* a boy. I *am* a boy."

Okay.

So I reassure her, once again, that everything's gonna be just fine. I still love her, and I will always. But could she just leave it with me for a bit? Because I needed a bit more time to get my head around this one.

So she goes off, and when she's gone I think, *Oh, my God. What am I going to do now? This can't be happening.* Half of me thinks, *This kind of thing only happens on Jerry Springer, surely.* But the other half of me thinks, *Yeah, sounds about right.* I didn't know anything about transgender. To be honest, I thought it was men in drag. I'd definitely never heard of a girl wanting to be a boy.

We actually didn't speak about it for quite some time. I was secretly hoping that if I didn't mention it, it would just all go away.

Some time later I tentatively broached the subject with her, and I say tentatively because I felt that if I broached the subject, I was somehow encouraging her to embark on this really difficult life. But difficult for who? I felt people would judge me, as a mother, as well as our family.

I said, "What do you want from life? Do you want surgery? You know, this is going to be really difficult for you. You probably won't ever have any children. And you may not even have a life partner. Could you not just be gay?"

I thought if I pointed out all the negative things that she'd somehow change her mind. But I didn't realise right then that it wasn't really a choice for her – it was just simply who she was.

I'm afraid things got a bit heated, and I said some things that I'm kind of ashamed of. You see, I'd always prided myself on being a really good mother. I was very liberal, and really open-minded.

But it's easy to say those things when the issues are outside your front door. When I was confronted with them, it made me take a very long, hard look at myself, and to be honest, I didn't really like what I saw. I kept blaming myself: *I should have insisted she play with girls' toys and I should have made her wear girls' clothes.*

Then I'd think, *What's so bad about this, anyway? I still have my child. She's not dead. She's not dying. So, why do I feel so sad? Why does it feel like a death?*

And I'd think back to the moment when she was born.

Myself and my husband, we were so excited, and we asked, "What is it?"

The nurse says, "You have a daughter!" And in that split second, like a movie running through my head, I see a toddler in a pink, frilly dress, and a 10-year-old schoolgirl in a pinafore and bobby socks. And then a young girl, sitting, having coffee with me.

But she'd never really worn the pink dress, or the pinafore. Instead she'd played with boys' toys and worn boys' clothes.

My friends had always commented what a tomboy she was, but I always thought it was a bit more than that. Now, I didn't know anything about transgender, so I definitely didn't think it was that, but I always thought there was something very different about her. She'd always played with the boys, and seemed kind of irritated by the girls, and asked why it was she could not go to the same school as her friends – the boys school.

Toilet training had been an absolute nightmare. Trying to convince her that she had to sit down to pee, she couldn't do it standing up like her brother Matt.

About a week after our heated conversation, I by chance heard a woman on the radio talking about being transgender in Ireland. And she gave details of a support group for parents of young people who were transgender.

So myself and my husband decided that we'd give it a go. To be honest, I wasn't crazy about going at all. They were really lovely people, but I didn't really want to be part of their group. I just wanted it all to go away.

But I also knew that no matter what, I was going to support my child. I just didn't know how to do it.

The support group organised a weekend away, a chance to meet with other families who had kids who were transgender, and speak with professionals who were in charge of the care of transgender people.

As we arrive at the hotel, I realise that my daughter already knows quite a few of the young people there. She's friends with them all on Facebook. But I also realise that these young people don't know my daughter – they know my *son*, Lucas. (I can't tell how much I hated that name.)

I quickly realised that if we're calling her one thing, and they're calling her something else, it's gonna be a bit awkward, so I pull her aside in the bar, and I said, "Look, for this weekend, we're going to try our best and call you Lucas, and use male pronouns."

The hotel was miles away from everywhere, and we didn't know anybody anyway. I thought it was a safe place where I could try out my new son. I know that sounds horrible, but I really needed to know what it would feel like.

She was – I should say, *he* was – delighted. I hadn't realised how much it would mean to him. And it did feel really strange and very difficult to do. But he was so happy, I couldn't but be happy for him too. And I thought . . . *okay.*

On the Saturday night, we all get dressed up to go to dinner, and Lucas dresses in a smart suit and a waistcoat. After the dinner, there's a bit of a sing-song going on in the bar, and Lucas spends most of the night up playing guitar and singing songs.

He was so popular. I couldn't get over how confident he was! As I was looking at him in the bar and admiring him, I thought, *Yeah, I'm still grieving the loss of my daughter, but I'm just loving my new son.* And I thought to myself, *You know, we're just going to have to do this.*

We live in a small town where everybody knows everybody. And I had expected a lot of resistance to my child's new identity. I had been quite prepared to move somewhere new if things got too difficult for him. I worried about how would I find the words to tell people, and how would I cope with their reactions.

I thought, *Gosh, we're gonna be the talk of the town.*

With the help of the support group, I found a way to tell a few close friends and neighbours. But what I found amazing was, most people weren't really that surprised by it at all. It seemed to quite make sense to them.

And of course I didn't get to tell everybody, so a good few people heard it from around, and what I thought was really lovely was that they found subtle ways of letting me know that they'd heard.

They'd say things like, "So, how's Lucas getting on?" And, you know, it opened the conversation so that we could get to talk about it. I got cards and I got texts from people saying how brave we were and they wished us well.

I really had underestimated people.

I knew at some point I was going to have to go down to the school and let them know what was going on, and I was anticipating quite a bit of a battle. I decided I wouldn't bring Lucas with me, in case there was a scene.

I walk into the principal's office, full of trepidation, and I'm ready to do battle for my son. But as I sit and start telling him about Lucas, the principal's already heard – he knows all about it. And all he's really worried about is, is he getting bullied or not?

I'm taken a bit off guard with this. I wasn't expecting this at all. They were in no way obliged to support my child at all, and yet, here they were.

He asks what bathroom Lucas uses, and I say, "Well, he doesn't really use any bathroom at school, because he doesn't feel comfortable."

The principal's horrified, and he says, "Well, make sure Lucas knows he can use whatever bathroom he wants."

I feel so indebted to him. I couldn't believe somebody could be so totally accepting of a situation that I had found so very difficult to come to terms with. I had arrived anticipating a confrontation, needing to advocate for my son's basic rights, but I left the office feeling I was walking on air.

So, we make plans to go to Dublin to change his name. At this stage, I'm getting used to it, and I think it kind of suits him.

So, myself and my husband, we get ready all the paperwork, and we get ready to sign off and renounce our daughter's name.

I'm feeling really emotional, but I try my best to hide it, because Lucas is so excited.

I can't sleep, so I end up tidying a few presses upstairs, and I come across a box of photographs of the kids when they were small. I sit on the bed looking at them and my husband and my oldest son, Matt, come in, and even they shed a tear or two.

I take out Lucas' Communion dress that I had made for him. And then his christening gown.

I realise the strange thing about the name Lucas was probably that I didn't choose it, and maybe that's why I hadn't liked it.

I find a letter he'd written to Santa when he was about nine. And he'd asked for a wrestling ring, and wrestlers, and a racing car track (there wasn't a doll in sight.)

And I think, *this is so the right thing to be doing. This is who he is, and who he's always been. And that the daughter I'm grieving is the daughter I had expected to have. And perhaps the loss of her, the pain of that, would ease with time.*

As I put away the photos and the dresses, I feel like I'm saying a final goodbye to my daughter.

And I take out the photograph of Lucas playing guitar in the hotel, and I admire him once again, and think about how very proud I am of him – I really do love my new son.

CATHERINE CROSS lives in the Midlands of Ireland and has two sons, Matthew and Lucas. She has worked as a bridal seamstress for the past 28 years, and recently graduated from Maynooth University with a Masters in Social Science. She enjoys singing in choirs and directs her own small choir in Rathangan Parish. She is currently secretary of the Parents support group TransParenCI, who support parents and family members of transgender youths. She presented to the Oireachtas Committee in the Dáil in October 2013 as part of the debate on the Gender Recognition Bill.

THIS STORY WAS TOLD ON APRIL 9 2015 IN THE **LIBERTY HALL THEATRE, DUBLIN**. THE THEME OF THE EVENING WAS *THE TIES THAT BIND*. **DIRECTOR: MEG BOWLES**.

To Face the Fear

Tony Wheeler

Adventures Without Borders

Travel has always been part of my life. I grew up in Pakistan, and then the Bahamas and then the USA. I never finished more than two years in the same school.

Then forty-two years ago my wife, Maureen, and I arrived in Australia. We were both British passport holders then—we're both Australians now. We didn't arrive on one of those last ocean liners that was still sailing out from the UK to Australia. We didn't fly into Melbourne's Tullamarine Airport, which had opened eighteen months earlier.

No, we turned up on a sailing boat out of Indonesia. We landed on the beach outside Exmouth on the North West Cape of Western Australia. We'd had a few times in the previous two weeks when we wondered if we were really going to make it down here.

We'd actually set out from London in an old car. We thought we'd just drive it as far east as it would go, and if it broke down we'd just walk away from it and leave it. But it got us all the way from London to Afghanistan. We sold it there in Kabul for a small profit. Then we carried on by every means of transport you could find, and eventually we went to Southeast Asia and we got down to Bali at a time when there weren't a lot of tourists.

We were hanging around in this little café one day, and we heard these New Zealanders say, "We only need two more crew, and we'll sail down to Australia." And we thought, *Well, that sounds like fun. Let's go.*

So we joined them, and we did sail down to Australia and landed on that beach. And if you needed the perfect introduction to Australia, our first twenty-four hours was absolutely that.

We stood at the side of town with our thumbs out, hitching a ride, and we watched kangaroos bound off into the bush. We got picked up by a Yugoslav truck driver and ended up at a pub. Then we hitched another ride, and travelled 400 km south to Carnarvon. Our first night we spent on a mattress in the back of a station wagon in a garage, with an orphaned baby Joey tumbling around in a burlap sack that was pinned up to the wall.

I mean, what a perfect way to arrive in this country!

A year later, we'd published the first *Lonely Planet* guide, and it was really the story of our travels getting out here. It was subtitled, "The Complete Guide to the Overland Trip." We'd come down through Iran, travelled around Afghanistan, and then gone through Pakistan. With those first books we realised there were a lot of other people who also had a taste for travelling to less conventional places. They're interesting, they're challenging.

You may sell more copies of books to the more frequently travelled places – I love Italy, I love France. But there's a bit more of a challenge to the out-of-the-way places in the world. I've taken shelter in an embassy in Kabul, in Afghanistan, because there was a riot going on outside and bullets flying around. I've been stopped for speeding in Zimbabwe. I've been arrested once in the Congo for taking photographs. I've even sneaked into Iraq without a visa.

So I've been to some places, and in a little way you could call them adventures. I've never been searching for danger; in fact, I'm quite a faint-hearted sort of soul. I get very concerned when I'm flying on tatty aircraft. I don't like dark alleys in violence-prone cities. Soldiers with big guns always make me feel very uneasy. I don't like swimming in deep water if there might be sharks down below. I've got to admit, I don't like big spiders either.

But we kept on doing this travel, and then children came along. By then this was no longer something I did just because I enjoyed it. I *did* enjoy it, but it was also how I made my living.

Maureen and I wanted to keep travelling together, so for a number of years our kids came with us. Every school holiday they were travelling somewhere. They'd been all around South America for a three-month trip before they were three years old. When our son was less than a year and our daughter was still two, we were in Kathmandu doing a little trek into the Himalayas. By the time Kieran was six years old, he'd been to every continent except Antarctica.

So they'd done some travelling. But I didn't want their travel to be ticking numbers off on a list. Because today there's so much misunderstanding in the world, and it's really by travelling that you meet people. You learn to understand them, and I wanted my kids to get some of that understanding. And that travel would be a way of connecting them to the outside world.

We were in Sri Lanka when Tashi had just had her third birthday in a garden in Kathmandu, and Kieran was still a baby almost. We stopped at a little place on the beach, and I was doing forays around the country from there.

One day I took Tashi, and we drove around the coast to Galle, a beautiful, old walled town on the coast. We were looking around, and I went to this one hotel. It was a building that dated from the late 1600s, and I'd been there before, so I knew what the hotel was like. All I really had to do was look at the changes—they'd added a swimming pool since the last time I was there.

As I was leaving, walking towards the car, Tashi took my hand and said, "Daddy, we haven't checked the bathrooms."

And I realised she knew part of what my job was all about – she knew that was part of what I had to do.

When they were six and nine they'd learned to take perfectly good nouns and turn them into verbs. There were things like, "We are *templed out*. We have seen all the temples we need to see." Or, "We have done too much *museuming* today – we don't want to do any more of that."

We were in Luxor in the south of Egypt. We'd just come out of Tutankhamun's tomb, and they both announced that they'd had quite enough tombing for the day, and they wanted to go back to the hotel. But heartless parents that we were, we intended to continue from the Valley of the Kings to the Valley of the Nobles, and we said not only are we going to go there, we're going to walk there over the hill that's in between them.

Nowadays, you're not allowed to do that, you have to take the road with a taxi or a bus. But we were going to walk up the hill and down the other side, and our kids said no, that they were on strike. They were not going anywhere at all, and they sat down by the path.

Well Maureen and I walked up the hill, expecting them to follow us very shortly. We got about half way up the hill and stopped to wait for them and looked down the hill ...

and there were our two kids coming up the hill riding donkeys.

They came by us, and our son said, "Oh we saw this guy coming down the hill with his donkeys, and we said, 'How much to take the donkeys over to the Valley of the Nobles?' Don't worry, Dad, I got him down from four Egyptian pounds to three."

And I realised they'd learned something without even being taught – I hadn't taught them how to bargain, they'd watched and learned it all by themselves.

Then when they were teenagers, Tashi was seventeen, and we were in Guatemala. We'd been up to the Mayan town of Tikal, in the jungle up in the mist-shrouded areas. Then we'd come back by bus down to a town called Flores on the lake, and we were going on from there to Belize. And we were just getting to the end of that bus trip, and Tashi said, "I'm not feeling very well."

In the afternoon she threw up, and when it was time for dinner, she said, "Look I'm really not feeling well. I'll stay home. You guys go out and have dinner."

We went out and had dinner, and when we came back she'd thrown up some more. And then she threw up again and again and again and again. And she was just looking terrible. By now she'd started to get diarrhoea, and her hands and feet were cramping, which is a sign of dehydration, and I was getting really frightened.

You know, you do things by yourself, and then you're responsible for yourself, but you're not supposed to get other people into trouble.

You're particularly not supposed to get your *kids* into trouble.

And this went on and on, and it just didn't get any better. She was limp. She could barely respond to us or answer questions.

It was getting dark by this time, and we were thinking, *What on Earth are we going to do?*

I thought, *I've got to go out and get some medical attention, because we can't handle this alone.*

So I went out into the street, and it was completely dark – there was nobody around. But one of those miracles that sometimes happens: a doctor lived next door, and I went to him. I explained what was happening, and even though my Spanish is terrible, I dragged out the best my Spanish could do. He came back to the hotel, and he diagnosed food poisoning.

He gave her an injection of an anti-spasmodic to stop her from throwing up, but it just didn't work, and he said, "Listen, I work at a hospital near the town. I'll get my car, and I'll drive there."

An hour later, he came back, and he set up a drip. We turned our hotel room into a little clinic, and plugged the drip into to Tashi and started giving her medication, and she gradually started to quiet down, and finally she went peacefully to sleep. He left, and we took turns staying up all night, keeping an eye on her.

The doctor came back at dawn, and in a day or so she had recovered. When you're travelling you often do encounter that kindness of strangers, and we'd definitely encountered it this time. I thought afterwards, *You know, you're very lucky there was a doctor living next door.*

He had pulled her back from the edge – we were really frightened.

And then I thought, *Have I put her off travel forever?*

But you know, a decade and a half passed, and the kids grew up, and we sold Lonely Planet. A lot of the money we got from that we put into a foundation, which we call Planet Wheeler. We've got seventy projects around the world, and somebody has to go out and check these projects. You know, check the water project in Ethiopia or the school in Tanzania, or a children's hospital that we help to fund in Cambodia.

And who goes to do it?

My daughter, Tashi.

TONY WHEELER wrote the original Lonely Planet guide after a long trek along Asia's 'hippie trail' in 1972 and went on to write and publish guides to just about everywhere. He has been described by the *New York Times* as 'the trailblazing patron saint of the world's backpackers and adventure travellers.' Today, Tony is mainly involved with the Planet Wheeler Foundation's work in Southeast Asia and Africa and Melbourne's Wheeler Centre for Books, Writing & Ideas. He is a director of Global Heritage Fund, which works to protect and develop archeological sites in the developing world. **www.tonywheeler.com.au**

THIS STORY WAS TOLD ON AUGUST 22 2013 AT THE MELBOURNE WRITER'S FESTIVAL IN THE **TOWN HALL, MELBOURNE**, AUSTRALIA. **DIRECTOR: SARAH AUSTIN JENNESS**

Kate Tellers

<<<<<<<<<<<<<<<<<<<<<<<<<<<<<<<<<<<<<>>>>>>>>>>>>>>>>>>>>

But Also Bring Cheese

In our little house on the north side of Pittsburgh, we had one television. It was black and white. We kept it behind the couch, and I was never allowed to watch it. Most nights it was my mother, my father, me . . . maybe some wooden blocks.

It was very *Little House on the Prairie,* but in the 1980s. One day, though, when I was about four years old, I snuck across the street to my neighbour's house, and she let me watch *The Love Boat.*

It blew my mind. When I think about it now, I can just picture Gavin MacLeod dressed in a captain's uniform, making out with all of these beautiful women with perfect perms. I *loved* it.

When I came home, I asked my mother why they kissed in that crazy way. That was a really difficult thing for my mother to explain, but finally she was like, "Well, um, when people love each other, like, a whole lot, that is the way that they kiss."

So when she came in that night to put me to bed, I grabbed her head and I smashed it up against mine, and I moved my head back, and I said, "I'm giving you *Love Boat* kisses."

I was *obsessed* with my parents.

When our friends were getting pets, they would get a guinea pig and name it Punky Brewster or a Chihuahua and name it Sting. I got two goldfish, and I named them Paul and Lisa, after my parents, because they were my rock stars.

When my sister was born, they named her Alice. We would go to parties, and they would introduce us, and people would laugh and say, "Oh, yeah, like *Kate & Allie.*"

And we would be like, "Uh-huh."

We didn't realise that *Kate & Allie* was a show on everyone else's colour TVs. It was like naming your kids Will and Grace.

But the rest of the world existed outside of our family, so much so that when my parents divorced, I didn't get angry, I didn't get mad. I was like, *Oh, this is the next thing we're doing together.* I wrote my college essay on how my parents' divorce made them my two best friends and took us on to our next adventure together. (I did get into college, though, despite that.)

The day before I was leaving for college, my mother and I were having lunch. She confessed to me that she had seen a doctor, and she was sick. And it wasn't a big deal, she was just going to have some chemo, and she would be fine.

And I really did, honestly, believe her.

But I couldn't unhear that. And I felt like I suddenly had to start considering a world with this big hole where my mom should be. I would go for months and months, and I wouldn't think about it, and then I would be reminded of it.

We'd be spending time together, and it's like my brain would split. And part of me would be completely present, and the other half of me would be taking all of these notes, so I could sear all of these specifics about her into my brain in case I ever needed them when she wasn't there.

After college I moved to New York. Sometimes on Friday afternoons, I would drive from New York City, across the state of Pennsylvania, to Pittsburgh to her apartment, and I'd get in really late.

She'd open the door, and she'd say, "Would you like a glass of wine?"

I would say, "Yes."

And we both knew that it wasn't *a* glass of wine, because it never was. We'd go into the kitchen, and she would have laid out all these mismatched blue-and-white plates, with homemade hummus and white cheeses and salty olives, and these huge globes that she'd fill with red wine. Somehow we would sit at the table and talk, and we would drink a lot of wine, but miraculously the glasses would never be empty.

One night we're sitting and we're talking, and she's laughing. She has just confessed to me that the hardest thing she ever had to do as a mother was to give me ipecac to induce vomiting, because when I was little, I accidentally ate a bunch of her asthma medicine. They were these little red-coated pills, and she could see the red in my mouth.

And *I* have just confessed to *her* that actually I'd gotten into the cupboard and eaten Red Hots. It was the only candy in our house, ever, and we used it once a year to put two eyeballs on a gingerbread man that we made. But I knew her reaction to me eating her asthma medicine would be better than her reaction to me eating refined sugar, so I let her just go with it.

So she's laughing about this, and she throws her head back. And my brain splits. And I start to take notes.

I note the way that she laughs so big that I can see the fillings in the back of her mouth. And that when she brings her head down, she pulls her turtleneck up to her chin, and then rubs her hand over the ribs on her lavender sweater.

And that her head is so small that she shops in the children's section at LensCrafters. I can tell because the candlelight catches the arm of her glasses, and they say "Harry Potter." We continue on like this until we're both so tired, and we crawl into bed.

For a while things are very good, and then things are bad, and then things are good.

And then one day she's visiting me in New York City. We're in midtown, and we're about to get on the subway. We've just seen a show.

She stops me, and she says, "You know what, Marian McPartland" – who hosts this show that she loved on public radio, *Piano Jazz* – "Marian McPartland is having an eighty-fifth birthday party at Birdland. And we should crash it."

This is my mom. She is the most elegant and gracious woman in the world. She wouldn't go to a block party without putting me in a dress and making homemade tabbouleh and bringing a bottle of wine, but okay, we'll crash this party.

We walk up to Birdland, and we just charge past the bouncers. We go right up to the bar. I squeeze us into some chairs, and I order the fanciest drinks that I can think of, which at the time were vodka gimlets. Because I really liked those glasses.

And we look around, and it's like an Al Hirschfeld drawing of what's happening in jazz at that time. I recognise Tony Bennett and Norah Jones. And there's Ravi Coltrane. The energy in the room is amazing.

We're seeing the show live, but in between all of these amazing performances people are loving up the birthday girl. And you can just feel that it's one of those nights that everyone in the room will remember, that could never be re-created.

Karrin Allyson, who my mother and I both love, takes the stage, and she starts to sing "Twilight World." I pick up my glass, and I turn to toast my mother, and I look – and she's *glowing*.

I take her in. My brain splits. And I think, *This is good. I can use this.*

Four Januaries later I'm back in Pittsburgh. The doctors have told us that it's time to come home.

I'm in my mother's bathroom. She's leaning on the sink. She's wearing these pink striped pyjamas that my sister has given her for Christmas the month before. I see her look up and look at herself in the mirror. I see a change come over her face, and I can tell that she's made up her mind. She tells me to call a nurse. She walks out of the bathroom, and she walks down the hallway and she lays down in her bed.

I know that this is the day that I have been afraid of for ten years.

My sister and I had made a calendar and scheduled my mother's friends and family to come visit her in these days, so that people could see her but that she would never be overwhelmed by too many guests.

And now we're calling everyone, and we're telling them, "Come over now, for what will probably be one of the worst nights of your life."

But because I'm my mother's daughter, I'm doing this as I'm pulling her plates off of the shelf and saying, "But also bring cheese."

And they do. People start coming. Aunts and uncles. My father. My mother's boyfriend. My sister's boyfriend. We all pile into her living room and sit on my mother's red velvet couch. Someone puts on a Miles Davis CD, and we're milling around. I've put food out, and I'm filling people's glasses of wine. My Aunt Jamie makes a pot of chilli.

People start to go in to visit my mother.

I hear her saying to them, as she's laid out in her bed, "Can I get you anything? Can I get you a cup of tea?"

And I'm like, "You're *dying. I* am going to do this right now." So I start handing people saucers and empty cups.

I'm like, "Just carry this in so she knows that we're okay out here."

In the living room, it feels very much like it does any other night that we're at my mother's house, except for I'm the one secretly refilling the wine and sneaking away the plates.

When the hospice first came to visit us, they gave my sister and me this pamphlet, a little blue booklet called *Gone From My Sight.* There's a line drawing of a ship on it. And it explains in somewhat poetic but also somewhat technical terms what happens to a body when a human being is starting to die. And I remember when they gave it to me, I was sort of furious. I thought, *There's no line drawing that can describe this very personal and very massive event in my life. This is my mom.* But on this night it's the only guide that we have. We've never done this before.

So my sister is reading and taking notes on my mom, and my sister comes in, and she can tell from the way that my mother is breathing that we don't have a lot of time. I go in to check on her, and she's gotten out of her bed. She's standing at her closet, and she's reaching up for a sweater. I ask her what she's doing.

She looks at me and says, "I have to pack."

And I don't know what to say to that.

So finally I say, "Mommy, where you're going, you don't need a suitcase."

She pauses, and she scrunches up her face like she always does when she's thinking. She nods. And she lays back into her bed, and she goes silent.

People continue to go in, and they start to say their good-byes.

Finally it's my turn. I go into her room, and I sit down on her bed and I start rubbing her calves.

I know that I should say I love her, and that I'll miss her. And that in twenty-eight years I can throw her the best eighty-fifth birthday party. Then, after that, maybe sometime we'll explode in one big fireball, so that neither of us would ever have to experience what it'd be like for one of us to have to live without the other.

But she knows all of that.

So I just tell her that the following November I'm going to be a bridesmaid in my friend from high school Jess's wedding . . . so that she knows that I have plans. And that I'm really excited that the dresses are green, because they'll bring out my eyes.

And then that's it. And I leave. And I'm on the phone with Jess in the hallway when I hear my sister. She's a classically trained singer, and I hear this Wagnerian wail hit all of these notes.

And I know that my mother is gone.

We all gather in the living room, and we drink all of the wine and we eat all of the cheese. I bring out this bottle of limoncello that my mother keeps for special occasions, because I figure that this one counts and I'm allowed. So we drink all of that. Everyone leaves, and I go to bed.

The next morning I wake up. And it's the day that I've been afraid of. I go into the kitchen, and I open up the front of the coffee machine and I empty out the grounds.

I realise that I still know how to make a pot of coffee.

I go into the living room, and I sit in her big blue leather chair. I open my computer, and I check my email. There's an email from my friend Nick, who I went to college with.

We email a couple of times a year, and he's asking me how I am and telling me about his new job.

I hit reply, and I type, "Nick, my mom died."

And it's real.

I wait for that big gut punch to hit me, for that big hole to open up. That emptiness. But instead I feel the strangest thing, the purest thing I've ever felt.

I just feel sad.

And it feels white.

And it feels hot.

And it envelops me.

And I feel full.

KATE TELLERS has been hailed as a "storytelling guru" by the *Wall Street Journal*. She is a writer, performer and teacher whose students range from fledgling eight-year-old stand-up comedians to Fortune 500 CEOs. In 2007 she discovered The Moth and has been a part of it ever since. She is currently working on a collection of essays about falling apart, tentatively titled, *We Always Knew You Would Be OK*. She lives in Brooklyn with her furry husband, baby and dog.

THIS STORY WAS TOLD ON AUGUST 27, 2014, AT THE **BYHAM THEATER, PITTSBURGH**. THE THEME OF THE EVENING WAS *DON'T LOOK BACK*. **DIRECTOR: CATHERINE BURNS.**

Jessi Klein

Tired, from New York

One of my happiest memories as a kid is staying up late to watch *Saturday Night Live* on this old black-and-white TV that I'd actually found in the trash area of my building and had convinced my parents to let me keep in my room.

There was something so magical and exciting about when the show would start, and the theme music would play over that cool, New Yorky montage of the cast. It made me feel really hip and alive, like I was part of a cool club. And not, like, a nerdy girl who was watching a black-and-white TV that I found in the garbage.

One of the highlights of my childhood was when I was ten years old, and my best friend's dad took us to 30 Rock to see a taping of *SNL*.

I remember that before the show started, I had to go to the bathroom. To get there I walked down the hallways of Studio 8H. And it was lined with photos of Gilda Radner and Bill Murray. I was like, *Oh, my God. Oh, my God. Oh, my God. They were here. I'm here. Oh, my God.*

When I got to the bathroom, I took fifteen paper towels and I put them in my pocket, to bring home and put into this little wooden box I had, where I kept all of my mementos. It had a unicorn on it. The only other memento in the box at the time was an acorn I had picked up on a trip to Woodstock.

On that visit to *SNL,* the host was Tom Hanks and the musical guest was Aerosmith. So it was awesome. And just when the night couldn't get any more perfect, afterwards my friend's dad took us to an incredible dinner at the Hard Rock Cafe, the coolest restaurant in the world.

I remember it so clearly. It was the first velvet rope I ever walked past, and as I was walking past it, I thought, *I feel fucking famous. I feel like Justine Bateman must feel all the time* (at the time she was the most famous woman in the world to me).

So cut to 2009. I am a grown-up. And I have achieved – largely because of the influence of *SNL* – my dream of becoming a professional TV comedy writer and stand-up comedian. I've been working in L.A. for three years, and I'm finally moving back to New York, mainly because L.A. is sunny and perfect, and I hate it, and I can't live there anymore. So I'm back in New York, and I need a job. And my agent calls me out of the blue.

He's like, "You know, *SNL* is actually looking for new writers right now. Do you want to submit some sketches?"

I say, "Oh, my God. Yes, of course I do. I just have to find them on my computer."

And by "find them on my computer," I meant I had to run to Starbucks and panic and write some sketches. It's really hard to write comedy at Starbucks, because there's no one around to tell you if your commercial-parody idea for a jockstrap for dogs is funny or not.

And if you're wondering, *Did you really submit a sketch that was a commercial-parody for a jockstrap for dogs?* The answer is yes. Yes, I did.

I thought, *All right. Well, I'm not gonna get this job.*

But then, a couple of days later, my agent calls me again. And he says, "*SNL* liked your packet. You need to meet with Lorne Michaels."

And I'm like, "Holy fucking shit."

I'll just give you a representative tidbit from the interview I had with him.

I'm a little nervous. But I go into his office, and it's one of those setups where there's a very large leather couch and then also a large leather chair. And I never know where to sit in that situation.

So I decide I'm gonna be endearing and honest, and I say, "So, uh, where do you want me to sit?"

And he says, "Well, why don't you sit on the couch, and I'll sit on the chair?"

"Okay."

Then we have a minute of small talk. And after a minute, he says, "Um, you know what? Actually, I want to sit on the couch."

And I look to see if he's joking, and he's not. We got up, and we switched.

I was like, *This is fucking weird.*

And then fifteen minutes later, I left, and I thought, *Not only am I not getting that job, I almost feel like I've been fired from the job.*

But then, a few days later, I am home and I am lying on my couch, watching Animal Planet, as is my wont. And I get another call from my agent.

And he's like, "Yeah, so you got the job. *SNL* wants you."

So I flip the fuck out. And I call my best friend, and he comes over. We order pizza. And I put Jay Z's "Empire State of Mind" on repeat.

I'm having one of those special moments in life – that window between when you get a cool job and you can tell everyone about it but before you've started the job and you realise what the job is going to entail.

And I was not prepared for what working at *SNL* entailed.

So I'll give you a brief picture of how the week works. It starts on Tuesday. And the writers stay up all night to write the whole show. *Literally all night.* You get there at noon, and you go home at 9:00 a.m. Wednesday morning. Like, at best. And maybe you'll go home and sleep for a couple of hours, but then you have to come back to prepare for Wednesday afternoon, which is this epic marathon affair in which Lorne and the whole cast, and all the writers, and everyone who works at the show, squishes into the writers' room and they read every single sketch that's been submitted.

There's about forty. It takes four hours. And afterwards Lorne goes off with his supervising writers, and they decide what's gonna go in that week's show, based on what got the most laughs.

They have this weird tradition where, even though there's email now, the way they let you know what's gonna be in the show is sort of high-school-play style, where the writers' assistant comes out with one piece of paper. And everyone has to crowd around to see what's been circled.

When I'd asked people why do we do it this way, they'd say, "It's just tradition." As if *SNL* is an Afghani village, untouched by time.

So my first Tuesday night – my first writers' night – I'm excited, but a little nervous, because I am not a night person. I am a morning person. I usually go to bed at 10:30 p.m.

But I think, *All right. I'm just gonna power through.* And I am powering through. And then, at about 10:35, I'm like, *I'm so sleepy.*

But my work was not anywhere close to done, because the host for that week was Blake Lively, the lead from *Gossip Girl.* I have to say that in addition to having the biggest boobs on the skinniest body I've ever seen in my life, she seemed super cool and funny and really nice. And I was writing a sketch where I decided she would play a wacky volunteer at an animal-adoption center.

So I was anal about making it perfect. I stayed up all night tweaking it. The hours were dragging on and on.

And in a nutshell, my first table read at *Saturday Night Live* – it bombs so badly. The sketch bombs in front of a room of people who I happen to think are the funniest people in the world.

I'm assuming that probably there are a few people here who have never bombed in front of the writers' room at *SNL*. So just to give you a sense of what it's like: imagine that you're having sex with somebody that you really like but they're not making any noise, no matter what you do to their body.

And then imagine that there's also a roomful of people watching it happen.

And they're not making any noise either.

And it's fucking terrifying.

It's so terrifying that I think, *This will not stand.* I'm determined that next week I'm gonna get something at least onto the dress-rehearsal show.

So a little background on that. Every Saturday, *SNL* actually does two shows. The first is in front of a studio audience, but it doesn't air. Any sketch that doesn't do well will not make it to the TV show.

So I'm like, *I'm gonna at least get that far.*

The host my second week is Taylor Lautner, who's the teen heartthrob werewolf from the *Twilight* movies. Which I have not seen, (1) because I am thirty-five years old and (2) if I want to see pale people being angsty, I'll look in the mirror. I don't need to spend money.

But he seems really nice. And he's very young. So I think, *I'll write something where he plays someone really young.*

So I write a sketch where he'll play Bristol Palin's ex, Levi Johnston. And all he's gonna have to do is wear a puffy vest and mumble like an idiot. Taylor Lautner nails this. And it gets laughs, and it goes to dress rehearsal.

I'm like, *Oh, this is a victory.*

Or so I think, until I realise what dress rehearsal means. Which is Mr Lorne Michaels sits under the audience bleachers during dress, and he watches the show on a monitor. And when your sketch starts, you slide into a chair next to Lorne, and you watch your sketch with him.

So my sketch starts, and then I watch Lorne watch my sketch bomb really badly. And I'm assuming there's a few of you who've never watched your sketch bomb in front of Lorne, so just to give you a sense of what it's like:

Imagine that you're having sex with Lorne Michaels. And he's not making any noise.

And I'm like, *Oh, my God!*

So this becomes my life, right? Week after week I am struggling to come up with material that I think will work on the show. And it doesn't always go terribly. But I can never get it to go great.

And I start to spiral. Because my whole identity, personally and professionally, up to this point in my life is that I can be funny. And I can't crack the code on this show. Before every table read, I am gripped with fear. Before every dress rehearsal, my stomach is in knots. I am walking around lost and confused, but in a foggy way. In a Keanu Reeves way.

It feels like there is a part of me that has become broken, and without it I'm becoming unhinged. I never see my friends anymore just 'cause of the hours.

And on the rare occasions when I do see them, they say things to me like, "You don't look very good."

Or, "Jessi, don't cry in this restaurant. We want to come back here."

I'm also not sleeping, because there's no time to sleep. And on the occasions when I might sleep, I'm too anxious, and I'm thinking about next week's guest, and what I should write for them.

I'll be lying there thinking, *Okay, Jennifer Lopez is gonna be on next week. What should I write for Jennifer Lopez?*

And then I'll be like, *Who the fuck knows what to do with Jennifer Lopez? Jennifer Lopez doesn't know what to do with Jennifer Lopez.*

And in the midst of all this stress, I'm trying to experience any kind of pleasure because I don't have pleasure in my life anymore. All I can do is go to the Anthropologie store downstairs at 30 Rock and spend too much money on some twee bullshit item. I spent $280 on, like, a sweater with a kangaroo pocket on it or some crap. Girls know what I'm talking about.

Or sometimes I'll get home really late, and I'll take an Ambien and I'll start to hallucinate just enough to send a vague sext to this guy I used to date in L.A.

Right when I was doing this, the Tiger Woods scandal broke. And I remember one of his mistresses talked about the fact that they Ambien-sexted.

Everyone at my job was like, "Ew, that's so gross."

And I was like, "Yeah, ew, that's so gross. I'm doing what Tiger Woods does."

I knew I was hitting rock bottom when the anxiety started to affect me physically. I started to feel like I was having heart palpitations, and because I'm a neurotic hypochondriac, I was like, *I'm dying.*

So I went to my doctor. I have a really good doctor, so he was immediately able to diagnose me as being an idiot.

He said, "You just need to relax."

I was like, "Okay, well, then give me some Klonopin."

And he said, "No, you should do this without drugs."

And I was like, "Why are you a bad doctor?"

Around this time a really good friend of mine sends me a link to a series of lectures by this British Buddhist monk named Ajahn Brahm.

She says, "Listen to this. It will make you feel better." I was sceptical, because generally the only self-help I will accept is from a very close girlfriend of mine named Oprah Winfrey.

But I'm desperate, so I'm like, "Okay."

I immediately fall in love with Ajahn Brahm. He has given a weekly talk for fifteen years about every aspect of human experience in the world. They're alphabetised on the website.

I start listening to these lectures in bed – literally I take my laptop and I put it by my pillow so his voice is in my ear.

One night I listen to a lecture he did about death and dying. The theme was accepting that life and death go together and are part of the same continuum.

I realise even though I'm not physically dying, maybe I can integrate this idea into the fact that my comedy is dying. If I'm gonna succeed at *SNL*, I have to make peace with bombing. You have to do that in life – make peace with bombing. But especially on that show.

I stop writing things from a place of fear. And I start to write things that I think are funny. I say fuck it, whatever, and I hand it in.

And things start to get better. On one of the last shows of the season, Tina Fey was the host. I love Tina Fey. And

I really wanted to get something on when she was on. I remembered on Tuesday night that I'd written this sketch when I was submitting to get the job.

I thought, *Maybe Tina would be good for this.*

I hand it in, and we do it at table read. And it doesn't kill, but it doesn't bomb. It turns out Tina wants to try it.

It's a commercial-parody, which means we're gonna shoot it Friday and edit all day Saturday. I remember sliding in next to Lorne right before dress. I was nervous that people weren't necessarily gonna get it, 'cause it was a weird idea.

It was a parody of a Duncan Hines commercial, the way they show lonely women substituting chocolate for sex. It was for a product called Brownie Husband. The idea was that it was a brownie shaped like a husband, and you could sort of fuck it and eat it at the same time.

The tagline that I had written was "It's the first dessert you'll want inside you . . . and inside you."

I was nervous. But then as soon as they started to play it, people started to laugh. And they were really laughing, like, rolling, hard laughter.

And Lorne is laughing. And if you want to know what it's like to make Lorne laugh, picture yourself having sex with Lorne and he's laughing.

When it airs, it's kind of a hit, and it becomes a trending topic on Twitter. People want a Brownie Husband.

And it was the first moment in the whole *SNL* experience when I thought, *Oh. This is what I thought it would be like when I was a kid.*

So the season ends. And the other *SNL* tradition is that they don't tell you until the end of the summer if you're hired back for fall. So you have months to stew. But I found myself worrying less about them not wanting me back than I was about, oh, my God, what if they DO want me back?

Because I was worried about going back to a place that had made me feel so crazy. But on the other hand, nothing felt crazier than the idea of leaving this job that every comedy person wants. That I had wanted since I was ten.

I started to think about what I would miss.

I thought, *Oh, I'll miss the approval of the audience laughing and Lorne laughing.*

But I remembered that, ironically, the sketch that got me that approval was one that I wrote at a Starbucks, by myself, before I thought I was worthy of even getting the job. And when I did get the job, I didn't have the glamorous experience that I imagined I would have when I was ten and I was watching that show on a shitty black-and-white TV.

But I actually had a much more important experience. Because what I learned was to be brave. *SNL* taught me that you can't be afraid to put something out into the world that's yours, something that's totally different and that you believe in.

So when *SNL* finally called, I had my agent respectfully say no.

And that fall I took my laptop back to Starbucks, and I started to write something new.

JESSI KLEIN is currently the head writer and one of the executive directors on the Emmy Award–winning show *Inside Amy Schumer*. She is a writer-performer who has written for Comedy Central, ABC, HBO and *Saturday Night Live*. She occasionally tweets but hates it.

THIS STORY WAS TOLD ON JUNE 28, 2011, AT CENTRAL PARK SUMMERSTAGE, NEW YORK CITY. THE THEME OF THE EVENING WAS *BIG NIGHT*. **DIRECTOR: SARAH AUSTIN JENNESS.**

Sasha Chanoff

◇◇

An Impossible Choice

I'm looking out a hotel-suite window in the capital of Congo, in the middle of Africa. There are bullet marks on the buildings out there, because war is raging. But it's nighttime and quiet. There's a nasty cockroach infestation in the kitchen, and a putrid smell in the air.

I've turned the TV volume up loudly, because the Congolese government has bugged our room. I turn and face Sheikha. She is a woman from Kenya with the brown skin of the coastal people and thick black hair and intense dark eyes. Tears are welling in her eyes, and she's pleading with me.

"Sasha, we have to take these people along with the rest. If we don't, they'll die here, and their blood will be on our hands. Please. You have to trust me."

I'm facing a terrible decision. And I'm afraid that no matter what I do, people are going to be killed. A month earlier in Kenya, my boss, David, had called me into his office at the International Organisation for Migration, handed me a list with 112 names on it, and told me he was sending me into the Congo on a rescue mission. The job was to evacuate 112 massacre survivors. He warned me really explicitly that under no circumstances could I include anybody else on that list. If I did, we would fail to get anyone out, and they would all die. David knew because he'd spent the past six months in the Congo, evacuating people.

I'd met one teenage girl that he pulled out. She had these nervous eyes. And she told me that the killing started when the president of Congo went on TV and said that all people of the Tutsi tribe are the enemy and needed to be hunted down and exterminated.

This was an extension of the Rwandan genocide in ways. The teenage girl went into hiding that day, but had to eventually come out to look for food.

And as she was sneaking around town, she saw a mob chase down and catch another woman. They put a tire over her body, pinned her arms to her sides, doused her in gasoline and set her on fire. They were killing people in terrible ways, because Tutsis were seen as the scape-goats for the Congo's problems.

The teenage girl had lost her own parents, but she had four brothers who were still alive, and they were on the list that David handed me.

David also warned me about Sheikha. She'd been on every previous mission with him, but he told me that I couldn't trust her – that she always tried to include additional people and I had to stop her from doing that.

Sheikha and I flew into the Congo, we rented a car and a driver, and went to the safe compound where the 112 were gathered. These big black gates swung open as our car drove into this two-acre compound with ten-foot walls and jagged shards of glass topping the walls. There were guards with AK-47s slung at their sides, standing around. A one-story building was in the middle, and a large tent off to the side, and latrines on another side. Somebody saw Sheikha, and all of a sudden there was a mob around our car. They were pushing it up and down and chanting her name.

And I remembered David telling me that "people are going to go crazy with relief when they see you, because they think they're going to die there. And when they see you, they'll know there's another flight."

But it felt really scary and out of control for me, because there were way more people than the 112 on our list. We set a table up on the top of a little hill, and the crowd gathered below. And I called people up one at a time.

And I took their name and their birth date and their photo. And I told them we'd be flying them out in a few days' time. I had to give this information to the Congolese immigration officials. I got really excited when I saw the four brothers of that teenage girl come up.

When we were done and trying to leave, a guy who was working in the compound said, "Before you leave, you have to go into that tent over there and look at the people who just came in."

And I thought, *I don't want to see anybody else. We can't take them, so why even look?* But my feet were walking towards the tent as I was thinking that, and I stepped inside.

And it was like time stopped.

It was really hot in that tent, and I remember the sweat trickling down the small of my back. But what struck me was how completely quiet it was, which seemed impossible because there were thirty-two widows and orphans standing and sitting in that tent.

The guy who brought us in leaned into me and said, "They were in a prison camp for sixteen months, where most of their family members were executed. We don't know how they survived." They all looked traumatised and emaciated. And they had these hollow stares like there was nothing behind their eyes.

Sheikha leaned down to a little girl holding a doll and said, "Let me see your doll."

All of a sudden, the doll's eyes popped open, and its tongue lolled out of its mouth. And we realised it was an infant child that looked more dead than alive.

I went over to a thirteen-year-old boy and said, "What's your name?"

And another smaller boy grabbed his hand and said, "He doesn't talk anymore. I talk for him." That thirteen-year-old had been brutalised so badly he just stopped speaking.

Sheikha and I left. And that night in the hotel room, she was holding the list of widows and orphans and begging me to take them. I said, "We can't."

But I wondered, *Can I live with myself if we leave these widows and orphans here and they're killed?* No, I didn't think so.

But could I live with myself if we tried to take them, and we failed to get everybody out and they all died? No.

And then I thought about who Sheikha was. She had this clear moral orientation. She did what was right in her heart and wasn't concerned about personal gain or recognition.

Then I wondered, who am I? My great-grandmother had come to the US as a refugee fleeing anti-Semitism in Russia. She was a widow who raised four children on her own. I'd been working with refugees since graduating from college six years earlier, but nothing had prepared me for this.

And then Sheikha said words that changed me: "Sasha, we're humanitarians. We're here on the ground now. If we don't do this, these people will be forgotten. And they'll die here. This is up to us. It's our decision."

In that moment I trusted her. So I called David. And he got really angry when we told him what we wanted to do.

He said, "Listen, I'll tell you exactly what's going to happen. You have to tell the Congolese immigration authorities, and then they're going to include their own people on your list. And then, at the last minute, maybe even on the plane, they'll pull your people off, and you won't get anybody out. You can't do this."

I said, "David, I get it. But we have to try." And he was quiet.

Then I heard him say, "Okay, then here's what you have to do. This is a US rescue mission. So get the US ambassador's approval. And try it."

We got the US ambassador's approval. Then, on the last night, as the sun was setting, we went to see the head of Congolese immigration, a stocky man with beady eyes who'd already told us how much he hated Tutsis.

When we told him we were taking the widows and orphans, he said that he had seven additional people we had to take.

We said, "That's fine."

Then he pulled out this whole new list and said he also wanted us to take all these other people.

We said, "We can't." We argued with him. We even tried to bribe him.

But as we were leaving, he said, "I'm in charge here. I say who leaves and who stays. We'll just see what happens tomorrow."

Those words terrified me. Back in the hotel, we realised we had another big problem. We had too many people for our flight.

But then we thought that the children all looked so emaciated that we could change the birth dates so that all the four- and three-year-olds would be under two and could sit in the adults' laps, and then we'd free up enough seats. So I spent the night doing that.

At 3:00 a.m., as I tried to close my eyes, I couldn't sleep. I was so wired with exhaustion and fear and the uncertainty of it all.

I thought, *Have we just condemned everyone to death with this decision?*

A few hours later, I went and got four buses, and I had four armed guards per bus. I went to the safe compound and we started loading everybody on.

And the people who weren't coming started yelling.

One man grabbed me, and he pulled my face close to his, and he said, "Sasha, you have to take me with you. Look at my face. I'm a Tutsi. I'll be killed here."

But we couldn't take him, or so many others. And their cries faded into the distance as our buses pulled out.

Now my heart jumped in my throat, because this was the most dangerous part of the entire mission. The Congolese government had told us that they would let us do this, but unofficially they didn't want us to succeed.

I worried that maybe a mob would attack our bus, or maybe gunmen would start shooting from around a corner. Hundreds of thousands of people had lost their lives already, and no one would notice a few more.

An hour later we finally pulled into the airport, and we stopped fifty feet away from the plane.

I thought, *There's the plane. Let's just get everybody on that plane.*

Congolese immigration police hustled me and Sheikha off the buses. And then they started checking people using the documentation we had given. As the widows and orphans came down, they stopped them.

I had this terrible thought:

Oh, my God. These people are witnesses to terrible atrocities. And the Congolese immigration police aren't going to

*let them leave, because they don't want them talking about
what they've seen.*

I thought, *Everything that David said is coming true
right now.*

And I felt so helpless. I looked around for Sheikha. She
was talking to the head of Congolese immigration and
waving her arms.

The seconds ticked by.

And then they let them off the bus. They boarded the
plane. We all boarded the plane. And I stepped on last.
The cabin had turned into a furnace, because the plane
had been sitting on the tarmac for a couple of hours.

It was so packed with people. There were so many
children sitting on laps of adults. The door shut behind
me. And I felt the plane engines rumble to life and cool
air came into the cabin. And we started down the runway,
and we lifted off the ground.

I'd imagined that in that moment people would erupt
into cheers of joy because they were finally safe. But
when I looked, everyone was crying for the people we
had left behind.

It was at once the most joyous and heartbreaking
moment. And in that moment I thought about Sheikha
pleading with me in the hotel. And I was so thankful. We
couldn't get everyone out, but we got those on our list
out, and those widows and orphans. And they were the
worst off.

I looked at the tiny infant, and there was the thirteen-
year-old boy. And there were the four brothers who were
going to be reuniting with their teenage sister soon.

And as their eyes met mine, I felt this incredible sense
of connection and shared humanity sink into the deepest core of who I am. And that feeling has motivated and
inspired me ever since.

SASHA CHANOFF is the founder and executive director of RefugePoint, a humanitarian organisation based in Cambridge, Massachusetts, and Kenya, which finds lasting solutions for the world's most at-risk refugees. He is a recipient of the Charles Bronfman Prize for humanitarian contributions and the Harvard Center for Public Leadership's Gleitsman International Activist Award, and is a White House Champion of Change. His book, *From Crisis to Calling: Finding Your Moral Center in the Toughest Decisions*, co-authored with his father, David Chanoff, relates the full story of the Congo rescue mission. Sasha lives in Somerville, Massachusetts, with his wife and two children.

THIS STORY WAS TOLD ON APRIL 11, 2014, AT THE **SHUBERT THEATRE, BOSTON**. THE THEME OF THE EVENING WAS *COMING HOME*. **DIRECTOR: MEG BOWLES**.

Moshe Schulman

<><><><><><><><><><><><><><><><><><><><><><><><><><><><><><><><>

Then You Will Know!

When I was a child, I was given a blessing to become the greatest rabbi of my time. But at fifteen years old, I was struggling in school and I felt like I couldn't live up to the pressure of my blessing anymore.

I'm the fourth of eight children, and I was raised in an ultra-Orthodox Jewish community in Monsey, New York. For those of you who haven't been raised Orthodox Jewish, it's kind of like growing up Amish, only we had electricity.

I wasn't allowed to watch TV, read secular books, eat non-kosher food or even talk to girls. And I was taught from a young age by my rabbis that if I disobeyed any of God's commandments, I would receive a punishment.

By punishment my rabbis meant that God would most likely, you know, kill me.

And here's the thing: *I believed them.*

I was a good boy. I got straight A's. I listened to my parents and my rabbis.

But as I got older, I started to question and wonder, *Would God really hurt me if I didn't obey him?*

So I started to test him. One morning at school, I moved my yarmulke from the back of my head to a few inches closer to the front of my head.

Now, that was a sign of modernism. That was like upgrading from a prepaid flip phone to an iPhone.

Then I started secretly listening to Howard Stern on the bus on the way to school. And I was wondering if the other boys were listening to him, too. It was fascinating to me to listen to someone who was discussing something other than the Talmud and the Torah.

Even more thrilling was the fact that this Howard Stern guy was Jewish. He was using Yiddish words and talking about Shabbos and the Jewish holidays.

And that got me thinking, *Wait a second, if Howard Stern is Jewish and he's practically sinning every day with the things I've heard him talk about, why hasn't God killed him yet?*

But even though I was starting to push back, I was still afraid of going too far.

At the same time, I was becoming disillusioned with my upbringing; things were falling apart at home. My parents were going through a pretty bad divorce, and I wanted to get away from them, and my rabbis, and the religious restrictions.

So for winter break that year, I planned a trip to Florida with my older brother, Israel. Israel had left the fold a year earlier, and moved in with my nonreligious Aunt Linda in Bellmore, Long Island.

The plan was to meet him at her house, and then we'd leave for the airport on Sunday.

Now, I had always wanted to go to my aunt's house. My brother told me she had things I could only dream of having one day: a grand white piano, a spiral staircase and *two* fifty-inch-screen TVs.

So I got to my aunt's house on Friday afternoon in time for Shabbos, and she was kind enough to buy me kosher food for the duration of Shabbos. But by the time Shabbos was over on Saturday night, there was no kosher food left, and I was hungry.

So we all get into the car to go graze for kosher food out on the pastures of Long Island.

Now, I was pretty good at searching for food, because being one of eight kids, I always felt like there wouldn't be enough of it, and I constantly paced the kitchen, looking in the pantry and the fridge for my next meal.

Sometimes I'd even go so far as to hide food out of fear that there wouldn't be any left.

And I always wished there was some sort of pill that would substitute a meal. Like the manna in the Torah.

When the Jews were in the desert, they complained to Moses and Aaron that they would rather have died with pots of meat surrounding them in Egypt than die of thirst and hunger in the desert.

And God, hearing their complaints, quickly answered and told them, "Look, guys, settle down. I'm going to show you how great I am. I'm going to fill the camp with bread and meat." I believe the direct quote was, "Because then you will know I am the Lord, your God."

And sure enough, my rabbis taught me that you could ask him for anything and it would literally drop from the sky. Anything you wanted – pizza, ice cream, candy – it would magically appear.

But nothing was magically appearing in Long Island, so we continued driving around, looking for a kosher restaurant, but none were open. I recommended we go to the local Stop & Shop to look for kosher frozen pizza. (For some reason, in my community, that's a delicacy.)

So we scanned all the aisles in Stop & Shop, but I couldn't find anything that had an *OU* marked on the package. (The *OU* symbol means that it has officially been certified kosher.)

If you were only allowed to eat food with an *OU* marked on the package, that meant you were most likely ultra-

Orthodox, which I was. But if you were only allowed to eat food that was watched over by a specific rabbi, then marked with an official stamp by that rabbi, that meant you were Hasidic.

But if you were allowed to eat food that had a "kosher but made with dairy" certification, then you were most likely Modern Orthodox, also known in my community as "a borderline Jew."

And if you were allowed to eat food that had a K marked on it, or worse than that, a capital K surrounded by a triangle, or even worse than that, the Hebrew National certification, you could forget about a seat next to God in the world to come, because you weren't even considered Jewish. Eating that food was just as bad as throwing your yarmulke to the ground, cursing God and biting into a bacon, egg, and cheese sandwich.

So having found no kosher frozen pizza, we all stood outside Stop & Shop contemplating what to do next. Our search for kosher food had been going on close to two hours, and we were all frustrated.

I was beginning to feel like the Israelites in the Torah. I would have preferred to die in Monsey with kosher meat surrounding me than die of hunger in the desolate suburb of Bellmore, Long Island.

My aunt asked me what I wanted to eat, and I didn't know. She asked me if it had to be kosher, and again, I didn't know. I was just wishing there was no such thing as kosher or non-kosher.

So my aunt pressed me again. "Does it have to be kosher or not?"

I was beginning to realise in the moment that even if I found something relatively kosher, I would have been disappointed. I secretly wanted something non-kosher, but I was too afraid to ask for it or admit it.

My aunt turned to my brother Israel for some help, and my brother said, "Look, I don't wanna force him to eat non-kosher if he doesn't want to."

My aunt was getting angry, so she said, "Well, what is with this kosher stuff anyway? It's just blessed by a rabbi, right? So why don't I buy some food and bless it. We'll just get this over with."

And I had to tell her, "Well, my rabbis taught me that women aren't allowed to bless the food."

That got her even more angry.

So she started to walk away, and I said, "Well, maybe I could eat something if I don't know that it's not kosher."

She quickly turned around and yelled, "How does that work?"

So I explained what I learned in Talmud class. Follow this, guys:

If a Jew is in an airport, and he buys a kosher hamburger, and while he's gone to wash and make a blessing on the bread, someone switches his burger out with a non-kosher one and he eats it, it's okay.

Now, that logic my aunt agreed with. She was excited about that. So she had a plan.

She told me that she'd go into the store and buy the food for me, and I wouldn't have any idea that it's not kosher. I agreed.

So we all got back into the car and drove to Stella's Pizzeria on Merrick Road. My aunt asked me what I wanted, and I told her a mushroom slice.

She said, "Just one?"

And I said, "Yes, just one."

(I didn't want to piss God off more by getting two.)

So my aunt and my brother went into the store, and I sat in the back of the car, waiting for God to blow up the pizza shop, the car, or both.

My fifteen-year-old mind was being filled with every rabbi I ever had in yeshiva yelling at me that I was going to be thrown into a pit of fire for sinning. I was in a *goyishe* car, in a *goyishe* parking lot, next to a *goyishe* store.

I watched closely as the counter boy put the slices into the oven. I was afraid it might touch pork. What if there's pork flavour in the oven, or what if he cut my slice with the knife that he cut a slice of pepperoni or bacon?

My heart raced as Aunt Linda paid the cashier, and I thought God was going to take her right then. He was going to take an arm off or sever her head.

I thought about that saying "Don't kill the messenger" to try and comfort myself.

But God was God. He could do whatever the hell he wanted.

I was scared for my brother, too, even though he didn't order or pay for the slices. But the fact that he was in the store, with my aunt, made him an accessory to my downfall as a kosher Jew. I started to get a stomachache, and I couldn't even tell if I was hungry anymore. The guilt was racking up pretty heavily.

I realised I wasn't that good boy that I used to be.

So my aunt and my brother walked out of the store and got back into the car. My brother held the pizza box with the slices in it. But I couldn't look at them or the box of pizza. I was too nervous. I just stared out the window as we continued down the street, afraid of the car crashing into a tree or a telephone pole.

I could already see the breaking-news headline: ORTHODOX JEW BUYS NON-KOSHER SLICE OF PIZZA AND IS IMMEDIATELY KILLED ON THE WAY HOME.

Then you will know I am the Lord, your God, I thought. *Then you will know.*

So when we got home, Israel placed the pizza box on the dining-room table. Aunt Linda went into the kitchen to grab some paper plates.

I asked Israel if he'd take my slice out, and he said, "No, I don't wanna get involved."

My aunt told us we were both nuts and she put my slice on a plate. My aunt and my brother had already started eating, so I felt a little encouraged. I figured if I was going be taken out, they'd go with me.

So I picked up the slice . . . and took the first bite.

I chewed it.

I swallowed it.

They asked me how it was, and I told them it was pretty good. But it was better than pretty good. Better than any kosher pizza I'd ever had – tasty tomato sauce, thin crust, fresh mushrooms and cheese.

But I didn't want to come off as too happy or cocky. I didn't want to piss off the Man Upstairs even more.

So I quickly finished the slice, and I checked to make sure I wasn't dead, and thought, *Please God, forgive me, just this once. Please. It's just a stupid slice of mushroom pizza.* I enjoyed the slice . . . but I had just broken a *major commandment.*

The next day Israel and I went to Florida, and it was over the course of that week that I traded in my yarmulke for a baseball cap. I was finally free from the pressure of my blessing, my rabbis and my parents' chaotic divorce. It was just me and my older brother, free to do as we pleased. We spent full days at Universal Studios, riding the roller coasters and playing arcades. We stayed up late in the hotel watching movies.

And I couldn't stop eating pizza that week. I think I had pizza for nearly every meal. Florida was my Sodom and Gomorrah.

But of course, it isn't that easy. It's not like I just ate that one slice and everything's all good.

It's been ten years since I ate that mushroom slice, and I've since made a full break from the religious fold. And yet I'm still scared that something horrible is going to happen to me for breaking the rules.

I imagine ordering a bacon, egg and cheese sandwich one day, and I can already see the breaking-news headline: FORMER ORTHODOX JEW ORDERS A BACON, EGG AND CHEESE SANDWICH AND IS INSTANTLY STRUCK DOWN BY LIGHTNING IN LOCAL DINER.

Then you will know I am the Lord, your God. Then you will know.

MOSHE SCHULMAN has written for the *Rumpus, Orange Quarterly, Vol. 1 Brooklyn*, the *Jewish Daily Forward, Tablet* magazine and elsewhere. The recipient of a scholarship to the Bread Loaf Writers' Conference, he lives in New York City, where he recently completed a memoir about leaving the ultra-Orthodox Jewish community of Monsey, New York.
mosheschulman.com

THIS STORY WAS TOLD ON FEBRUARY 6, 2015, IN THE GREAT HALL AT **COOPER UNION, NEW YORK CITY**. THE THEME OF THE EVENING WAS *SECRET HEART: STORIES OF CLOAKS AND DAGGERS*. **DIRECTOR: MEG BOWLES**.

Navreet Chawla

<><><><><><><><><><><><><><><><><><><><><><><><><>

It's a Box

I go into the phone box and I put 20 pence in. I call my boyfriend, and he answers. So I put the pound coin in, and before we begin to talk, I give him the number of the pay phone so he can call me back, just in case my money runs out.

Just as we're about to speak, I suddenly feel the door behind me open.

And a hand appears out of nowhere.

And I watch it press down the switch hook of the phone.

And I hear the pound coin drop to the bottom.

And I watch the hand remove the coin.

Earlier that evening, I'd actually been staying at my boyfriend's flat on the main university campus. He was away on work experience, and I had the keys to his flat, which was great for me because I actually lived off the main campus.

But after spending a few days there, I suddenly had this urge, this yearning to go home. I wanted fresh clothes, to sleep in my own bed, hang out with my girlfriends. I just needed to go home and be in my own space.

As soon as I thought it, a voice in my head said, *Don't go*.

But I want to go home. And again, the voice said, *Don't go*.

I wasn't really sure what to do with that. I didn't know what it meant. I was living in the city, and of course it can be a bit weird at times. But it did make me feel anxious, and so I really had to think about what I was going to do. Eventually I decided, *No, I'm going to go home*.

But to appease the voice, I decided to remove my jewellery. Remove my watch. Leave my cards and my cash, but just take enough for the bus fare to get there and back the following morning, and call my boyfriend from the pay phone.

I set off. It was about 8 o'clock in the evening.

I was living in Birmingham at the time, and it's full of subways, and certainly when I was there, it had the reputation for being quite seedy and unsafe. I'd actually been flashed a number of times down there.

But this evening was different. As I walked along the subway, I saw a female police officer just ahead of me.

I remember thinking, *This is a really good sign. See? I'm safe*.

I break my stride so I'm almost walking in tandem with her, but without making it too obvious. And then I exit the subway, and I get to my bus stop. The bus arrives unusually early, and again, I think, *This is great. Everything is flowing as it should be. I have nothing to worry about*.

I sit near the bus driver, because I think this is the most sensible thing to do, and then I get to my stop.

I'm now on the home stretch. I'm probably about 200 yards away from my flat. All I have to do now is get home.

As I start to walk, I notice a pay phone on the corner, and I think to myself, *I'm gonna call my boyfriend from here*, because the pay phone on my campus is always ringing off the hook, so this is a great opportunity.

I remember thinking as I walked into the phone box, and felt the door close behind me, *I'm safe in here. It's a box*.

I call my boyfriend. And before we speak, the door opens behind me, and a hand appears out of nowhere, and I watch it press down the switch hook of the phone. I hear the pound coin drop to the bottom slot and the hand removes the coin.

I don't remember dropping the receiver. But I do remember seeing it swing from side to side. And suddenly, these arms tighten around me, and I can feel something sharp against my neck.

I'm scared. I'm so fucking scared.

My heart is beating. It's beating so fast it's pulsing in the back of my throat, and it almost feels like it could tear my throat open. My mouth is dry, and I'm choking and I can hardly breathe. I can feel my legs wanting to buckle.

And I keep thinking to myself, *Is this happening?*

Is this really happening to me?

I think I'm told not to move or make a sound, but I can't be sure.

He asks me for money, but I don't have any money. No wait, I do, I have 75 pence.

But he thinks that I'm taking the piss out of him. He pushes me up against the phone, and he grabs my bag, and now I'm panicking. I don't know how I'm going to get out.

And then all of a sudden, something happened to me. I was suddenly overcome by a strange sense of calm, presence and clarity. My senses were completely heightened, and I felt like I embodied every cell of my body. I could feel and sense everything. And the voice in my head said, *So what happens now? How does this end?*

I started running through different scenarios in my mind. Maybe I'm stabbed and I die. Or maybe I'm raped, stabbed, and then I die. Or maybe I'm stabbed, but I end up in intensive care, and then I go into a coma and then I die.

And the voice said, *Well, it doesn't sound like you have anything to lose, then. But if you do survive, the police will want a description. You need to get a description.*

So I raise my hands calmly, and I slowly turn around to face him. And I tell him he should check my pockets for money if he doesn't believe me. And so he does. And I look at him, and I take the image of him in – the colour of his eyes, his hair, his clothes.

And the Stanley knife in his hand.

He looks up and he notices the tracking movements of my eyes, and he quickly spins me round and pushes me up against the phone. This time, the grip around me is much tighter, and his hands are moving over my breasts.

And the voice says, *Don't move. Don't even flinch. Let him touch you. Let him think he has you.*

So I do. I let him touch me. And all the while, I keep thinking to myself, *How did I get into the phone box? Which hand did I use to open the door? Did it open from left to right or right to left? Which hand did I use to get into the phone box?*

His hands are travelling downwards towards my groin. And in that moment, I decide I'd rather die.

I raise my hands, and I grab his arms, and I force my weight against him and push him back into the door. And I swing to my right so that I can swing to the left and use his weight to leverage the door open.

And the door opens.

So I run.

And then I stop running because I notice he's not chasing me. I turn around, and I think it must have been the adrenaline running through my body, because all I can think about now is wanting to find him so I can stab him and kill him.

But I can't find him anywhere. Instead, I notice an Indian man standing in the driveway of his house, watching me.

I ask him, "Which way did he go?" He says he doesn't know.

I start running down a side street, and he says, "I don't think that's a good idea," and he runs after me.

He asks me if I'm okay.

Of course I'm not okay. I've just been mugged.

He walks me back to the phone box and I pick up my bag. The phone is replaced on the hook, and it rings immediately.

It's my boyfriend – I forgot. He tells me he's been ringing me for two minutes.

Two minutes. Is that all it was? Two minutes?

I hang up because I just can't talk. The Indian man offers to drive me home, and I tell him he's crazy.

"I'm not getting in a car with you. You're a stranger. You're a man."

He offers to bring his wife along so I feel safer, she just has to get ready and get her purse. While I'm waiting, every single member of the family appears at the door, wanting to know what happened, wanting to come along for the ride. Eventually, everyone is seated in the car.

Everyone except me. (Someone has to get out of the car so I can get into the car.)

The drive is excruciatingly slow, and I burst into tears.

The grandmother says to me, "What are you crying for? It's not like you were raped."

"Oh, wait a minute," she says. "He didn't touch you down there, did he?"

"No."

"Well, that's all right then, because otherwise you would have been spoiled."

I just want to get the hell out of here.

We eventually arrive at the campus, and as the car drives off, I stand in the silence of the evening and realise, I'm home. I made it home.

Before, I always took my intuition for granted, and after this, I realised, I don't get to negotiate with it. But I always know now that its love and its care for me is completely unconditional.

NAVREET CHAWLA is a practising pharmacist and an expert in complementary medicine. In her eclectic career, she has also been a stand-up comedian and, as a trained clown, has performed for patients with dementia. Navreet writes and blogs on subjects including the history and culture of medicine and well-being; the doctor-patient relationship and its impact on therapeutic outcomes; the schism between scientific biomedicine and complementary medicine; and the use of language in health and illness.

THIS STORY WAS TOLD ON OCTOBER 5 2015 AT THE **UNION CHAPEL, LONDON**. THE THEME OF THE EVENING WAS *LEAP OF FAITH*. **DIRECTOR: MEG BOWLES**.

Hasan Minhaj

Prom

The first time I fell in love, I was in the first grade and it was with this girl named Janice.

I went up to her on the playground, and I said, "Janice, I love you!"

And she said, "You're the colour of poop."

I grew up in a small town called Davis, California, and I was one of the few brown people there.

All I wanted as a kid was to fit in. I remember we had this assignment in the third grade.

The teacher said, "Write down what you want to be when you grow up."

So all these kids said, "I want to be an astronaut" or "I want to be an NBA player."

I wrote, "I want to be white."

The teacher said, "Honey, what do you mean?"

And I was like [*points to the palm of his hand*], "I want *this* part of my skin to be *all* of my skin."

My father had emigrated from a small town in India called Aligarh during the early eighties, and he was the only brother from his entire family to make it here to the States. He felt it was his duty to establish the American dream here in America by securing a financial future for his family.

I was his first and only son. So that means the rules were very, very strict. That meant no fun, no friends, no girls. Go to school, come home, study – you can have fun in med school. The simplest things became this huge debate with my dad.

"Dad, I want to go to the movies."

"What?"

"I want to see *Lethal Weapon 4.*"

"Hasan, *humnay Aligarh se nay aye* Lethal Weapon 4 *ke liye!* I didn't leave Aligarh for *Lethal Weapon 4.*"

My dad was willing to forsake my fun to secure the American dream.

Now, by the time my senior year of high school had rolled around, I had been cut from the basketball team for the third year in a row, I had just gotten off of Accutane, so my skin was slowly peeling away, and I had yet to go to a football game or school dance. So I was just killin' it. I was just like *crushing* high school.

But there was one bright spot, and her name was Bethany Reed. Her family had just moved from Ohio to Davis, and her father was a very successful cardiologist. So they had this gorgeous house with a beautiful white picket fence. Her family looked like it had been cut out of a J.Crew catalog.

She was small, cute, and dainty; she had this curly hair that bounced up and down when she would walk; and she always smelled like Big Red cinnamon chewing gum, even after PE. It was incredible.

We had AP calculus together, and she didn't know about the Davis High social hierarchy and where I stood on it; she just thought I was funny and charming, and she really liked my AIM game. My AOL Instant Message game was so tight. Whatever I lacked in real-life game, my online persona was *on point.*

So we'd have these study groups together for AP calc, and for the most part they were always at her house. And

I just remember going over to her house, and we'd be sitting at the dinner table, and it was just like, "Hahaha! Have more mashed potatoes."

And I'm like, *Oh, this is tight.* You know? *This is so cool.*

One day Bethany says, "When are we gonna study at your place?"

And I was like, "Ugh."

I had this cardinal rule. I would never invite school friends over to my house, because I didn't want to open myself up to ridicule. You know, have a person come over and be like, "Why do your parents talk like that? What language are they speaking? What's that smell?"

I just didn't want to be embarrassed. But by the end of the school year, I felt really close to her. So I broke that rule, and I invited her over to my house to study.

I remember I told my parents, "Everyone, please be normal."

And my dad was like, "Hasan, we're normal. ... Samosa?"

I'm like, "Jesus."

So we're at the dining-room table doing integrals. You can hear the hiss of samosas frying in the kitchen and Hindi playing on Zee TV. My mom and dad are arguing in Hindi.

I'm looking up from my textbook, looking at Bethany, thinking, *Please don't say anything, please don't say anything, please don't say anything.*

And she looks up and says, "Wow, this seems really nice."

And I was like, *I'M IN LOVE WITH THIS WOMAN. I am going to marry you, YOU ARE MY WHITE PRINCESS. When can we get married? Can I put a ring on it right now?*

She kept coming over, and we kept doing integrals on the dining-room table. One night I walked her back to her car, and as I was walking her to the end of my drive-way, before she got in her car, she turned and just kissed me, right on the lips. No tongue, but ... it was *amazing*. Fireworks, the whole thing. It was incredible.

Then she got into her car and drove off.

And I loved her for that. She knew the rules. She knew – no fun, no friends, no girls. And definitely no girl-friends. She knew that my father would never allow us to be boyfriend and girlfriend, at least while we were in high school.

She didn't say, *Hey, can we hold hands at school? When can I see you again?* Nothing. *Finally, someone who gets it.*

Now, by the time spring quarter had rolled around at my school, my AP calculus class was a pretty tight-knit group of overachievers, and Mr B, our calculus teacher, really wanted us to try to have a semblance of a normal life.

So he got in front of the class that seventh period and he said, "All right, you guys are all killin' it academically. You're gonna go to the country's best institutions. But I want you guys to have normal lives, which is why I'm making it mandatory for every single person in this class to go to prom."

One of the kids was like, "Are we getting extra credit for this?"

And Mr B's like, "No, you're getting *life* credit. There's no extra credit. You're going to prom."

I was sitting in the back, and I'm just like, *Yeah, right, Mr B, there's no way you're gonna get the kids in this class to go to prom. That is just not happening.*

The Jehovah's Witness girl, she's not going to prom. There's the Korean exchange student, he's definitely not going to prom. You have to be able to speak English to say, "Can you go to prom with me?" He's not gonna be able to do that.

They used to sell Cup O' Noodles at my high school, right? There was this kid named Meelan, and kids would eat the Cup O' Noodles, then leave the broth on the lunch tables. Meelan would go to the lunch tables and drink people's lukewarm broth.

I was like, *There's no way Broth Breath is getting a date to prom*. Impossible.

But Mr B was focused. He pulled down the whiteboard, and there was this bracket with all of our names on it. It led to prom. The big dance. This was like March Madness for nerds.

But I thought, *Look, no one's gonna go, I'm fine, I don't have to address this problem*.

But the weeks went by, and slowly, one by one, everybody got a date to prom.

The Korean exchange student managed to ask somebody to prom. The Jehovah's Witness girl, her parents all of a sudden became cool. She was able to go. Even Meelan popped an Altoid and asked someone and got them to say yes. It was crazy.

Three days before prom, Mr B pulls down the whiteboard, and the last two names on the board are Hasan Minhaj and Bethany Reed. And the whole class goes crazy, hooting and hollering, you know?

I was so embarrassed. I looked down at my calculus book, 'cause I couldn't handle the pressure, but again Bethany was so cool; she didn't say anything in front of everybody. And then the bell rang. Seventh period was over.

We walked to my locker, and as I was putting my calculus book away, she turned to me and said, "Hey, you've been my best friend ever since my family moved here from Ohio, and my senior year wouldn't be the same without you. So will you go to prom with me?"

And I said, "Yes. Yes, I will go to prom with you, my white princess." (I didn't say white princess, but in my mind I said that.)

Now, I'm not a bad kid. I love my parents. I love my dad. We had a tumultuous relationship, but I really did love him. And I had seen a lot of sitcoms. I'd seen *Full House*. I know the drill. Go upstairs, talk to Danny Tanner, pour your heart out, cue emotional music, hug, and we'll figure it out.

I go home, and I say, "Dad, can I go to prom?"

He says, "Hasan, *me tumara mou torthunga*" which translates to "Hasan, I will break your face."

Duly noted, Father.

So I go with Option B. I call up Beth, and I tell her, "Look, here's the deal: I'm gonna have to sneak out to go to prom with you. It's too late to get a limo and tux, so I'm just gonna wear a normal suit, and I'm gonna sneak out of the window, and we're gonna take your dad's car, and we're gonna go to prom, and then I'm gonna sneak back into my room, and if I get beat up and I die, well, YOLO, you only live once, you know what I mean? So this will be the night of our life."

And she says, "Cool, let's do it."

So the night of prom rolls around, and I'm getting ready in my room. I put on my JCPenney suit, put my Geoffrey Beene tie on, I spray two puffs of Michael Jordan cologne on, you know? I'm ready.

I live on the second story of our house, and I climb out the window, and my trusty Huffy's to the left of the house. I get on my bike, and I'm balancing the corsage in one hand.

I made sure I was biking fast enough that I'd get to her house on time, but slow enough that I wouldn't get pit stains. And I was riding extra wide with my knees out –

that way my slacks wouldn't get caught up in the chains. I made it to her house in time.

I got to her door, and I was like, "Man, I did it. I'm going to prom with Bethany Reed. This is the American dream."

And I knock on the door, and her mom opens the door ... and over Mrs Reed's shoulder I see Erik Deller, the captain of the water-polo team, putting a corsage on Bethany.

Mrs Reed looks at me and says, "Oh, honey, I'm sorry. Did Bethany not tell you?

"See, we have a lot of family back in Ohio, and we're gonna be taking pictures tonight, so we don't think you'd be a good fit.

"Do you need a ride home? Mr Reed can give you a ride home."

I said, "No, it's okay. I got my bike." I rode home, and I climbed up on the roof and into my room, and I played video games the rest of the night in my suit. It was the best I've ever been dressed playing Mario Kart.

The next day at school, Bethany stopped me at my locker before first period and said, "Hey, listen, whatever you do, please, please don't say anything. Please. Okay? My parents are good people. The rest of the class, they wouldn't understand. Please don't say anything."

And I said, "Okay."

Seventh period rolled around, and Mr B, in front of the entire class, said, "So, lovebirds, how was prom?"

Everybody turned and looked at me, and I said, "Yeah, you know, I decided not to go. I just wasn't really feeling it." And everybody looked at me, and they were like, "Wow, you dick. You stood up the new girl from Ohio. You're a jerk."

And there it was – I got socially crucified for this girl that I love in front of the whole class.

Bethany and I never spoke after that. We just went our own separate ways.

But the hardest part about it was that as I stood there on her porch that night, I felt like her family was right. It wasn't just some toothless yokel yelling "Camel jockey!" from the back of his truck. I could let that roll off my back. Her father was a respected cardiologist. They were a well-to-do, successful family. So I just accepted it as true that I wasn't good enough. Who was I to ruin their picture-perfect American prom? After all, prom wasn't an event for people that look like me.

It really kind of messed with my notions of self-worth, for a long time.

A few years passed, and my father suffered a heart attack – a quintuple bypass. When he was lying in his hospital bed, I drove up from L.A. to come visit him, and he was the most vulnerable he'd ever been in his entire life, emotionally and physically. I told him the story. And he said, "Hasan, I'm mad at you."

I said, "Why? 'Cause I snuck out? 'Cause I lied to you?"

He said, "No, because you didn't forgive Bethany.

"See, when I first emigrated from Aligarh, I was scared. I was scared of everything that America had to offer. I was afraid that you were gonna get caught up in the wrong crowds. I was afraid that you were gonna get into drugs, which is why I tried to protect you from everything.

"And see, Bethany's family, they were scared, too. They were scared of people that looked like us for whatever reason. And you were scared of me, and Bethany was scared of her parents. Everybody was scared of everybody. But, Hasan, you have to be brave, and the courage to do what's right has to be greater than your fear of getting hurt."

There are days where I feel like I can forgive Bethany, and there are days where I feel like I can't. I'm working on it.

But I'm gonna try to be brave. I'm gonna be brave for me and Dad.

HASAN MINHAJ is a comedian, actor and writer, based in New York. He is a correspondent on the Emmy Award–winning program *The Daily Show with Trevor Noah*. His critically acclaimed one-man show, *Homecoming King*, recently returned to Off-Broadway. A 2014 *Just for Laughs* "New Face," he was selected by the Sundance Institute to develop his solo show and feature film at the prestigious New Frontier Storytelling Lab. He hosted the documentary special *Stand Up Planet,* produced by the Bill and Melinda Gates Foundation. His viral web series, *The Truth with Hasan Minhaj,* has been featured in the *New York Times* and other publications. He has been seen on a variety of other television programs, including *Arrested Development* on Netflix, HBO's *Getting On* and @*Midnight* on Comedy Central. **www.hasanminhaj.com**

THIS STORY WAS TOLD ON MARCH 8, 2014, AT THE **MUSIC HALL, PORTSMOUTH,** NEW HAMPSHIRE. THE THEME OF THE EVENING WAS *COMING HOME.* **DIRECTOR: SARAH AUSTIN JENNESS.**

Noreen Riols

◇◇◇◇◇◇◇◇◇◇◇◇◇◇◇◇◇◇◇◇◇◇◇◇◇◇◇◇◇◇◇◇◇◇◇◇◇◇◇

The Price of Freedom

During World War II, I was a pupil at the French Lycée in London. But on reaching the ripe old age of eighteen, I was obliged to abandon my studies and either join the armed forces or work in a munitions factory.

Well, that option did not thrill me. So I decided to become a member of the Women's Royal Naval Service. Because I liked the hat. I thought it was most seductive.

But when I went to sign on, I was taken aside and closeted in a kind of windowless broom cupboard with a high-ranking army officer, who began asking me an awful lot of questions which had nothing to do with the navy. He was leaping like a demented kangaroo in and out of four languages. And he seemed very surprised that I could keep up.

He sent me to a large building in central London. Oh, I knew it well. But like the hordes of people who passed by every day, never had I imagined or even suspected that this was the headquarters of Churchill's secret army. And that behind those walls, members of every occupied country were organising acts of sabotage, and the infiltration of secret agents into enemy territory at night, by parachute, fishing boat, felucca and submarine.

Without realising what had happened, I had been recruited into the hidden world of secret agents on special missions. (But I never got my seductive hat.)

I was assigned to "F" for France section. It was an exhausting but exciting, thrilling, exhilarating life, full of action and emotion. We lived some very intense moments.

I got to know an awful lot of agents. And I shared many confidences with those who were about to leave. They told me of their concerns for their families – many of them were married with young children – and of their own apprehension of torture and of death.

They knew they only had a fifty-percent chance of coming back. And they were afraid.

Brave men are always afraid. Courage isn't the absence of fear. It's the willingness – the guts, if you like – to face the fear. They faced their fears. And they left.

I remember one. He was a Jew. A radio operator. And he was going in on a second mission. Well, for a Jew to go in at all was extremely dangerous. But many did – we had quite a few Jewish agents. But a radio operator? A second mission? A radio operator was the most stressful, hazardous, dangerous mission of all. He lived on his nerves. He could never relax. He was always on the run, always with the Gestapo just a couple of steps behind him. He needed nerves of steel, because once infiltrated, his life expectancy was six weeks.

I was with this agent on the night before he left. Oh, there was no romantic association; I was just keeping him company. After all, he was an old man – he was almost thirty-five.

During the evening he drew out of his pocket a small velvet box. And inside there was a gold chain with a Star of David and a dove of peace hanging on it.

He said simply, "I'd like you to have this."

"Thank you so much," I stammered. "I'm terribly touched, but I couldn't possibly accept it."

He looked so sad. So disappointed.

He said, "Please do, oh, please do. All my family in France has perished in a German concentration camp. I've nobody left in the world. And I'd like to think that somebody remembers me. Somebody perhaps even thinks of me when I'm over there."

So I took his little box, promising to look after it and give it back to him when he returned.

But he didn't return.

Those who did return were taken immediately for a debriefing, and I often accompanied the two debriefing officers. For me it was a revelation to see their different reactions. Some returned with their nerves absolutely shattered, in shreds. Their hands were shaking uncontrollably as they lit cigarette after cigarette.

Others were as cool as cucumbers. And I realised then that we all have a breaking point. And we can never know until we're faced with the situation what that breaking point actually is. Perhaps that is why departing agents were strongly urged if arrested by the Gestapo to take the cyanide pill, which was always hidden somewhere around their person before they left. It would kill them within two minutes.

I grew up attending those debriefing sessions.

Many of those agents weren't very much older than I. Hearing their incredible stories, witnessing their courage, their total dedication, I changed almost overnight from a teenager to a woman.

One snowy Saturday evening in early February, I was told that I was to leave and go down to Beaulieu. Now, Beaulieu was the last of the many secret training schools. These training schools were dotted all over England. And the future agents attended each one in turn during their long, tough, six-month training. Beaulieu, or Group B as it was called, was in Hampshire, deep in the New Forest.

Only six women worked there during the war, and I am the last survivor.

We were used as decoys. We worked in the neighbouring seaside towns of Bournemouth and Southampton. My pitch was usually Bournemouth. It was there that we taught future agents how to follow someone – find out where they were going, who they were seeing – without being detected. How to detect if someone was following *them* and throw them off. How to pass messages without any sign of recognition or even moving our lips. This took place on the beach, in the park, on benches in the town, in telephone booths, and in the tearooms above the Gaumont Cinema.

The last exercise was reserved for those future agents whom the instructors thought might talk. Now, the instructors were with them all the time. They watched their every movement. They analyzed it all. And if they thought that they might talk, they would have a carefully prearranged setup meeting between a decoy and a future agent in one of the two grand hotels in Bournemouth.

(Of course, if I had taken part in the earlier exercises, I couldn't take part in that one, because they would know me, and then one of the other women took over.)

The meeting would take place in the bar or the lounge, followed by an intimate dinner tête-à-tête. It was our job to get them to talk – to betray themselves, in fact.

The Brits didn't talk much. Foreigners sometimes did, especially young ones. Oh, I understood. They were lonely. They were far from their homes and their families. They didn't even know if they would *have* a home, or even a country, to go back to once the war was over. And it was flattering to have a young girl hanging on their every word. Before they were returned to London at the end of their month in Beaulieu – and it was in London, in their country section, that their fate would be decided – each one had an interview with our commandant, Colonel Woolrych. (We called him Woolly Bags behind his back.) He had all the reports from the different training schools, and he made his final report that went back to London and carried a lot of weight.

Now, if they had talked, during the interview a door would open and I, or another decoy, would walk in.

Woolly Bags would say, "Do you know this woman?" And they would realise they'd been tricked.

Most of them took it well. But I'll never forget one. He was a Dane – oh, a glorious blond Adonis. I think he was rather taken with me. (At the time I weighed about twelve kilos less, and I didn't have white hair.)

When I entered the room, he looked at me with surprise, and then almost pain.

Finally, blind fury overtook him. He half rose in his chair and said, "You bitch!"

Well, no woman likes being called a bitch.

But as Woolly Bags said to me afterwards, "If he can't resist talking to a pretty face over here, he's not going to resist when he's over there. And it won't only be his life that is in danger, it will be many others."

I think it was then that I realised my whole life was a lie. I lied to everybody. I had to. To those agents. To my friends. To my family.

My mother thought I worked for the Ministry of Agriculture and Fisheries. She died at eighty without ever knowing the truth, because all of us at the secret army were under the Official Secrets Act for sixty years, until those files were opened in the year 2000. And by then most of us were dead.

On the eve of my nineteenth birthday, I fell madly, hopelessly in love with an agent. He was one of our best agents. A crack. He'd just returned from a very successful second mission, and he was adulated. He was a legend in the section. I'd heard all about him, but I never thought I'd meet him. Then, suddenly one evening, he was there. Our eyes locked across a crowded room. And it was as if a magnet drew us irresistibly towards each other.

I couldn't believe that he could love me. He was handsome. He was twelve years older than I. He was a hero.

He must have met many beautiful, sophisticated, elegant, gorgeous women. (Oh, he had – he told me. But he said he'd been looking for me.) Our idyll lasted three months, until he left on his next mission.

I was terrified. It was a very dangerous mission. They said only he could carry it off. I was so afraid. But he reassured me. He said he was a survivor. And he promised me that this would be his last mission, and when he came back, he'd never leave me again. We'd grow old together.

The day he left, we had lunch, just the two of us, in a little intimate restaurant. We both knew that it would be many months perhaps before we'd be together again.

We kept emotion out of our conversation. I think we were both afraid of breaking down. I know if we hadn't, I would have broken down, and I'd have begged him not to go.

I imagine you've all been in love. Can you picture what it's like to be terribly in love, and know that all you have is a few hours, this moment in time?

He took me back to the office, and we said good-bye at the bus stop. I don't think we even said "good-bye."

As I walked through the door, I turned. He was standing on the pavement, watching me. He smiled and raised his hand to his red parachutist beret. A final salute.

He was infiltrated that night.

I never saw him again.

The mission was successful, but he didn't return. And I was left with a little cameo of a perfect love. Perfect, perhaps, because it had been so brief.

When the news that I'd dreaded came through, they tried to comfort me. They told me I should be proud. He was incredibly courageous – a wonderful man, who realised that there was a force of evil in the world that had to be annihilated, but that freedom has a price tag. He paid that price with his life.

But I didn't want a dead hero. I didn't want a medal in a velvet box. I wanted Bill.

All those agents in the secret army were volunteers. They didn't have to go. But they went. Almost half of them never returned. Like Bill, they gave their youth, their joie de vivre, their hopes and dreams for the future.

They gave their all, for us. They gave their today, so that we might have our tomorrow.

NOREEN RIOLS was born in Malta of English parents. After the war she joined the BBC, where she met her husband, a French journalist with the BBC World Service. She is the author of eleven books, has written for numerous newspapers and magazines, and broadcasts often. She was awarded the Médaille des Volontaires de la Résistance, and in 2014 was awarded a Chevalier de la Légion d'Honneur, France's highest honour. Her most recent books are her memoir, *The Secret Ministry of Ag. & Fish: My Life in Churchill's School for Spies* (2014), and the novel *Autumn Sonata* (2014). She lives in a village near Versailles.

THIS STORY WAS TOLD ON AUGUST 28, 2014, AT **THE UNION CHAPEL, LONDON**. THE THEME OF THE EVENING WAS *EYEWITNESS*. **DIRECTOR: MEG BOWLES**.

By Every Claim of Love

Amy Biancolli

The Weight of a Ring

It was a few minutes before 10am in late September 2011, when I heard the doorbell ring. I was in the attic, where I sometimes worked on movie reviews. At the time I was working as a film critic.

I had been procrastinating on this one review, so when I heard the door, I was annoyed. But I went downstairs, and went up to the front door, and went up on my tiptoes, and peered through the glass.

As soon as I saw them, I knew. Because we all know from the movies what it means to see two cops at your door. It means that something horrific has happened to someone you love. But I let them in. It was a man and a woman. They were kind, I remember that. I don't remember who said what. They must have asked me my name. I must have told them. They must have asked me if I was married to Chris Ringwald. I must have said yes.

They told me to sit down. And they said that a man had been found at the base of a hospital parking garage a mile from my home.

I said, "Did he jump?"

And they said, "Yes."

"Is he dead?"

"Yes." And in that moment, learning of my husband's suicide, I felt my whole world shear away from me. I felt cleaved in two.

That day I did the toughest thing I've ever had to do. I told our three children. Our oldest was seventeen at the time, and on a gap year in Ecuador. Our younger daughter was a sophomore at Albany High. She was fifteen. And our youngest, our boy, was eleven. He was in sixth grade.

That first night, my kids and I didn't want to be apart. So we lay on the living-room floor in sleeping bags and watched *Battlestar Galactica* (the new one, the really good one, the reboot).

We turned it off after a little bit and tried to sleep. Mainly I just lay there thinking about all that I had lost – my husband of twenty years, who I was with him, our future together. All our dreams, some of them really mundane. We had always talked about becoming old farts together – walking the neighbourhood holding hands – and that was gone, too.

Yet I knew I had to have a future, even though we weren't going to be buying that convertible after our youngest went off to college. I just didn't know what that future would be.

I couldn't curl up into a ball. There had to be a next morning when I would get up, and then a next, and then a next. But what was the next?

The week unfolded the way these weeks do, in a whirl-wind of loving people coming by with casseroles and plates of ziti and meetings with funeral directors. The funeral. The wake.

At one point one of the funeral directors came up to me with a question that caught me off guard. He wanted to know what I wanted done with my husband's wedding ring.

Did I want to take it home, or did I want it cremated and buried with him?

And I said, "Thank you, but I want that ring."

I loved that ring. That ring was me on his hand for two decades. That hand held our vows, and it was a beautiful hand. He was a writer, but he had worked for years before that in carpentry and construction, and he had these big, thickly muscled hands. It was a big ring on a big finger, and it had warped to his finger. And I loved the warp. The warp was our life together.

So I brought it home, and I decided I didn't want to stuff it into a drawer in the dark. Instead, I put it on a chain, and hung the chain on a hook in the back of my bedroom closet door. And that felt right, to have it present. Because he was so present to me. I was so madly in love with him. Right from the beginning, we knew from the first date. Four months after that first date, we got engaged. He didn't have the engagement ring with him when he proposed, but he went down to Manhattan on the train and saw a jeweller named Bobby Satin, of all things. We used to laugh about it. It's like his name was out of the movies: Bobby Satin.

He came back up by train – actually got off in Hudson, and we had dinner there.

And before he gave me the ring, he explained that the central stone was not a diamond. He said there were smaller stones that were diamonds that were flanking the central stone. But he said, "I decided you're not a diamond. You're a ruby, because rubies are rarer."

And that was the start of our life together.

Six months later we were married, and for the whole time I was with him, he was the most extraordinary, charismatic, brilliant, interesting, giant-hearted man. And he was also the sanest – until he wasn't. He left his job, became anxious. The anxiety led to insomnia, which led to worsening anxiety and depression, and it all spiralled away into suicidality. After six months, I lost him.

And having lost him, there I was with these rings on my hand that I didn't know what to do with. I didn't know how long to wear them, because there was nobody to tell me. When you lose your spouse, no one comes up to you and says, "Welcome to widowhood. Here's the guidebook."

There's no guidebook. There's no etiquette. There are no rules. All we have are musty old expectations, clichés based in large part on movies and literature.

We have the idea of the old ladies in black sackcloth dresses, murmuring over their rosary beads and maybe banging themselves on the foreheads with Bibles. And I'm Catholic – I own rosary beads and I own Bibles – but I wasn't doing that.

Instead, I was hauling myself through every day, schlepping my kids, caring for them, writing. Doing my best, laughing with my friends when I was able to, and all the while grieving my husband like crazy.

As I was doing those things, I had these rings on my hand that implied he was alive. And I didn't know how long to wear them.

People would say, "Well, do what feels right."

But I didn't know what felt right. Nothing felt right. How could anything feel right?

I'd found these two online support groups for young widows, and I went on and I checked. And sure enough, there were whole conversations about this. Some widows and widowers said they removed the ring right away, as soon as their spouse died. Some people said they melted them down into a new piece of jewelry. Some said they wore them on a chain around their necks.

And some said, "It's been five years, and I still feel married. I'm still wearing the rings. I'll always feel married."

And I did feel married . . . the first couple of weeks. You just do. But as the weeks turned into months, and the reality of my husband's absence set in, it became more and more painful.

When I say painful, I mean it literally. That's one of the things nobody tells you about widowhood, is that you'll feel a head-to-toe literal body ache. The loss of intimacy, both physical and emotional. The touch deprivation. It all makes you want to lie in bed at night, wanting to be held by the person who's not there.

That hurt.

And what made it hurt even more was the fact that it disagreed with the rings on my hand. The disconnect was too much.

So finally, about four months after my husband died, I took the train down to Manhattan to see a movie. Because periodically studios would make me go down there. Mostly I saw movies up here in Albany, but now and then there'd be a movie that they really didn't wanna screen for me up here. Sometimes it was because the movie wasn't very good.

In this case it was a film called *The Grey*. It was a thriller starring Liam Neeson and a bunch of computer-generated wolves behaving in very non-wolf-like ways. I thought it was pretty silly. Other critics liked it. But in any case, I was down there at this screening, chatting with a colleague.

I don't remember who he was or who he wrote for. But in the course of this professional chitchat, it occurred to me that if he saw the rings on my hand, he would assume that I was married. That I had a living, breathing spouse somewhere. And I did not.

And this was not me worried about dating. That's not what this was about. It was just the pain of knowing that my husband wasn't there and my hand said something different.

So I went home and I talked to the kids. I wanted to make sure it was okay with them. And it was. They totally got it. I went and I bought a very nice gold chain. As I removed the rings from my hand, my hand felt lighter and naked and really weird. And it hurt.

But it was an honest pain. It was a pain I knew I had to learn to live with. And I did. I learned over two years.

Then about three months ago or so, I don't know what impulse made me do this. Just a random impulse. Curiosity. I sat down on my bed with my rings and put them back on my hand. And I held it out. And it was an alien hand. It wasn't my hand any longer.

With those rings on my hand, it looked like a hand from another life and another me. Too much time had passed.

And so I removed the rings, put them back on the chain and hung them on the hook on the back of my bedroom closet door, with my late husband's.

AMY BIANCOLLI is the author of *Figuring Shit Out: Love, Laughter, Suicide, and Survival* (2014), a memoir of life after the death of her husband, writer Christopher D. Ringwald. An arts reporter and columnist for the Albany *Times Union*, she previously served as film critic for the *Houston Chronicle*. She is also the author of *Fritz Kreisler: Love's Sorrow, Love's Joy* (1998) and *House of Holy Fools: A Family Portrait in Six Cracked Parts* (2004). She lives in Albany, has three children, and blogs at **www.figuringshitout.net**

THIS STORY WAS TOLD ON MARCH 22, 2014, AT THE KITTY CARLISLE HART THEATRE AT **THE EGG, ALBANY, NEW YORK**. THE THEME OF THE EVENING WAS *LOST AND FOUND*. **DIRECTOR: MEG BOWLES**.

Omar Musa

<><><><><><><><><><><><><><><><><><><><><><><><><><>

The Hat

My mother moved from New South Wales to Malaysia in the 1970s to work in theatre, and got put in charge of directing the first Malay language version of *Hamlet*. They were auditioning all these different guys for the main role of Hamlet, and no one was quite cutting the mustard until this guy walked through the door. He had long, black hair. He was a bit mysterious. He came from Borneo, the land of headhunters and pirates and orangutans and jungles. And he auditioned for it, and he was perfect, and he went on to become the first Malay Hamlet. He also went on to become my father (which, to me, was a far more auspicious achievement).

He moved to Australia around 1980, so I guess less than 10 years after the White Australia policy properly ended. As I was growing up, I was definitely in between worlds. I was wearing sarongs at home and speaking Malay and praying five times a day and eating food with my hands.

And my father always told me, "You will be an outsider in this country. If you want to get anywhere, you will have to work twice as hard as the white kids. You will have to be fearless and ferocious and fierce."

He also told me, "You should be proud of your culture. You should be proud of being Malay. You should be proud of being Muslim, even if people tell you that you shouldn't be."

And so when I got into my teens, and I was trying to find my feet in this world and in this country, I decided, yes, I'm going to own this. I'm going to *own* being Muslim. And I want to display it in some kind of outward, physical way.

My father had told me that a Muslim man should always wear a hat – it's a very seemly thing for a Muslim man to do. So I decided to go out in Queanbeyan in Canberra, and find my great Muslim hat.

If any of you are from Canberra, you might remember the Community Aid Abroad shop. It was in Civic Interchange, right next to that old takeaway that's still there, selling the same battered savs and chiko rolls. And I went in amongst all the incense and the mats and the wooden carvings and the white do-gooders, and there, shining like a beacon, was the hat rack, and there I saw my great Muslim hat.

It was a majestic thing, made out of this black cloth. It had gold threads through it, and green and red. It was *shining*.

And I decided I would wear this hat. I bought it for $22. I had saved up my ducats from working at Kingley's Chicken in Queanbeyan, across from the Royal Hotel.

I would wear my hat every day, and at school, if my teachers told me to take it off, I would say, "You are being very culturally insensitive."

I would even wear it when I was running track. For a brief period in my life, I harbored this ambition to be an Olympic runner (before genetics and laziness caught up with me.) So I was standing there, about to run the 800 metres at the starting blocks, and I used to train with this really good friend of mine, and I was wearing my hat.

He took one look at it, and he gave me this withering look I'd never seen before, and he said, "Man, I can't stand it, how you wear that hat all the time. Why are you always trying to be so *ethnic*? Why can't you just be like the rest of us? Why can't you just be like a normal Australian?"

I remember, I was running around the track, and I was furious. I was also a bit sad. I was trying to figure out why it was that me just repping my culture, repping my heritage, had offended him so much.

Looking back on it now, I don't think I was exactly repping my heritage, because I think that my great Muslim hat had actually been woven by some indigenous Guatemalan tribespeople. But I was 14 at the time, man! You know, I was trying my hardest.

My father and my mother had told me that there was a rich tradition of performing poetry in the archipelago, and that you perform it with full body – it's not just isolated to a dusty old ivory tower for academics. It's something that lives on the streets and in the villages.

I was looking for all these Muslim role models. I came across Malcolm X and the Black Muslims, and Muhammed Ali, who was the coolest man in the world, and he was a Muslim and a poet.

And on SBS, they played this documentary about the Black Muslims, and I taped it to VHS. (I'm sure some of you remember what that was.) I would watch it every few days, because I loved the oratory, I loved all the speeches.

But there was this 30-second clip right at the end, where these two guys got on stage, and they started speaking a very percussive type of poetry over a heavy drum beat. Now, one of them had a very deep, distinctive baritone voice, something like a preacher. The other one was a little bit more of a wildcard. He had his hat back, and he had sunglasses, gold teeth and a massive clock around his neck. So, of course it was the famous rap group Public Enemy.

I was sitting there just astounded, and I thought to myself, *This is the coolest shit that I have ever seen in my life*. I decided right then and there, that this was the sort of poetry my father was talking about. *This* was the sort of poetry that I would one day make.

The years passed, and then one day I decided that I needed to save up some ducats and go to Malaysia for the first time since I was a child. I'm ashamed to say that when I was there when I was nine, the whole time I was complaining that I wanted to eat some Western food, which stands at odds with me now, because I'm a great laksa and durian hunter these days.

So I went to Borneo, and I saw my grandparents for the first time in years. They were getting very old, and they insisted that we go to this small plot of land that was on the border of Brunei and Malaysian Borneo. These were my grandmother's ancestral lands. Her people had come hundreds and hundreds of years ago from Java, to teach the Sultan of Brunei to cultivate wet rice.

We got dropped off in the middle of the highway, and I'll always remember my grandfather, he was wielding this *parang*, which is the Malay word for a machete, and he was cutting his way through the undergrowth.

Now the machete, in Borneo, is seen as a very dangerous thing, part of headhunting culture or piracy. But at that moment, as I saw him cutting through the undergrowth, forging a lane from the road to this old, dilapidated hut in the middle of the jungle, suddenly in my head I realised that the *parang* can be a very constructive tool. It can be something that forges a path between places that don't usually connect, places that don't usually communicate with each other.

So we get to this hut in the middle of the jungle, and there's a family of orangutans living there, and we have to shoo them out of the house. And my grandparents tell me that when my father spent time at this little piece of land, he would sit in front of the hut and he would read the Koran with his very deep, mellifluous, beautiful voice, and suddenly, dozens of orangutans and families of monkeys would start climbing down from the trees and sit in front of him like a rapt audience, listening to him reading the Koran.

We were dragging water from the river, and it was then that my grandparents were telling me about their lives of hardship and about their family history.

My family history.

And I decided at that moment, I would start going back to Malaysia every year, because it anchored my soul in some way.

And then a few years ago I went to my cousin's wedding on the outskirts of Kuala Lumpur. We all had to dress in this traditional *baju melayu*, which is a traditional Malay Muslim outfit. It's long pyjama pants, very colourful, and a long *baju* with fake diamonds at the chest. And then you wear this kind of sarong that is woven with gold, and you turn it into a thick band of fabric and lift it up over your bellybutton.

Now, I didn't know how to do it, but everyone else could just do it so easily – it came so naturally to them – and it suddenly exposed this rift between me and my family. But they all gathered around me, and they made me suck my big Western belly in, and they tied the sarong perfectly.

Then they said, you need one more thing.

And they gave me a jet black *songkok*, which is the traditional Malay Muslim cap. They perched it jauntily on my head, tipped it to the side, and of course I got some jet black Ray Bans, so that it will look extra boss, you know?

Then we went to the wedding, and we were sitting there, eating our *ayam masak merah*, and the *durians*, and the *rendang*. There was a special display of the ancient form of Malay martial arts, which is called *silat* – so people flipping and rolling around and fighting each other.

But then at a certain point, someone decided to bring out a more modern form of entertainment, which was the karaoke machine. So they bring it out, and all these people start singing these really saccharine love songs. I couldn't understand a word, but I knew exactly what they were talking about.

Then suddenly, my cousin says to me, "Hey, Omar, I want you to get on stage. I want you to do that thing that you do in Australia, that type of poetry, that hip-hop. I want you to perform for us.

Now, I'm shitting myself speaking in front of all of you here at the Sydney Opera House tonight, but I think that *that* was the scariest show that I've ever had to do. It was a family reunion, and I was standing there, bared, completely exposed before my family for the first time, performing something that I loved.

And I said:
I set sail on a river of thoughts, a dreamtime,
Neverland, carry the torch for my fam.
I light it up, stand up proud,
Try to represent my folks the only way I know how.
So I honour them every time I jam on the drums,
To work for my fam in the shanties and slums.
Do it for my people, the ordinary people. . . .

I stood there, and they were cheering and applauding and clapping their hands.

I went and I sat down next to my grandmother, and she looked at me with these piercing eyes, and she said, "You know, I never learned how to read or write."

I said, "I know."

She said, "I've been illiterate my whole life. I was kicked out of my home at the age of nine and tapped rubber and lived on the streets."

I said, "I know."

She said, "But I have 150 poems in my head that I created when I was living out there. A-B, A-B, *pantuns*, the traditional improvised form of Malay poetry. This poetry that you're doing now is like the poetry that I used to help me get through those hard times."

And it was then that I realised I had found my own *parang*, my own machete. My words could cut through worlds, could cut paths through time and even generations.

OMAR MUSA is a Malaysian-Australian author, rapper and poet from Queanbeyan, Australia. A former winner of the Australian Poetry Slam and the Indian Ocean Poetry Slam, he has released four hip hop records, two poetry books, appeared on ABC's Q&A and TEDx at the Sydney Opera House. His debut novel, *Here Come the Dogs* (2014), was long-listed for the International Dublin Literary Award and Miles Franklin Award and he was named one of the *Sydney Morning Herald*'s Young Novelists of the Year in 2015. He is currently working on a new album and a novel that is set in Malaysia and Indonesia.

THIS STORY WAS TOLD ON SEPTEMBER 6 2015 AT FESTIVAL OF DANGEROUS IDEAS AT THE **SYDNEY OPERA HOUSE**, AUSTRALIA. THE THEME OF THE NIGHT WAS *RAZOR'S EDGE*. **DIRECTOR: MAGGIE CINO.**

Bethany Van Delft

Light and Hope

I had a perfect pregnancy. I saw a specialist every week, though, because I was an elderly primigravida, which is a sweet way of saying they felt I was too old to be carrying my first child.

I saw a maternal foetal specialist every week. And every week the doctor and nurses would gather around the ultrasound and look at the baby and say, "What a perfect baby. This is a miracle at your age."

I spent nine months wondering what this was going to be like. What was it going to be like to give birth? What was it going to be like to see this person I had been growing all this time?

Especially – what was that rush of love that new mothers talk about? What was that going to be like? And of course, being a stand-up comedian, I relished the new market that motherhood was going to thrust me into.

But most of all, the thought of leaving the house one day as the two of us and coming back home as a family filled me with wonder.

When the time came, they told us to prepare for a very long labor. But no, I pushed for twenty minutes. And Lucia Esperanza was born at 10:59 p.m. that evening on 10/11/11 (not 11/11/11, the birthday that we hoped for, the perfect birthday), just to let us know that she would do things when she wanted to.

They put her on my chest and I soaked in this little person I'd been carrying around. I saw her little chin and her heart-shaped mouth, her button nose and her folded ears. I saw her almond eyes, and my heart stopped.

I asked my husband, Jayme, "Does she look like she has Down's syndrome?"

Jayme said, "No."

Instead of the rush of love, I felt a wave of fear and anxiety.

They brought me to our recovery room and they took the baby to do some routine tests. Jayme went downstairs to get everyone. It felt like I was alone for hours.

My worry turned to fear, and my fear turned to panic and I finally rang for the nurse, hysterical.

I was like, "Why is it taking so long? Is there something wrong? What is wrong with my baby? Can you bring her back to me?"

She brought back the baby, and I called Jayme, sobbing, and I asked him to please, keep everybody away just for a few more minutes while the nurse helped me calm down.

Then fifteen people came in to meet her, and they said, "How are you feeling?"

I said, "Wonderful." But I was terrified.

The next day the pediatrician came in our room, and he said, "Congratulations! Your baby is perfect."

It was such a relief. I could breathe again.

He said, "Her Apgar score was great."

And her hearing was fine. And she had ten fingers and ten toes – and he suspected that she had Down's syndrome.

He gave us a packet with a number on a Post-it note on top for us to call.

As he was leaving, he said, "You know, now is the time to have these babies, what with all the research. I mean, some of them even read."

We spent our days in the hospital in the room with the door closed, and the shades pulled. At night Jayme slept in the single bed with me, behind me. And he held me really tight. I think he held me so tight so I wouldn't fall out of the bed from crying so hard.

It was confirmed. She had trisomy 21, which is three copies of her twenty-first chromosome instead of two. That first few weeks was just a blur of tears and forms and doctors' appointments and lists I made of all the things that were never going to happen now – all the things that she would never do.

I slept on the couch with her for four months, with her skin on my skin, so she could feel loved. But every time I looked at her, all I thought is, *Where is my baby? Whose baby is this? When do I get to see my baby?*

I had begged Jayme to please let me change her name. Esperanza was my grandmother's name, and Lucia was just a cute reason to call her Lulu. Together it means light and hope. But I didn't call her Lucia. I didn't call her Lulu. I didn't call her anything, because she wasn't my baby.

That made him so, so sad, but he said, "Just give it some time. She's our Lulu. Just give it some time."

Jayme went back to work, and I was a wreck. I was pining for the little family that I thought we'd be, for the home that I thought we'd have. And I hated the place we lived now, filled with all the baby-shower gifts and the strollers and the bassinets and all the stuffed animals. The things that used to make me daydream and smile, but now just wrenched my gut.

I felt guilty when I looked at the shower presents. I felt like somehow we had deceived our friends and family, and that I should return all the gifts and apologise to everyone. I felt deeply, deeply ashamed that I wanted a baby at my age and didn't get the testing.

The tests come with a risk of miscarriage. And I had already had two miscarriages after the age of forty.

I was terrified to have another miscarriage and maybe never have a baby. So Jayme and I told each other that, no matter what, this was our baby, and everything would be fine. But now I knew that, for me at least, that was not true. I lay in bed at night with my stomach in knots, and the broken record playing in my head: *I cannot do this. I am not supposed to be this kind of mother. I am not cut out to be this kind of mother.*

I knew that no matter whose baby we had, she had to be cared for. She had to be raised. It wasn't her fault I felt the way I did. She didn't deserve to suffer for it.

Robot Bethany kicked in.

I went to every conference, every workshop, every lecture about Down's syndrome. I read so many books, and I would go with an armful of my books, filled with neon tabs, to every specialist appointment and I'd ask a hundred questions.

I got every service I could get from early intervention. At three months old, she had a massage therapist.

At night I'd watch YouTube videos of children with Down's syndrome reciting the alphabet, or playing guitar, or driving a car, until I fell asleep.

I learned what sorts of activities could benefit children with Down's syndrome, and I took her to everything. I took her to music classes. I took her to swim classes. I took her to the museum, to play groups, all with typical kids, as if that would make the world see her that way. I joined a mom group.

As a rule I never talked about Down's syndrome, just the things that new moms talk about. But one time I was feeling bold, and I started to talk about the particular concerns that my family had.

One mom said to me, "But why don't you have her with her own kind?"

I thought of Jim Crow, and I thought how separate is never equal. Only equal is equal. And I told that mom, "She is a child. This *is* her own kind."

But I learned to never talk about what I was feeling again. I never talked about how scared and lonely I was. I never talked about how I ached. I never talked about how much I hated Down's syndrome. I never talked about how ashamed I felt about that.

At the time I was still performing. There was a burgeoning market for mom comedy, so I just kept writing about new-mom things, never about what my personal challenges were.

I landed an audition for a mom TV comedy in Los Angeles. I went. The audition was fine. But as I was walking out, I heard the other mom comics having a conversation.

One said, "I mean, you know my kid's a little retarded, right?" They all laughed.

She said, "I mean, you've seen her, right? You have to admit she's a little bit Downsy."

My heart broke into a million pieces, but I didn't put the comics in their place. I made an excuse. I told myself that sometimes comedians say really nasty things (like that time a comedian said to me, "Aren't you too old to be pregnant? Isn't your baby gonna be retarded?").

Back at home my loneliness consumed me, and it turned to anger. At family members who lived a mile away from me, but were never around. At friends who disappeared. I had friends who were there, but acted as if everything was fine. I was angry at anyone who had a typical child, or a typical baby, or anybody who was pregnant and joyful.

My anger turned to despair; I was completely hopeless. Doing the right thing for the baby was my only motivation, and I went from activity to activity like a zombie.

I felt that I couldn't be the mother that she needed me to be and be a good wife to Jayme. I told him that I wished I could move out. But really, I wished I would just die, so they could find someone better.

Then some friends invited us to vacation with them in Key West, with friends of theirs. It was all couples, with no children. I was very worried about being the one to bring the kid to the party, especially our child.

I didn't know what the couples had heard about her. I didn't know what they would think of her. I had no idea what to expect. I walked in the door, and they had a gift for her. They had a little book about vacations.

They all tried to play with her, but she's a little shy. She's afraid of strangers, so she cried. When night came, we put her to bed, and the Jameson came out, and we started telling stories and getting to know each other.

I gravitated to one woman in particular, and over the course of seven days, I told her everything. I told her I was afraid that we could never travel again, and that the baby wouldn't love the beach the way I love the beach.

I told her how I was afraid that I wasn't doing enough for the baby and that I would never be able to do enough for her. And I was afraid that she would never appreciate the things that we *do* do for her and how ashamed I was about that feeling.

She didn't judge me. She didn't say, "Well, at least . . ." or "It could be worse. . . ." She just listened. She did point out that actually we *had* travelled – we were in Key West. And that it was on the beach, and the baby was loving the beach. She said that things were going to be however they were going to be – because of us and in spite of us.

And that was such a relief to hear her say. She lifted a weight off my soul.

On the last day, the baby played with everyone. She threw her beach ball, and they'd catch it, and everyone would cheer. They said this was the best day of the vacation.

I had watched them get to know her, and I watched her through their eyes.

She was hilarious.

She was fun, she was warm, she was smart and she definitely did things when she wanted to. She was our Lulu. Our light, and our hope.

When I returned home, I didn't see the people who weren't there. I saw the people who *were* there, and who wanted to be there.

And when we got to talking, it turns out that none of us knew what to say or how to say it. But now they listened, and they said that they loved our perfect little family.

They thanked us for showing them the way, by just treating her as a child, because that's what she is.

And once I stopped fearing being this kind of mom, I realised that all moms cry a lot. All moms doubt their ability to raise this child. All moms worry about the future.

I used to wish I could go back in time and get that test after all, but now I wish I could go back in time and allow myself to feel the joy that a new mother feels. Because that's what I was.

It's a lot easier to talk about this stuff now. Now if somebody asks me if I was shocked when she was born, I say, "Of course I was shocked. I never expected a daughter of mine to have straight blond hair." (I definitely thought she'd be rocking the Afro puffs.)

We still go to our music classes, and we still go to our play groups and the museums, with typical kids. And we go to places just for kids with Down's syndrome, too.

After our long days filled with fun, we come back to the apartment.

When I put my key in the door, Lulu always says, "Home, Mama."

And I say, "Yes, Lulu. We are home."

BETHANY VAN DELFT's "hip & grounded, laid-back delivery" has earned her the honour of performing at the prestigious *Just for Laughs* festival in Montreal and appearances on Comedy Central, TV Guide Channel and NickMom. A former model, she is a co-creator of the comedy showcase *The Dress Up Show* and has her own monthly show, *Artisanal Comedy.* Unashamedly in touch with her inner nerd, Bethany also enjoys being a panelist on *You're the Expert* and *Literary Death Match.*

THIS STORY WAS TOLD ON APRIL 11, 2014, AT THE **SHUBERT THEATRE, BOSTON**. THE THEME OF THE EVENING WAS *COMING HOME.* **DIRECTOR: SARAH AUSTIN JENNESS.**

Gil Reyes

‹›

Kidneys and Commitments

I'm sure the woman on the other end of the phone identified herself as being from the clinic I'd been to the day before. Maybe she said her name. Maybe she asked if I was sitting down. But I don't remember any of that. In my memory I just pick up the phone, and this voice says, "Go immediately to the emergency room. Your kidneys are failing."

And as I get up and get dressed, there's this voice in the back of my head saying, *This is absurd. I'm in my twenties. I'm invincible. I'm immortal. I don't even need health insurance.*

I don't even have health insurance.

Sure, I'd been feeling bad for a while. But my swollen ankles, those were because I was waiting tables, working double shifts, trying to save up money, not because my body wasn't processing water waste, right?

And those splitting headaches, those were because I was really stressed out, trying to get into grad schools, and not because your kidneys regulate your blood pressure.

When I had finally collapsed a few days before, I didn't have any more excuses. That was when my boyfriend, Sean, made me go to the clinic.

Sean and I had been dating for a year and living together for a few months. It was moving a little bit fast, but either of us could go to grad school at any minute, so it was fine. We had sort of a day-by-day mentality. We were keeping each other just at arm's length.

In fact, I was able to convince him not to go with me to the emergency room. I mean, why should we both sit around all day waiting for some doctors to tell me that that's not what it is? That it's something else – something that can be fixed with a pill?

So I went. Alone. Terrified, but hiding it well. And this trait of mine, this sort of crazy independence, maybe it stems from when I came out to my Southern Baptist mother from Alabama and my Catholic Hispanic dad from Texas, when I was a teenager growing up in Kentucky.

If you're thinking this didn't go well, you're right.

There were Bibles manifesting from nowhere (even though I'd been to church more than they had throughout my life). There was screaming and yelling, and I left that night thinking, *I'm one of the damned.*

Because they told me, "You're going to hell."

We didn't speak for a while – over a year. And when we began to try to put our relationship back together, the damage was pretty done. How close can you get when there's this whole part of your life that somebody wants nothing to do with?

I remember once, out of the blue, my dad, said, "I never want to meet anyone you're seeing. I don't ever want you to bring anybody home."

But as my emergency-room visit became a ten-day stay in the hospital, I had to let a lot of people know where I was.

In fact, that hospital room was where my parents first met Sean. I learned my kidneys were functioning at less than ten percent. I learned that I would probably have to go on dialysis.

If you don't know much about dialysis, it's a way to live. It's not a *great* way to live. It's not pleasant. It's very time-consuming. It's expensive.

No, what you want in this situation is a living donor, a kidney donor. You could get on the national transplant list. That is going to take time, maybe years, waiting with a bag packed by the door.

And cadaver kidneys have other issues; they're not the best choice. If you can get a living donor, though, usually family – somebody who's a perfect match – that's the ideal situation.

Well, my relationship with my parents had left me a little bit wounded. I had trouble trusting people. This is one of the things I was bad at in my twenties. It used to be at the top of the list.

Now the top of the list was kidney function. But the not trusting people was still up there. I had this trouble with accepting help. And if you have trouble accepting help, imagine trying to accept a kidney.

People stepped up to get tested. My dad, despite our differences. My mother wasn't eligible. My best friend, his dad. Friends from college, high school, work.

But there was one more person who really wanted to get tested: Sean.

Talk about a commitment.

He eventually wore me down. He said, "You know, whatever happens, whether or not we're together in the future – if I can do this for you now, I want to."

As the months began to pass, and I did go on dialysis, and my father was disqualified as a donor because of kidney stones, I went on Social Security and food stamps because I was too weak to work.

Friends were disqualified for various reasons.

I wasn't going to be going to grad school. I spent a lot of time thinking about how I was going from twenty to eighty overnight. Comparing blood-pressure medicines with my grandmother. I spent a lot of time alone, sleeping, mostly.

But I remember this one day where I made it out to the park, and I was sitting alone. It was a cool day, a fall day. I was praying, meditating, considering this entire process. And I found this really strange peace that's hard to describe.

I found this kind of acceptance of myself, and where I'd been, and I thought, *You know, it's fine. If this is what it is, if this is it, I'm okay with that. I can die in my twenties.*

I stopped praying to get better, and I thought about the thing that I'd want. If I could pray for one thing, it was to feel worthy of that love that I hadn't felt for so long.

I stopped asking for time, and thought about time *well spent.*

It was December when Sean called me from work and said, "I have an early Christmas present for you."

He was as good a match as my dad.

He said, "Would you let me give you a kidney?"

And I said, "Yes."

And we spent time well. Sean's a big language geek, so we named it: Renée, after the renal system, and Renatus, for rebirth.

We would tell people, "We're having a kidney!"

Our friends convinced us to have a party. We had a kidney shower. (Sean really wanted to register, but I thought that might be going a little far.)

Nevertheless, people brought us gifts: pyjamas for recovering, and bad movies. (Sean *loves* bad movies.)

And we played games, like "kidney bean bingo" and "pin the kidney on Gil."

We got this big red-velvet sheet cake shaped like a kidney. And we wore medical masks, and we cut it together, and fed each other pieces and took lots of pictures.

The day of the surgery came in May, and they had us both on gurneys, ready to go. We're surrounded by Sean's family and my family.

My parents are there. And my mother starts crying.

We never talk about this, but we cry the same way. We scrunch up our cheeks in the same way, and we hold back those tears. I can see it in her face when she's trying to work something out.

She leans down and takes Sean's hand and says, "Thank you."

I think she's seeing him differently, and maybe she's seeing me differently.

The surgery goes great, and we recovered together for weeks and weeks in a strange little honeymoon.

A year later we get a card in the mail. Now, it's not unusual for my mother to send cards. (She sends cards for the strangest occasions, even though they live fifteen minutes away.)

But this one was addressed to Sean. It said what a blessing he is. And it recognised our anniversary. They asked us to go to dinner with them, like couples do with their parents.

And I never asked for any proof, because you're supposed to rely on faith, but I have a family where I have parents and a partner – a perfect match – where before I had a boyfriend.

And a ten-inch scar across my abdomen to remind me every day that I am loved.

GIL REYES is a director of live theatre, so mostly tells other people's stories from behind the scenes. He is a co-founder and co–artistic director of Theatre [502], a member of the Fairness Campaign's Leadership Council and a Kentucky Colonel. Post–kidney transplant, his life path took him from Capitol Hill to championing education-focused nonprofits. Gil, Sean and their dog, Herman, share a shotgun home in Louisville, Kentucky.

....

THIS STORY WAS TOLD ON OCTOBER 28, 2013, AT THE **ZELLERBACH HALL, BERKELEY,** CALIFORNIA. THE THEME OF THE EVENING WAS *THE BIG BANG: THE MOTH AT THE BAY AREA SCIENCE FESTIVAL.* **DIRECTOR: JENIFER HIXSON.**

Cathy Olkin

◇◇◇

On Approach to Pluto

It was the Fourth of July this past summer, and I was really looking forward to a day off. I had been working hard for a long time on NASA's New Horizons mission to Pluto, and there was always something to do. But I was going to take the Fourth of July off. So I slept in, I read a little. I decided to check email.

Never check email on a day off.

There was a message there from the mission operations manager, Alice Bowman. My eye immediately went to it. It said that the spacecraft had gone safe. It called home, which is basically saying, *Help me, I'm broken.*

That's the worst possible thing that can happen. I was like, *How could this have happened? It was gonna be a simple day – a day off.*

I had been working on this project for more than a decade. In 2004 I had relocated my family from California to Boulder, Colourado, to work on this mission.

This was a once-in-a-lifetime opportunity. I'm an astronomer and I had been spending decades looking at Pluto through ground-based telescopes. And it's just this fuzzy dot. There's not much to see – you can't make out any surface details. We kept looking through these ground-based telescopes – even through the Hubble Space Telescope – but it's still just a fuzzy dot, because Pluto is really far away.

So we moved. My husband started telecommuting for his job, and we moved our three-year-old and our five-year-old.

We were here, we were settled.

All we needed to do now is build a spacecraft, test it, launch it and fly it three billion miles to Pluto.

So we did. It worked out. We built a small spacecraft, about the size of a baby grand piano, and we launched it on the largest rocket we could get, an Atlas V. It's about twenty stories tall.

So you've got a *small* spacecraft, a *big* rocket, and what you get is the fastest spacecraft ever launched – it's going at thirty-four thousand miles per hour.

To put that in perspective, when the Apollo astronauts went to the moon, it took over three days. For New Horizons the spacecraft passed the moon in just *nine hours*. We were *flying*. (It's an unmanned spacecraft, so I mean that figuratively – there's no one on it.)

But it will take the spacecraft nine and a half years to go from earth to Pluto, so we've got a lot of time on our hands. We think about what data we're going to collect, how we're going to do it, and we make contingency plans in case something goes wrong. We considered more than two hundred different scenarios. What do we do if this breaks? What do we do if that goes wrong? We had this huge binder full of contingencies.

So I find myself on that Fourth of July. It's just ten days before our closest approach to Pluto.

You see, we can't stop and orbit Pluto. We don't have enough fuel to slow ourselves down, because we're going really fast. So we just have to go right by and take the best images we can as we're flying past.

It's a once-in-a-lifetime opportunity. We have to get it right at this time.

And the spacecraft has just gone safe.

I rush over to the Mission Operation Center and I settle in the situation room. This is a conference room right outside the mission operation center. You can see the operations people through the window, but they like to keep the scientists a little separated so we don't get in the way.

I'm sitting with my colleagues, and, interestingly, I'm starting to feel calm. That sick feeling in the pit of my stomach is relaxing, because I've been working with these people for more than a decade and everyone knows what they need to do. We all know what our responsibilities are and how to make this work. We have three days to get the spacecraft back in working order. By July 7 we have to have it up and ready to start executing those commands, so that when it flies by Pluto, we get the data that we've been waiting more than a decade for.

We start to get information back, but it takes a while.

It takes the signal four and a half hours to travel from earth out to the spacecraft, and then it takes *another* four and a half hours for it to come *back* so we can hear what the spacecraft had to say. So it's like a really slow conversation. Imagine you say "hi" to someone, then you go watch three football games, and you come back and they say "hi" back. That's the kind of data rates we were getting.

We start to find out what went wrong. We had overtaxed the computer on the spacecraft. Remember, this computer is ten years old. (My guess is that none of you use a computer that's ten years old on a daily basis for really important things.)

But we planned for that, because we sent two computers. So we overtaxed the prime computer, but before it crashed, it started up the backup computer and said,

"Call home." So now we're on the backup computer, we kind of know what went wrong, and we've got a big question in front of us: do we try and get back on the prime computer, or do we fly through closest approach on our relatively untested backup computer?

The whole time we've been flying across the solar system, we've never turned on the backup computer. The last time it was on was on the ground when we were testing it a decade ago.

So we make the logical decision to switch back over to the prime computer. But we're worried, because if we really messed it up, it may not start, and we're getting short on time. At this point we've been in the situation room for three days. People are taking naps in the conference room; many orders of pizza are coming in and being eaten.

We don't have a lot of time left. We send up the command to switch back over to the prime computer and then we wait.

I find myself nine hours later back in the situation room looking through the glass window at the operations people, hoping this works.

When I hear mission operations manager Alice Bowman's voice over the intercom say, "We are back on the prime computer," I see people erupting in cheers – everybody was so elated.

I let out this huge sigh of relief. I didn't even realise I had been holding my breath. It was amazing.

We managed to get the spacecraft back in working order, everything was going right and we had four hours to spare. It was outstanding. We started going back through our main sequence and getting data.

It was absolutely stunning, views of Pluto like we had never seen before.

I couldn't believe the beauty and the details that were awaiting us at Pluto. We would have never expected the unusual terrain we've seen. We saw a heart-shaped glacier made out of nitrogen and carbon monoxide ices. At the edge of the glacier there were huge mountains – mountains as tall as the Rocky Mountains – made out of water ice. Pluto has a large moon named Charon, and on that moon there's a deep canyon, deeper than the Grand Canyon.

All these wonders awaited us.

When I had previously looked at Pluto through our ground-based telescopes, they were there; I just couldn't see them. We had accomplished our objective of transforming Pluto from a fuzzy point of light to a complex, rich geologic world.

It was miraculous.

CATHY OLKIN is a planetary scientist at Southwest Research Institute in Boulder, Colourado. Her main topic of research is the outer solar system, specifically planetary atmospheres and surfaces. As a deputy project scientist for NASA's New Horizons mission to Pluto, Cathy has been soaking in all the new information about her favourite planet. After more than nine years and 3 billion miles, the New Horizons spacecraft made it to Pluto and took the first-ever close-up pictures of Pluto and its moons.

THIS STORY WAS TOLD ON SEPTEMBER 21, 2015, AT THE **BOULDER THEATER, BOULDER**, COLOURADO. THE THEME OF THE EVENING WAS *HIGH ANXIETY*. DIRECTOR: MEG BOWLES.

Taylor Negron

<><><><><><><><><><><><><><><><><><><><><><><><><><><><>

California Gothic

I was born in Los Angeles, in a house in a canyon.
It was resting in a stand of palm trees that cast thin,
unmoving shadows ... like prison bars. It was very
California Gothic. *I* am very California Gothic.

I am the child of those people that you would see in
ads for cigarettes in the back of *Life* magazine – those
handsome people who were always wearing terry-cloth
robes and penny loafers, smoking cigarettes, and looking
like they just heard the funniest joke of their life. The
Virginia Slims woman married the Marlboro Man and
had me.

It's very California Gothic to have your best friend's
mother, who is a movie star, keep her Oscar in her kitchen,
next to the salt and the cumin and the Coumadin.

It's very California Gothic to see Joan Didion crying
in her green Jaguar at a stoplight on Moorpark ... below
Ventura.

It's also very California Gothic to have a cousin who is
a rock star. My cousin is Chuck Negron, the lead singer
of the group Three Dog Night. And he bears a startling
resemblance to Charles Manson.

Now, when you were a kid like me in 1970, growing
up in Los Angeles, you knew that you shared the city
with Charles Manson and his family, because that grizzly,
murderous night of mayhem and helter-skelter was all

anybody could talk about. And for those of you who are too young to know what helter-skelter is, it was kind of like twerking . . . but with blood.

It was really scary. And really horrifying.

And my parents were always going out on the town; they were never at home. They were always getting dressed up and leaving, like in *Mad Men*. I'd be home alone.

One night they went out the door.

My father stopped – and he said, "I want you to close every door and window in this house, because I don't want these hippies to come in here and degut you."

That was an option in my childhood. To be degutted. And it left a tremendous psychic scar on my soul about the world being very scary and horrible. That I needed *protection*.

I'm still very disturbed by hippies and longhairs and headbands, and large candles, and beads, and bandannas. I just don't like any of it.

I was twelve years old at the time. I was a tween. I was a changeling . . . because I was changing. Into a man. But childhood is a place where your fears are disproportionate. My fears were *so huge*.

But so were my goals. And . . . and that's where the magic can happen, in these goals.

Now, my goal – my particular goal in my childhood – was to own a gorilla or ape. Anything from the monkey family that I could just, you know, play hide-and-go-seek with. Shoot dice. Swimming. Light ironing.

My parents were from New York, from the Bronx. They didn't have any connection to animals.

And they were like, "You're *never* going to get a monkey. You will never have an ape in this house. So get over it."

But something really magical had happened that Christmas of 1970. My Uncle Ishmael – that's his real name – was a trucker, and he owned his own flatbed truck. This meant that he could go around and get stuff that fell off of *other people's* trucks. He would arrive at our house one day in that flatbed truck, and it would be full of boxes of Roma tomatoes. Then, the following day, there'd be stacks of Eve and Lemon Twist cigarettes.

Well, one day he was closing down this raggedy-ass Circus Vargas in the parking lot of the Hollywood Bowl on Highland, and he discovered a monkey that had been left behind.

A live monkey. Named Carroll. Two *r*'s, two *l*'s. And we knew that because it was written on the cage. *A free cage.*

And that's what clinched the deal. Because my parents were like, "Well, if it's free . . . how bad could it be?"

Carroll arrived on that flatbed truck, in his cage, surrounded by boxes of grapefruit. I was so excited. When I looked into that monkey's round eyes, I knew that he would understand everything that I had to say and think. And that I would experience unconditional love.

Well, the monkey promptly squatted, shat into its hand, and then threw it into my face . . . underpaw.

And from the shadow I heard the ice clink in my mom's drink. And she said, "Well, it's your monkey."

And it *was* my monkey. I loved my monkey so much, and I stuck with my monkey when everybody turned against him. Sometimes they even put a sheet over his cage. I stuck with him when he willfully and intentionally fucked my grandmother's mink hat, missionary style. (I took the blame.) I never gave up on that monkey. Because Carroll was my most treasured early Christmas present.

But he was not our only unexpected gift that holiday season. That Christmas, in 1970, the Santa Ana winds blew too hard against the glass in cold, frightening Los Angeles.

I fell asleep on Christmas Eve, and when I awoke, I looked out the upstairs window at the driveway and saw a van pull up in front of the house and turn off the lights and just stop. Nothing happened, for thirty minutes. It just sat there.

I realised, *This is it. This is my nightmare, it's going to come true.*

And I thought to myself, *Well, I'm twelve. At least I made it to twelve.*

Then eventually the doors opened up, and this big plume of smoke came out. And these hippies staggered out on wobbly feet and started slinking up to the front of the house – Charles Manson and the family. I felt vulnerable lying there in my Charlie Brown sleeping T-shirt. And I waited for the physical and emotional attack to begin.

There was a knock on the door and I heard my mother's voice, muffled.

I knew she was dead, throat cut. I'd read the papers.

But then I heard her say, "Grilled cheese sandwiches for everyone!" And I'm thinking, *Why is my mother offering protein to serial killers?*

Then my father bursts in the door, and he says, "Your cousin Chuck is here. Come down."

I timidly follow my father down the stairs. I see what appears to be Mama Cass Elliot, Jim Morrison and assorted longhairs devouring Christmas cookies.

My cousin stood by the record player, shyly holding a new Three Dog Night album. He told us he was going to play a song none of us had heard before. Side A, Song 1:

"Jeremiah was a bullfrog. Was a good friend of mine.
I never understood a single word he said, but I
helped him a-drink-a his wine."

And on that cold, windy night, everyone stood up and started to dance. My father grabbed my mother, and they started dancing. I looked over and Jim Morrison – *the* Jim Morrison – was dancing the jitterbug with my grandmother on the coffee table.

It was so extraordinary. It was magnificent. The hippies and the longhairs were all singing along to choruses of:

"Joy to the world, all the boys and girls now."

And then the song was over, and someone picked up the needle and put it back at the beginning. And the song continued, and the dancing continued. And there's something emblematic about certain California Christmas memories, and here is one that was *transcendent.* Rock and roll.

And this is what made my monkey legendary.

Carroll came hurtling down the stairs. He'd escaped his cage. He went right up to the stereo and started dancing. Had we forgotten? Carroll was a *circus monkey.* And this was his cue:

"You know I love the ladies."

His arms outstretched like rubber bands. And he started picking off ornaments from the Christmas tree.

"Love to have my fun."

And the monkey started to juggle.

"I'm a high night rider and a rainbow flyer, a straight-shooting son of a gun. I said a straight, shoot – "

And if you could have seen the expression on those stoned-out (on, we found out later, LSD) hippies, as Carroll, *my* monkey, rightfully claimed the spotlight. *Glee* is a very good word to use. That's what it was – pure happiness and glee.

Because I was twelve years old, and I was alive. I had escaped Manson's knife. And I had a monkey with talent. And as everybody danced and laughed and ate cookies, I looked at my family, and all of their crimes, past, present, and future, seemed to just spill out and dissolve into the contours of the blue shag rug.

And as Carroll balanced an ashtray on his nose, it was as though I was looking into my own future. Because I saw all the glorious things that could happen with music and with joy.

That Christmas, the last one that I was ever a child, I learned a very important lesson:

No matter how horrible your day is, and no matter how scary your night is, everything can turn on a dime.

When there's a knock on the door.

And music,

and joy,

arrive.

TAYLOR NEGRON was a veteran stand-up comedian, actor and writer. He starred in his own HBO special and appeared on *The Tonight Show*, in films such as *Stuart Little*, *The Last Boy Scout*, *Fast Times at Ridgemont High*, *The Aristocrats* and *Punchline*, and on *Curb Your Enthusiasm* and *The Wizards of Waverly Place*. He performed regularly across the United States and was a founding member of the UnCabaret. Taylor was diagnosed with liver cancer in 2008, and on January 10, 2015, just a few months after he told this story, he died at the age of fifty-seven at his Los Angeles home, surrounded by family. We miss him very much.

THIS STORY WAS TOLD ON MAY 28, 2014, AT THE **WHARTON CENTER FOR THE PERFORMING ARTS, EAST LANSING**, MICHIGAN. THE THEME OF THE EVENING WAS *TWIST OF FATE*. **DIRECTOR: JENIFER HIXSON.**

Hector Black

Forgiveness

My story begins in the late sixties, when my wife and me and our three little girls moved to Atlanta because we wanted to be a part of the civil-rights movement. It seemed like the most promising thing happening in our country.

We found a job working with the Quakers in a very poor neighbourhood. A lot of kids used to come over to our house and play, and one of them was named Patricia. She was eight years old. Looked like her hair hadn't been braided in ages – just terrible. Impetigo sores down her legs.

She told me she never knew when she went home from school whether she would have an apartment to live in or not, because her mother was an alcoholic and sometimes drank up the rent money. Often they had no place to sleep. Patricia started spending the night with us whenever her mother lost their apartment.

She was one year older than our oldest girl and she became very much a part of our family. When we moved away after two and a half years, she asked if she could come with us, and we were happy to have her. We moved to rural Georgia, and she lived there with us and blossomed.

She grew into this beautiful young woman. She had a great sense of beauty and art and colour. She made her

high-school-graduation dress. Painted a mural on the high-school wall. She went on and graduated with highest honours from Fisk University in art. She went back to Atlanta and earned her master's degree in library science and worked in the public library, with children who were often unloved and uncared for, such as she had been.

She bought a house in a changing neighbourhood. One night in November, she came home late from work. A crack addict who was stealing for his habit saw no light on in her house and went around the back. He broke in the window, stole some things, and took them to the local crack house. Got his first hit of crack.

Later he was walking around the neighbourhood, and there was still no light on, so he entered the house again. He was a heavy user and wanted another dose of crack, so he took a whole bunch of things.

Trish came home while he was gathering them up.

He hid in a closet. She opened the closet door and fell backwards. He tied her hands behind her back. I learned later that they had a conversation, which sounded exactly like Patricia.

She told him to get help with his drug habit. She told him where there was food in the refrigerator. He told her to put burglar bars on the back of the house and always leave a light on.

He asked about the sewing dummies that were in the house. And she told him that a woman named Susie – my wife – had taught her how to sew, and she made bridal gowns as a sideline income.

He got a lot of stuff, and then went back out onto the streets and got a massive hit of crack. Coming by the house again, he thought she would be free by now. But the lights were still out. So he went in again.

He asked for sex.

She said, "You'll have to kill me first." And so he strangled her and violated her body.

When we learned about this, it was the darkest thing that had ever happened to our family. We'd known death. But not like this, at the hand of another human being. Not this . . . brutality. We were all devastated.

I'm a Quaker. I don't believe in violence.

And I yelled out, "I'll kill the bastard!"

I was furious at what he had done to our child. I wanted him to hurt.

It's very beautiful where we live in Tennessee, along a state scenic wild river. I'd go walking, and these visions of what had happened to Trish would come crashing in on me. I couldn't control them.

They would come and haunt me, no matter where I was or how beautiful it was around me. It was like he had control over me and was pushing my head in the mud.

As I said, I'm a Quaker, and part of what's important to us is that we find God in every human being. And I knew I had to find that in this man.

My first instinct had been that he was a monster. He was no human being. He deserved no compassion from me. Then I wanted to know what had happened to him that made it possible for him to do such a deed.

Little by little I learned a bit about his life.

His name was Ivan Simpson. He was born in a mental hospital. When he was eleven years old, his mother took him and his younger brother and little sister to a swimming pool, and declared that God was asking her to drown them because they were enemies of God.

He and his little brother escaped, and he stood there while she drowned his little sister in front of him. He said he felt relief that his sister was not going to be tormented any longer.

I couldn't help thinking that here we are, the richest country the world has ever known – the most powerful. And there was no one for this little boy. What would I be like if the woman who brought me into the world had tried to destroy me? It wasn't that I was trying to excuse what he had done. But I felt for him . . . as another human being, suffering.

There was a hearing in Atlanta. The final hearing in his case. I had written to the judge earlier, and told the judge how much we loved Patricia, and how much a part of our life she was. My youngest girl couldn't remember life without Patricia.

At the hearing they read all the charges against him. And I just sat with my wife, Susie, and held her hand and cried. I was thankful I was deaf, and that I couldn't hear a lot of what they said. Susie noticed that we had a lot of friends in the courtroom, and there was nobody for him . . . no one.

After he was sentenced to life without possibility of parole, those of us who knew Trish were given an opportunity to say how the crime had affected us.

Her cousin got up and said, "I hate you, Ivan Simpson. I hate you because you took my beloved cousin away from me. I hate you because you'll see the dawn, and she'll never see the dawn again. And I hate you because my taxes are going to feed you." She was weeping.

And then it was my turn. I'd printed out a statement, because I didn't know how steady I would be.

I said how much we loved her. That she was not our daughter by any claim of birth, but she was our daughter by every claim of love.

How sometimes when you do what you think is a kind thing, like taking in a needy child, you can pat yourself on the back. But how we received far more than we ever gave. She was God's gift to our family. I described how she's buried on our farm, and when our family got together to try to think of what to put on her tombstone, we found this saying: "All the darkness in the world cannot extinguish the light of a single candle." I said to the judge, "Love is that candle. Love does not seek another death. Love brings life and healing and wholeness."

At the very end I said, "I don't hate *you*, Ivan Simpson, but I hate with all my soul what you did to my daughter."

And then, it was almost as if two hands were on my shoulders, and I turned around and faced him when I said my last words.

I said I wished "for all of us who had been so wounded by this crime, I wish that we might find God's peace. And I wish this for you also, Ivan Simpson."

And our eyes met for the first time. The tears were streaming down his cheeks. I'll never forget the look – like a soul in hell.

He was being led off, and he was sentenced to life without possibility of parole, so he knew he was going to die in jail. He asked to come to the microphone.

Twice, with the tears streaming down his cheeks, he said, "I'm so sorry for the pain I have caused. I'm so sorry for the pain I've caused."

There was a woman sitting next to us, whose job was to help people through these painful moments. She turned to me and said, "There's something we rarely see: true remorse."

That night I couldn't sleep. I kept thinking about what had happened in the courtroom. I could have just said, "You murdered my daughter ... and you're sorry? Big deal."

But I couldn't. He was a man off the street. He had nothing. But he'd given me the only thing he had. He had nothing but his apology. With those words he'd asked me to forgive him.

And he could have walked out of that courtroom and said, "To hell with all of you. My life is over."

But he didn't.

I knew then that I had forgiven him. And I felt a peace that I hadn't had in a long time. I felt a great burden lifted from me.

I wrote him a letter. He wrote back. One of the things he said was that he missed God's touch. Ever since he had killed Patricia, he felt as though God had abandoned him. But he said he felt he heard God's voice by way of compassion in what I'd said in the courtroom.

We sent him a Christmas package. And I thought, *My God, what are you doing? What are you doing, sending a Christmas present to the man who murdered your daughter?*

But I knew I had to do it. Because I think when you forgive someone, you start to care about them. And I knew he had no one. No one in the world.

We had a small group of people in Cookeville, Tennessee, where we live. We thought we'd maybe get together with other people who had lost loved ones to violence like this.

I remember one woman whose brother had been killed fifteen years before, coming and telling her story. Her brother was a doctor. He was killed by a man off the streets – to her, a nobody. And she was as angry as if it had happened the day before.

And I knew that was no way to live. That was not life. A friend of mine told me that when you hate, you take poison and you expect the other person to die. And I think that's true. Revenge and anger hold you in the past; forgiveness can free you to go into the future.

My wife and I went to south Georgia to visit Ivan in prison. It took a long time to arrange it. But we felt it was, again, something we needed to do.

So we sat down together and talked for two and a half hours. It was just extraordinary. Because I'm very deaf, I was sitting very close to him. He was unshackled.

When it got time for us to leave, he stood up, and I did, too. And it seemed the most natural thing in the world that we had our arms around one another.

It was an unbelievable moment, that I could have my arms around the man who murdered my daughter.

I think forgiveness is possible, even for the worst among us.

And I do believe we all need forgiveness, God knows.

HECTOR BLACK was born in Brooklyn and grew up in Queens. He served in the US army during World War II and graduated from Harvard in 1949. He worked in an interdenominational ministry in New Haven for a year, lived in a communal Christian community for eleven years and later moved to an impoverished Atlanta neighbourhood to work with Quakers. He founded Hidden Springs Nursery in rural Georgia and later moved the business to Tennessee, where he still lives with his family.

THIS STORY WAS TOLD ON APRIL 16, 2013, AT **THE PLAYERS, NEW YORK CITY**. THE THEME OF THE EVENING WAS *COMMITTED: STORIES FROM THE INSIDE*. **DIRECTOR: CATHERINE BURNS**.

Afterword

Afterword

Catherine Burns

Artistic Director THE MOTH

I first started hearing about the Moth in the late 1990s.
Word came that a gentleman named George Dawes
Green and his friends were fluttering about New York
City, telling stories onstage in front of packed crowds.
It was described to me as a moveable feast – a floating
nightclub of sorts – devoted to first-person storytelling.
The shows took place in bars and restaurants, museums,
parks, speakeasies. It was a completely different group of
storytellers every time, with legends like George Plimp-
ton, Mira Nair, Vernon Reid, Andre Gregory and Candace
Bushnell sharing the stage with firefighters and accoun-
tants, dog walkers and trapeze artists.

George always had a keen ear for fabulous raconteurs,
and the charm to get them to sign up to be on stage. He
surrounded himself with friends and collaborators who
knew how to make things happen. Soon a community of
talented curators, producers and directors sprang up.

It's hard to overstate how low-tech it all was. If you
were lucky enough to manage to get on their mailing list,
you'd receive a gorgeously designed (but inexpensively
produced) postcard in the mail, often just days before the
event. There were no advance sales, so you had to show
up early, stand in a massive line and claw your way in. It

was always worth it. (This was your only chance to hear the stories – there was no podcast to download afterward.)

The first Moth I attended in person took place on the deck of an old boat parked on the Hudson River. I was mesmerised. What a thrill to hear a story directly from the person who lived it. The tellers were so vulnerable and funny and brave. They spoke without notes in front of a single microphone on a stand, simply lit by a spotlight.

I had never seen anything like it. It was the complete opposite of the film world that I'd been a part of for a decade, where even on an "indie" film the stories would unfold on sets surrounded by dozens of crew. Maybe I wasn't the only one who was worn out by stories that could only be told with the help of thousands.

George and his merry band of friends and collaborators were pushing for just the opposite, and in doing so brought on what can only be described as a modern storytelling movement, where "dinner party stories" were moved to the stage and recognised as art. This renaissance has inspired tens of thousands of shows worldwide in places as diverse as Tajikistan, Antarctica and Alabama. And The Moth itself has flown abroad, with regular monthly shows now taking place in London, Dublin, Sydney and Melbourne. We're thrilled that stories from those evenings can be read in the pages of this, our second, book.

We go to print on the cusp of our twentieth anniversary. The stories in this book were all originally told live at Moth events around the world, then transcribed and lightly edited for the page. Each story was crafted with the help of one of the Moth's directors (many of whom have been with the Moth since nearly day one, starting out as volunteer story coaches and curators when there was no budget to pay them). The title of the book, *All These Wonders,* comes from Cathy Olkin's story, which puts us in the room at the moment she and her fellow NASA scientists first gazed at the surface of Pluto, a huge payoff that had, as is often the case, come only with great risk. And while most of us aren't rocket scientists, we all have moments in life when we are forced off the map. Sometimes it's by choice, metaphorically stepping into uncharted waters ("Here Be Dragons" as the sixteenth-century globes claimed). Other times we get shoved there against our will by another person or by the Fates. But the stories in this book show us that when we dare to face the unknown, we usually discover that we have more grit and tenacity than we thought. And we often land in a place that we couldn't even have imagined when we started out.

The number-one quality of all great storytellers is their willingness to be vulnerable, to tell on themselves in front of thousands. Each story told is a gift to the listeners.

But the audience brings a gift of its own. We live in a world where bearing witness to a stranger's unfiltered story is itself an act of compassion. It takes courage to listen with an open heart and an open mind and try to understand what it's like to be them – why they think like that, dress like that, made the choices they did.

Some of the stories are lighthearted and fun, but others are more challenging – a boy soldier trying to recover what's left of his childhood, a humanitarian worker deciding who will live and who will die in a refugee camp, the Holocaust seen through the eyes of a nine-year-old. But we look away at our own peril. For what wonders await us when we don't turn away. Sometimes it is easier to try to make sense of the world one story at a time.

And when we dare to listen, we remember that there is no "other," there is only us, and what we have in common will always be greater than what separates us.

About the editor

CATHERINE BURNS is The Moth's long-time Artistic Director. She is a frequent host and producer of the Peabody Award-winning The Moth Radio Hour, and the editor of both Moth story collections. As one of the lead directors on the Moth's MainStage for more than a decade, she has helped hundreds of people craft their stories. She is the director of Edgar Oliver's solo show *Helen & Edgar*, as well as Adam Gopnik's *The Gates*. Born and raised in Alabama, she now lives in Brooklyn with her husband and six-year-old son.

About Lemn Sissay

LEMN SISSAY MBE – who introduces this volume of The Moth – is the author of several books of poetry, as well as articles, records, public art and plays. He is the current Chancellor of the University of Manchester and was an official poet for the London Olympics. His Landmark Poems are installed throughout Manchester and London, in venues such as The Royal Festival Hall and The Olympic Park. Sissay is associate artist at Southbank Centre, patron of The Letterbox Club and The Reader Organisation, inaugural trustee of World Book Night, and a regular contributor to the BBC. His new book, *Gold From the Stone*, will be published in August 2016.

About THE MOTH | www.moth.org

THE MOTH is an acclaimed not-for-profit organisation dedicated to the art and craft of storytelling, and a recipient of a 2012 John D. and Catherine T. MacArthur Foundation MacArthur Award for Creative & Effective Institutions (MACEI). It was founded in 1997 by the novelist George Dawes Green, who wanted to re-create the feeling of sultry summer evenings in his native Georgia, when moths were attracted to the light on the porch where he and his friends would gather to spin spellbinding tales.

EACH SHOW features simple, old-fashioned storytelling on thoroughly modern themes by wildly divergent raconteurs who develop and shape their stories with The Moth's directors. Through its ongoing programs – The Moth Mainstage, which tours internationally; The Moth StorySLAM program, which conducts open-mic storytelling competitions in twenty-two US cities plus London, Dublin, Melbourne and Sydney; The Moth Community Program, which brings storytelling workshops free of charge to underserved populations; The Moth High School StorySLAMs, which brings the thrill of competitive storytelling to high schools across the country; and The Moth Corporate Program, which offers industry-specific storytelling solutions – The Moth has presented more than twenty thousand stories, told live and without notes, to standing-room-only crowds worldwide.

THE MOTH PODCAST is downloaded over 44 million times a year, and the Peabody Award-winning **THE MOTH RADIO HOUR**, produced by Jay Allison and presented by PRX, The Public Radio Exchange, airs in special runs on the BBC, and weekly on both The Australian Broadcasting Corporation, "ABC RN"; and over four hundred and fifty radio stations in the US. The first Moth book, *The Moth: 50 True Stories* is an international bestseller.

Thanks

THE MOTH would like to thank:

Our founder, George Dawes Green. Our Board of Directors: Serena Altschul, Lawrence C. Burstein, Deborah Dugan, Joan D. Firestone, Alice Gottesman, Eric Green, Ari Handel, Tony Hendra, Courtney Holt, Anne Maffei, Dr Alan Manevitz, Joanne Ramos, Melanie Shorin and Roger Skelton.

Everyone who has ever worked, interned, or volunteered at The Moth and helped us achieve our goals, particularly our talented and tireless staff: Catherine Burns, Sarah Haberman, Sarah Austin Jenness, Jenifer Hixson, Meg Bowles, Maggie Cino, Kate Tellers, Jennifer Birmingham, Inga Glodowski, Anna Katrina Olujimi, Micaela Blei, David Mutton, Sarah Jane Johnson, Kirsty Bennett, Larry Rosen, Catherine McCarthy, Jenelle Pifer, Michael La Guerra, Jemma Rose Brown, Michelle Jalowski, Sam Hacker, Nadine Tadros, Timothy Lou Ly, Chloe Salmon, Jodi Powell, Anna Martin, Lauren Fiorelli, Betsy Perez, Bonnie Levison, Casey Donahue, Miles Smith and Suzette Burton.

The Moth StorySLAM community, where each week, hundreds of five-minute true stories are shared around the world. Many of the stories in this book are from people we first met at The Moth StorySLAMs.

Our talented musicians who light up the stage with their sound. And our incomparable Moth hosts, who bring their nimble wit, emotional intelligence and fiery energy to audiences night after night in twenty-six cities across the globe – you are our ultimate ambassadors.

Our collaborators, friends and partners in crime: Jay Allison, John Barth, Meryl Weinsaft Cooper, Adam Gopnik, Joanne Heyman, Kerri Hoffman, Matthew Inman, Dan Kennedy, Viki Merrick, Paul Ruest, Jake Shapiro and Kathleen Unwin.

The BBC, the Australian Broadcasting Company and the hundreds of public radio stations around the United States who air The Moth Radio Hour; all of our national partners for both the MainStage and StorySLAM series; and all of our regional StorySLAM crews for their tireless dedication.

Our overseas crews, who have been our eyes and ears on the ground in their countries, helping us avoid stepping on a lot of toes and acting like clumsy "Yanks" as we we spread our Moth wings across the oceans. In London: musician Cathy Fox and the team at the Union Chapel, Islington, as well as producers Ben DeVere, Christine Andres, Anna Lumsden, Polly Scates, Clare Wadlow and our hosts Charlie Partridge, Sara Barron and Robin Clyfan. In Dublin: Julien Clancy and Colm O'Regan. In Melbourne: Merrilee Mccoy and Cal Wilson; and in Sydney: Alli Sebastian Wolf and Andy Leonard.

Our gifted agent, Daniel Greenberg, and his colleagues Elizabeth Fisher and Caspian Dennis.

The entire team at Serpent's Tail (Thank you for truly being our partners in the UK – we could not be more thrilled to be a part of the Profile family): Andrew Franklin, Hannah Westland, Hannah Ross, Sarah Ward, Drew Jerrison and most especially our extraordinary editor, Mark Ellingham, who has patiently held our hand and smartly guided us as we figured out together how to make The Moth fly in Britain and Australia, both on and off the page.

Storyteller photo credits

Adam Mansbach – *Jessica Taves*; Amy Biancolli – *Allen Onderchain*; Arthur Bradford – *Eli Dagostino*; Auburn Sandstrom – *Sean Carter*; Bethany Van Delft – *Dare Kumolu-Johnson*; Bill Simon – *Mark Arrigo*; Bliss Broyard – *unknown*; Carl Pilliteri – *Jason Falchook*; Catherine Burns – *Aly Nicklas*; Catherine Cross – *Mark Arrigo*; Cathy Olkin – *Jason Falchook*; Chenjerai Kumanyika – *Allison Evans*; Christian Garland – *Jason Falchook*; Christof Koch – *Jason Falchook*; Cole Kazdin – *Sandra L. Dyas*; Dan Ilic – *Victoria Baldwin*; Dori Samadzai Bonner – *Jessica Taves*; George Dawes Green – *Jason Falchook*; Gil Reyes – *Noriko Shiota Slusser*; Hasan Minhaj – *Christian Leonard*; Hector Black – *Sarah Stacke*; Ishmael Beah – *Sarah Stacke*; Jessi Klein – *Jason Falchook*; John Turturro – *Jason Falchook*; Josh Broder – *Jason Falchook*; Joshua Bond – *Allison Evans*; Jung Chang – *Mark Arrigo*; Karen Gearon – *Erin Hermosa*; Kate Braestrup – *Brewster Burns*; Kate Tellers – *Jason Falchook*; Lemn Sissay – *Mark Arrigo*; Louis C.K. – *Jason Falchook*; Magda Szubanski – *Carla Gottgens*; Mary-Claire King – *Jason Falchook*; Melissa Lucashenko – *Carla Gottgens*; Moshe Schulman – *Jason Falchook*; Navreet Chawla – *Aron Klein*; Noreen Riols – *Jason Falchook*; Omar Musa – *Victoria Baldwin*; Peter Pringle – *Jason Falchook*; Samuel James – *Joseph Michael*; Sara Barron – *Mark Arrigo*; Sasha Chanoff – *Allison Evans*; Shannon Cason – *Renee Rosensteel*; Stephanie Peirolo – *Heather Immoor*; Suki Kim – *Victoria Baldwin*; Suzi Ronson – *Braden Moran*; Tara Clancy – *Allison Evans*; Taylor Negron – *Dare Kumolu-Johnson*; Tim Fitzhigham – *Mark Arrigo*; Tomas Reichental – *Mark Earley*; Tony Wheeler – *Carla Gottgens*.